Margaret Dibben edited the personal finance pages of *The Guardian* from 1982 to 1986 and has closely followed the changes affecting the financial services industry for many years.

She is now self-employed as a freelance journalist, writing about personal finance in a wide range of publications. Her columns appear regularly in several national and local newspapers and consumer magazines.

She also appears on television advising older people about how to handle their money problems.

Margaret was named Insurance Journalist of the Year in 1983, the first time the award was made, and was runner-up Consumer Insurance Journalist of The Year in 1987, which is awarded by the British Insurance and Investment Brokers' Association.

The Guardian MONEY GUIDE
NEW EDITION

MARGARET DIBBEN

COLLINS

To Ted

William Collins Sons & Co. Ltd
London · Glasgow · Sydney
Auckland · Toronto · Johannesburg

First published in Great Britain 1984
Third edition 1988
© Margaret Dibben 1984, 1986, 1988

British Library Cataloguing in Publication Data
Dibben, Margaret
The Guardian Money Guide.—[Updated ed.]
1. Finance, personal
I. Title
332.024   HG179
ISBN *Limp edition* 0 00 410447 1
ISBN *Hardback edition* 0 00 410449 8

Photoset by Rowland Phototypesetting Ltd, Bury St Edmunds, Suffolk
Printed and bound in Great Britain by Hartnolls Ltd, Bodmin, Cornwall

CONTENTS

Acknowledgements

The detailed checking of a book like this is a monumental task. I hope I have expressed adequately my deepest gratitude to the very many people who provided and checked the facts and figures.

But, in particular, I would like to name the following who generously gave an enormous amount of time and care to reading individual chapters of the manuscript. Without them, the book would have been only halfway useful:

The Automobile Association; British Gas; Association of British Insurers; British Insurance Brokers' Association; British Telecom; Trisha McLaughlin of the Building Societies Association; Stephanie Cooper; Department of Health and Social Security; Electricity Council; Hinton & Wild; the Law Society; Legal & General Assurance Society; Lloyds Bank; National Girobank; National Savings; Office of Fair Trading; the Post Office; the Royal Institution of Chartered Surveyors; Royal Insurance; Trustee Savings Bank; Unit Trust Association.

Tim Good patiently demystified the subject of tax. And David Simpson bravely and scrupulously read the whole manuscript. My thanks to everyone.

The author and publishers have made every effort to ensure that all information in this book is correct at the time of going to press. However, it should be remembered that *The Guardian Money Guide* is intended as a general guide only and the author and publishers accept no responsibility for any consequences arising out of the use of this book.

It is strongly recommended that professional advice is sought before any financial planning is undertaken to provide up-to-date information suited to individual circumstances.

FOREWORD TO THIRD EDITION

What an eye-opening experience it has been to compare the first edition of *The Guardian Money Guide*, published four years ago, with what is happening in the world of personal finance today.

There has been so much substantial new legislation and technological advance that no single aspect of our money has escaped attention. From pension rights to the way life insurance is sold; from the services of a building society to social security and housing benefits.

But in many other instances the changes in personal finance have been more subtle than simply a solid new Act of Parliament. Most obvious, of course, is the increased number of small investors who have been buying shares. The Government's privatisation programme, despite the BP set-back, has totally changed the public attitude to investing in the stock market. At least as far as new issues are concerned. Add to that the growth in home ownership which, with house price rises, has created wealth for many for the first time and you will understand why people are taking a keener interest in their money.

So, this is not simply an updated version of the original *Money Guide*. Many sections have been substantially rewritten to reflect the new situation. Personal pensions are now here; a complete shake up of social security and housing benefits has taken place; banks and building societies have changed their roles; and investor protection has been strengthened. I have also added a completely new chapter on being self-employed, for those thinking of starting their own business.

Such is the extent of this very enormous upheaval in financial services that there are bound to be problems. Some institutions are trying to do too much too soon. When a crash happens, it will put the new investor protection legislation properly to the test and we can judge whether the new Financial Services Act has been worth all the effort and expense.

Instead of pointing to new opportunities on the horizon, this edition of the *Money Guide* brings them into focus. The changes planned over the past few years have now become a reality. The restructuring is still not complete, however. The end of the decade promises to be almost as eventful as the start.

MARGARET DIBBEN
MAY 1988

CHAPTER · 1

BUDGETING

Humans come in two forms: one can manage its money and enjoys budgeting; the other can't, and doesn't. Most people belong to the second category and it is for them that *The Guardian Money Guide* has been written.

If you are totally incapable of keeping tabs on your finances but nevertheless muddle through life quite happily, then the distress of trying to balance 'cash in' with 'cash out' is not worthwhile. However, if you really do want to feel in control of your finances but do not know how to go about it, then read on.

The first step in learning how to sort out your money problems is discovering exactly how much you have coming in each week or each month. Surprisingly, many people cannot say with any precision.

You then need to work out a fairly accurate idea of how much you will be paying out regularly. If you do not know the exact figure, make a guess, but remember to make an allowance for inflation. Bills have a habit of growing larger, rarely smaller. This is how to start:

Write down and then add together: per month

- [ ] net pay after all deductions   £..........
- [ ] dividends and interest from savings   £..........
- [ ] occasional bonuses   £..........
- [ ] social security payments   £..........

         £..........

Next, total your regular expenses:

- [ ] mortgage or rent   £..........
- [ ] rates   £..........
- [ ] ground rent   £..........
- [ ] water rates   £..........
- [ ] telephone   £..........
- [ ] gas   £..........
- [ ] electricity   £..........
- [ ] oil or coal   £..........

☐ season ticket or commuting costs   £..........
☐ insurance premiums – house building   £..........
                        – house contents   £..........
                        – life insurance   £..........
                        – mortgage protection   £..........
                        – car   £..........
☐ road fund licence   £..........
☐ TV licence   £..........
☐ TV and video recorder rental   £..........
☐ hire purchase and credit repayments   £..........
☐ credit card bill   £..........
☐ subscriptions to – publications   £..........
                     – associations   £..........
☐ school fees   £..........
☐ children's pocket money   £..........
☐ other   £..........

                                                               £..........

The next main item to allow for is:

☐ food   £..........

followed by the other necessities of life; estimate how much for:

☐ cleaning materials   £..........
☐ dry cleaning and laundry   £..........
☐ kitchen and bathroom accessories   £..........
☐ dentist's and optician's bills   £..........
☐ vet's fees   £..........
☐ travelling   £..........
☐ petrol   £..........
☐ car repairs   £..........
☐ household repairs   £..........
☐ haircuts   £..........
☐ medicine   £..........
☐ other   £..........

                                                               £..........

**Next come the less essential expenses; items that you can manage
without, or delay buying, if you really have to:**

☐ meals out   £..........
☐ drinks and cigarettes   £..........
☐ sweets and toys   £..........

☐ books, magazines and newspapers £..........
☐ records, tapes, video cassettes £..........
☐ theatre, cinema, music, gambling £..........
☐ postage £..........
☐ evening classes £..........
☐ birthday and Christmas presents £..........
☐ holidays £..........
☐ clothes £..........
☐ hobbies and sport £..........
☐ decorating £..........
☐ cosmetics £..........
☐ garden tools £..........
☐ miscellaneous items £..........

£..........

Add together all the outgoing totals and subtract this from your income.

If you have already run out of money before you reach the end of the list, then hopefully you will, on the way, have seen areas where you can cut back. Each of us has our own priorities.

If you are fortunate enough to have money left over after allowing for these predictable outgoings, the next step is to start an emergency fund. Build up a pool of money, say up to £500, perhaps in a bank or building society where it will earn interest but where you can get hold of it quickly.

This is money to tide you over when the unexpected happens: the car breaks down or you receive a large bill from the vet.

With that taken care of, you can please yourself. You can save a bit more, you can gamble, or you can spend it.

This is how an average family divides its money:

☐ housing	15·8%	☐ durable household goods	7·6%
☐ fuel, light, power	6·2	☐ other goods	7·8
☐ food	20·7	☐ transport and vehicles	15·0
☐ alcohol	4·8	☐ services	11·5
☐ tobacco	2·8	☐ miscellaneous	0·4
☐ clothing and footwear	7·4		

At least 80 per cent of the population reckons it saves regularly and, on average, people save 11 to 12 per cent of their disposable incomes.

HOW TO PAY THE BILLS

Now you know where you stand, the next step is to discover how to manage your money. There are various ways.

You could, for example, line up half-a-dozen empty jars and every week put a few pounds in each. But apart from the safety risk, you are losing money. If the money were put in a deposit account instead, it would be earning interest. There are many kinds of convenient savings schemes which you will find in Chapter 3: Savings.

Here are some better ways of spreading the costs of living.

Rates

Most local authorities will let you pay your rates on a monthly basis instead of all in one go at the beginning of the year. When you receive the bill, you can ask to pay either in two halves or, better still, in ten monthly instalments.

Look at it this way. If you regard rates as a monthly instead of annual expense, you can fool yourself that you have two 'free' months out of twelve. This is not true, of course, but the trick can help you feel richer.

You can pay the bill by standing order from your bank account, by sending a cheque each month through the post, or by calling in person at the town hall.

A few local authorities have introduced savings stamps and some have made arrangements for payment through post offices or gas and electricity showrooms. Ask at your town hall if your authority has any such scheme.

The advantages of spreading the cost of the rates bill are that it helps you budget and delays payment; you are holding on to your money for as long as possible and paying only at the last moment. The situation is different if you spread the cost of gas and electricity bills because you are paying in advance for these.

Rates will be abolished from April 1989 in Scotland, and a year later in England and Wales, to be replaced by the poll tax.

Gas and electricity

Gas and electricity bills are far higher in winter than in summer and, to even out the expense, you can buy savings stamps at gas and electricity board showrooms whenever you can afford it. This is called a pay-as-you-go scheme. The disadvantage is that you are paying for the fuel before you use it. The gas and electricity boards get their hands on your cash sooner than if they had to wait for settlement of a quarterly bill.

Another way of smoothing out big bills is to open a budget account and pay in an amount each month. The board estimates your annual bill and divides by 12. You pay the same amount each month so that in summer you pay for more energy than you use but in winter you pay less.

If you start the account at the beginning of winter at least you are immediately getting the benefit of paying less for the heavy winter bills.

The monthly payment can be made either by standing order, direct debit, or in cash at the showrooms.

Both gas and electricity board showrooms sell stamps at £1 each. They are interchangeable between the two and a few sub-post offices also sell them. The savings stamps scheme is a poor way of managing your money unless you really have difficulty meeting the quarterly bills. In effect you are giving the gas or electricity boards an interest-free loan: except in the coldest months they collect your money sooner than they otherwise would but they do not pay you any interest.

The same criticism applies to a budget account although this is a popular way of paying. You would be better off opening a building society account, depositing the same monthly payments there and earning interest on the money.

Some electricity boards allow payment by Access card. If you pay off your credit card bill in full each month, you will not pay any interest and gain another six weeks of free credit.

The gas board does not permit this and argues that because you pay for the gas after you have used it anyway, it sees no reason to give you yet more time to pay up.

You can also pay gas and electricity bills through Transcash at the post office but it will cost you 50p unless you are a customer of Girobank (see p. 24).

Meters

If you find paying your fuel bills very difficult, you can have a slot meter installed. There is no charge for the meter but the running costs are higher. Unless you use fewer than 30 therms a quarter (about the amount a gas cooker takes a quarter) it will work out more expensive.

Scotland

The Royal Bank of Scotland runs its own savings stamps scheme. These stamps can be used towards paying gas and electricity bills or they can be cashed in.

The stamps are sold in denominations of 50p, £1 and £2. They can be bought at bank branches or in the showrooms. At the bank, they can be exchanged for cash or used to pay any bill you would otherwise settle through the Giro system (see pp. 17 and 37 for an explanation of the Giro system).

Water

The regional water authorities will let you spread the bill over eight months of the year. One or two of them issue savings stamps and some allow payment by credit card. Water used to be a utility that qualified for social security assistance but this was stopped in April 1988.

Telephone

You can buy savings stamps at the post office or a British Telecom shop to go towards paying the telephone bill. British Telecom issues the stamps in

£1 and £2 denominations. Like gas and electricity board stamps, these are a bad buy.

Television licence

You can buy 50p savings stamps at the post office to help pay for a television licence.

Road fund licence

Car tax can be paid half yearly but it costs more this way. A six-month licence is half the cost of a 12-month plus 10 per cent. One year costs £100, six months £55. There is also the chance that the fee will go up during the year. If you have already paid for the full year, you will avoid the increase until your licence is due for renewal. If you pay half yearly, you might get caught for the second six months. However, if you cannot meet the whole cost all at once, paying in two halves is a help.

The licence for a motorbike has to be paid in one go unless the bike is larger than 250cc. That costs £40 a year.

Season ticket

You may be able to persuade your employer to give you an interest-free loan to buy an annual season ticket: if you can this is a very good deal.

Otherwise, a British Rail annual ticket costs the same as 40 weekly tickets; a quarterly costs 11.52 weeklies; and a monthly 3.84 weeklies. A weekly is 15 per cent cheaper than ten single tickets.

BANK BUDGET ACCOUNTS

Some banks, but not all, will organise a budget for you. You add together everything you expect to spend on regular bills for the coming year, add the service charge, and divide by 12. You pay this amount each month into a special account at the bank.

You can write out cheques from this account using a special cheque book, without worrying if there is enough money to meet the cheque.

Under the Midland Bank's system, there is a £10 annual service charge. When the account is overdrawn, you pay interest charges calculated at 19 per cent or 20·3 per cent APR. However, you receive nothing at times when the account is in credit.

The National Westminster Bank's scheme works differently. You are not charged interest, neither do you receive any. But there is a service charge of £35 a year to cover the first £500 you will be spending. Above that, there is a £1 charge for every £50 you spend.

Some banks offer a 'save and borrow' account. You pay a predetermined amount each month and then can automatically borrow 30 times that figure. This is called 'roll-over' credit; as your monthly cheque is paid in, your borrowing limit is topped up. Again, you will pay interest charges when the account is in the red.

For paying bills, it is economically sounder to deposit the money in a building society or bank deposit account to benefit from the interest.

Shopping

There are various other ways of stretching your money further when you go shopping. These include paying by credit card, mail order or joining a store's own credit scheme. You can learn more about buying on credit in Chapter 4: Borrowing.

> The gas and electricity boards and British Telecom can ask you to pay a deposit if they know you to be a bad payer, or if they know nothing about you. The amount is likely to be between £50 and £100 but on the plus side they do pay you interest on the money.

CHAPTER · 2

BANKING

Many people are nervous about approaching a bank manager; the pin-striped image which bank managers have cultivated can frighten away potential customers before they have even taken the first step through the door. But despite feeling more like robbers than customers, a bank account is a convenient medium for moving money around.

On the other hand, now that some of the larger building societies offer a full cheque account, perhaps one of these would suit you better.

HOW TO CHOOSE A BANK

It is difficult to advise anyone how to choose a bank since you must weigh up the relative merits of each one and decide how important these are to you. Most often people pick the bank that their parents used, or the one with the most convenient branch to their place of work.

If you want to compare bank charges, 'free' banking is now offered by all the banks, as long as you stay in credit. But if you do go overdrawn, you will find the charges steep. Most banks are also open on Saturday mornings, so there is not much to choose on that score either.

The charges that a bank adds to your statement are, to a large degree, at the manager's discretion: a formula is programmed into the computer but the manager does not have to keep to those charges if he does not want to. He will usually let the computer work out the figure. But, if he does take a personal interest, he will weigh up the amount of money you have in credit in your current account (this money is, in effect, a free loan to the bank) against how good a customer you are. Does he have to bounce your cheques regularly? Do you call into the branch frequently to pester him? You are not a 'good' customer if you do.

If you think you have been charged too much on your statement, telephone the manager and tell him so. He may reconsider if you point out an inequity in the calculations.

The bank already has the upper hand because the bank manager deducts the charges directly from your account before telling you, and without asking your permission. You then have to persuade him to reimburse your account if he agrees to waive the charges. No other system of payment works this way.

Always, a bank manager will respond more positively to a reasoned request rather than an irate outburst pointing out the injustice of such a large profit-making institution having the audacity to milk its impecunious customers.

Some banks have an account which allows small automatic overdrafts with no charges but at an annual fee.

How the banks line up

The best-known banks, the Big Five, are: Barclays, Lloyds, Midland, National Westminster and TSB.

Next in size and familiarity come the Co-op Bank, Yorkshire Bank and Girobank which operates through post office branches.

Scotland has the Bank of Scotland, Clydesdale Bank and Royal Bank of Scotland. The Scottish banks produce their own bank notes. Scottish notes are acceptable in England and Wales but if you cannot persuade a shop to take them, go to any clearing bank branch and they will exchange them.

If you are unhappy with the service you receive from your bank, you can always change. You can move banks, but it may be that **by simply switching to a different branch you find a more sympathetic manager.**

Girobank

There are various services provided at post offices by the Girobank including an ordinary banking service which includes cheque books, cashing facilities, easy household bill payments, travellers cheques and Postcheques. Girobank is a separate organisation from the post office and it pays a fee to use post office counter services such as staff.

BANK OR BUILDING SOCIETY?

Since the building societies have been allowed to move into new areas, a few have started offering proper cheque books with the same clearing facilities as banks, and overdrafts if you want one. Some already had cheque books but with no cheque guarantee card or overdraft. But the new breed, led by the Nationwide Anglia and then the Abbey National, brought out accounts which could not be bettered by any bank.

Indeed, as the building societies pay interest on credit balances, albeit a low rate of interest, this makes them even more attractive.

CURRENT ACCOUNTS

The main use of a current or cheque account is to be able to move money around safely and conveniently. This is known as money transmission.

To pay for goods in a shop, though, you need a cheque guarantee card. The card enables you to shop almost anywhere and pay by cheque, up to the maximum mostly of £50 a cheque. Without a cheque guarantee card, you are mainly limited to paying household bills.

Then, with a bank current account you can run up an overdraft. A bank manager will usually allow you to do this if you ask him politely first, or if you have obviously had an unusually stressful month which will be offset by a regular salary cheque.

For more information about overdrafts see p. 57 and for high interest cheque accounts see p. 39.

Writing out a cheque

You must write clearly in ink and you must ensure that no one can add a few noughts to your figures. If you make a mistake when writing the cheque, you can tear it up and write out another, or you can correct and initial the mistake.

Cheques are either 'crossed' (two vertical parallel lines drawn through) or 'open'. 'Open' cheques, now rarely used, can be cashed only at the branch where they are drawn. Crossed cheques can be paid into a bank account or they can be cashed at a local shop by endorsing, that is signing your name on the back.

If a cheque has been made out in your name but you want to pay it into someone else's account, you can shorten the procedure of paying it into your bank and writing out a separate cheque if you endorse the back of the cheque.

Always remember to fill in the cheque stub or record sheet so you can check your bank statement when it arrives.

Cheque guarantee card

Provided the number of the cheque guarantee card is written on the back of the cheque, anyone who accepts it knows that, whatever happens, he will receive his money up to the usual £50 limit. When you use a cheque guarantee card, you cannot, under any circumstances, stop payment of the cheque. Remember this if you are buying goods that you might change your mind about.

Even if the card is stolen and misused, or you do not have sufficient funds in your account, the bank will have to pay up. But you should not write the number on the back of the cheque yourself. This must be done by the person accepting the cheque or the guarantee is invalidated. **Do not keep your cheque guarantee card with your cheque book: if both are stolen together, fraud is easier.**

If you write a succession of cheques for £50, using a cheque guarantee card, to buy a more expensive item and the cheques bounce, one for £50 will be honoured by the bank but not the rest.

If someone steals your cheque card and uses it fraudulently, you are not responsible once you have reported the loss. Until then, you are liable up to £25, although banks do not in practice impose this penalty. The bank and retailer take responsibility for accepting the counterfeit signature.

Stopping a cheque

If you have not used a cheque guarantee card to support a cheque, you can telephone and instruct the bank not to pay up when the cheque is presented. You need to act quickly and it will cost you around £2 or £3. If you have simply changed your mind about buying an item, although the bank will obey your instructions not to pay, you still legally owe for the goods.

Standing orders

Your bank will automatically make regular payments on your behalf by standing order. You simply fill out a form which can be cancelled at any time, give it to your bank and then you can forget about paying mortgage instalments, insurance premiums, annual charity subscriptions, or whatever.

Direct debiting

This is a similar system to standing orders but is more popular with the banks because it is cheaper for them to operate. The amount of any regular payment which you make is bound to change (usually upwards) from time to time.

For payments such as annual subscriptions you might have a variable direct debit which authorises the bank to pay a different amount when the recipient asks for it.

For regular payments which do not change very often, such as monthly insurance premiums, you could have a fixed direct debit under which the bank will need your permission to pay a higher amount.

Paying-in

Most people choose to have their monthly salary paid directly into their bank account; indeed you often do not have any option about how you are paid. (See p. 149 about being paid in cash.) Both banks and employers prefer paying you this way because it is cheaper and avoids the enormous security hazard of handling large amounts of cash.

If the bank manager knows that you have a regular pay cheque arriving each month, he is more likely to agree to your request for overdrafts and loans.

For other amounts of money, you will be given a paying-in book with your cheque book, or you can pick up an individual paying-in slip at the branch. If you are paying into a bank which is not your own, you may have to pay an extra charge. To avoid this you could, for the cost of a second-class postage stamp, send it through the post.

If someone has sent you a cheque which is crossed, then you can convert this to money by paying it into your bank account. If it is not crossed, you can exchange it for cash at the bank, but only at the issuing branch. And so too could anyone who found the cheque if you lost it.

Bouncing cheques

If you write out a cheque but have no money in the account, unless the manager allows you to be overdrawn, he can bounce your cheque.

When the payee, that is the person to whom the cheque is made out, pays the cheque into his account he will not get the money as he expected. Instead, the cheque is returned to him with the invitation: 'refer to drawer, please represent'. This gives you, the bad payer, a few more days to come up with the money, and the next time he presents the cheque, the manager may authorise payment.

But sometimes the cheque has the blunt message, 'refer to drawer'. This tells the payee that he is not going to get his money, so he better speak to you urgently.

Joint accounts

Many couples open joint accounts. There are various permutations. You can both sign cheques separately, or you can arrange that one can sign alone, but the other can sign only jointly. Or, very restrictively, you can insist that neither can sign a cheque without the other's signature as well.

Statements

All banks will send you a statement of your account, monthly if you ask for it, or every few months if it suits them better. The service is free unless you ask for a statement too frequently, in which case you can be charged.

You should always check your statement against the cheque stubs or record sheet because mistakes can, and do, happen. If you discover you have wrongly been credited with someone else's £1000, do not rush out to spend it. When Customer B discovers the shortfall he will demand it back and the bank will trace it to your account.

Unless you can prove that you genuinely believed the money was yours and you have already spent it, you will have to give it back.

If you are visually handicapped

All the banks will send Braille statements to blind customers and there is no charge for this. They will also issue large print statements and have Braille booklets. National Westminster and Lloyds have a Braille office which transcribes blind customers' correspondence.

The banks will supply free cheque templates which guide you to the correct position for filling out cheques and a note gauge to help you identify your bank notes.

GETTING CASH

This is the most frequent transaction you will conduct with your bank. You can withdraw cash from a bank even if you hold your account at another by using a cheque book supported by a cheque guarantee card, but there will probably be a charge of 50p for doing this. Barclays charges other banks' customers £2 on Saturdays.

At your local branch you can withdraw as much cash as you like (as long as you have enough money in the account), but at other branches of your own bank or other banks, you are limited to the £50 a day rule under the cheque guarantee scheme. You can make special arrangements if you regularly withdraw large amounts from one particular branch of your own bank away from your home branch.

Cash dispensers have become an indispensable part of most people's lives. They are machines which give you cash at any time of the day or night (except at Lloyds Bank which closes the machines from 11.30 p.m. to 6.30 a.m.).

Customers have shown that they would rather queue outside in the rain to use the cash machine (known in the business as automated teller machines or ATMs) than face a cashier inside. One reason may be that you can withdraw up to £100 a day, or £250 from a building society ATM, rather than £50.

Cash machines are mostly sited on the outside wall of a bank branch, but they are increasingly being installed inside and also in factories and shopping centres. By using a plastic card, you can withdraw cash, order a statement or cheque book and check how much you have in your account.

These machines are now becoming even more sophisticated: they can hand you a printed statement; take in cash; and obey your instructions to pay bills.

If your cash card is stolen, you can be responsible for the first £25 or £50 of fraudulent use until you inform the bank, which you should obviously do immediately.

How to get cash when the banks are closed

1. use a cash dispenser: your Visa and Access credit cards will also work in the machines.
2. cash a cheque at your corner shop or garage.
3. use a tourist *bureau de change*: these are mostly in London and are extremely expensive.
4. raid the children's piggy bank.
5. exchange a recent purchase from Marks & Spencer.
6. look under the stairs for returnable bottles.
7. have a meal with friends, pay the bill by cheque or credit card and collect their contributions in cash.
8. use the Co-op Handybank for longer opening hours.
9. some hypermarkets have facilities for cashing cheques.
10. open a Girobank account at the post office (this is open longer hours than a bank).
11. write a cheque in exchange for the contents of the church offertory plate!

To operate the machines you must remember a four-figure number. This is your Personal Identification Number or PIN which you key into the cash machine. The computer then matches your PIN against the code in the magnetic stripe on the back of your plastic card to make sure you are who you say. You have three chances to key in the right number, then the machine swallows your card.

Do not, whatever you do, keep your PIN with your cash card because if you were to lose them together, anyone finding them could easily get the cash. In fact, you should not keep your PIN written down anywhere. If you do not trust your memory, try disguising the number, preferably more cleverly than by simply reversing the order.

LOANS

A bank manager is one of the first people to go to if you want a loan. There are various types of loan, from a small overdraft to start-up finance for a new business.

For more details on borrowing, see pp. 55–65, p. 166 for business loans and pp. 69–76 for mortgages.

NIGHT SAFES

If you regularly have a lot of cash which you would like to bank after the branch has closed, you can ask for access to a night safe. Small shop-keepers, for example, do not like keeping the day's takings in their premises overnight. Night safes are installed in the outside wall of a bank and can be opened only with a special key. You then simply drop the money in a bag down the chute.

The next working morning the cashier will check the cash and send you a receipt. If the cashier's reckoning differs from yours, the bank will sort this out the next time you call. If you regularly use a night safe, the branch staff will know you well and you should be able to clear up the discrepancy.

There are two systems. As well as having your money or cheques counted by the cashier the next morning, you can have the bag of money kept intact for you to collect. The cost is around £3 a quarter for each wallet you have, plus 80p every time the wallet is used.

STORAGE – SAFE CUSTODY

Any valuables you own, jewellery, silver, documents or whatever, that you feel would be more secure in the bank's vault than in your own home can be deposited for safe custody.

The charge will be about £10 a year plus VAT for small deed boxes and parcels, or £30 for large ones. The more space you take up, the more you will pay.

If the bank is burgled and you lose your valuables, the bank is not responsible for compensating you. You should, therefore, make sure you have insurance cover. Only if you can prove that the bank was negligent will you stand any chance of claiming against it.

DEPOSIT ACCOUNTS
All the banks have various savings schemes. See pp. 37–9 for details.

BUDGET ACCOUNTS
Your bank may offer a budget account to help spread the cost of household bills. You estimate how much you expect to pay out over the next year, divide by 12 and pay this amount in regular monthly instalments to the bank.

At some periods you will be in credit and at others in debit, but the bank will honour all cheques paid out of a special account. You pay a charge for the service. Two banks mainly offer this service: Midland and National Westminster. See p. 14.

WHAT YOUR BANK MANAGER CAN DO
The role of the bank manager has changed substantially under the Financial Services Act. Branch managers now are really just salesmen for their bank rather than the fount of all financial knowledge they used to be.

Certainly, they can no longer be the friendly adviser to widows and orphans with a few thousand pounds of investments. The Financial Services Act has put paid to that.

But even before this, it had become impossible for a bank manager to know everything about all forms of investment. The range was too wide, and the pressure to make profits too intense. Bank managers had to devote most of their time to the most profitable customers.

Small savers could not expect their bank managers to spend valuable time sorting out their investment problems. So, in fact, the Financial Services Act has made official what was happening in practice anyway.

Under the Act, banks have had to decide whether they want to sell only their own investment and life insurance products or whether they will sell a wide range from all of those available. This is called the 'polarisation' rule (see p. 132).

All, except for National Westminster, have chosen to be tied to their own products. National Westminster is independent and sells what it considers the best available for each customer.

These rules only apply to investments, which include life insurance and pensions. Banks are still free to do what they like on other services and other forms of insurance.

The definition of investments includes shares, unit trusts, gilts, options, commodity futures and life insurance policies, both endowment and unit linked but not term or health insurance.

However, the banks have made sure they do not lose out by only selling their own products. Those that are tied also have insurance broking subsidiaries which are independent. The manager can pass on business within the group.

If they sell their own investments, they make a profit. Or, when National Westminster, or one of the other banks' broking subsidiaries, sells you an insurance policy, it earns commission. They are larger than the high street broker but otherwise no different.

Aside from investment advice, you can reasonably expect your bank manager's attention for half-an-hour and there will be no charge. If he then arranges a loan for you, or helps you to set up a company, the arrangement fee and his investigation time will be charged.

However, if you treat a bank manager as a problem counsellor and use up a great deal of his time, he will mentally list you as a time waster and might very well raise your bank charges in revenge.

Transcash

Even if you do not have a Girobank account yourself, you can pay bills to anyone who does by Transcash. Just fill out a slip at the post office and hand it to the clerk with the money. There is normally a fee of 50p. You can send money abroad through Transcash; it costs £3.50 for each transaction. Using Transcash or Freepay you can order and pay for goods advertised on television, in the press or by direct mail, free of charge.

If you are not a Girobank customer you can pay your gas or electricity bills by Transcash at the post office, but you pay a 50p fee. If you are buying something on mail order, this could be through a Freepay account, in which case the company pays the fee.

Tax advice

The bank manager will give advice on simple tax problems. There may be no set scale of charges for this, but if you have complicated affairs, the branch manager will refer you to the bank's taxation specialist who will give you a quote for the likely cost.

Executor

A bank can act as executor of your will. You may prefer the idea of leaving this chore to the bank rather than putting the onus on a friend or relative. **But a bank's fees for this can become very expensive.**

There is a set scale relating to the value of the estate and banks will charge accordingly, regardless of how much or how little work is involved. But you can be confident of continuity. If you appoint your own executors, they may die before you, but there is always another bank manager to succeed the present one. As a guide, you might pay 5 per cent plus VAT on the first £50,000 and 2 per cent plus VAT above that with a minimum fee of £500.

If the estate remains unsettled after one year, the bank will take over as trustee and probably charge 1 per cent of the total amount a year.

SENDING MONEY ABROAD

This can be extremely expensive, particularly for small amounts. There are various ploys to keep down the cost but, with the cheapest ways, there is a greater element of risk.

If you ask your bank to transmit the money, it is guaranteed to arrive safely but the charges run as follows: cable transfer is the fastest system; it costs 25p per £100 but there is a minimum charge of £6 and a maximum of £30 plus the cost of sending a cable, which is probably a couple of pounds.

Money going to Europe is sent by a special electronic interbank system called SWIFT. This costs 25p to send £100 with a minimum charge of £6 and a maximum of £30. The money will take about three working days to arrive.

An international payment order can be sent in any currency but travels airmail, so it is slower. The charge is the same, 25p per £100 with a minimum of £6 and a maximum of £30. Both telegraphic transfer and international payment orders are sent to foreign banks and not to individuals and named for the recipient.

Another way to send small sums overseas is through Girobank by Transcash which costs £3.50. See opposite for more details.

A cheaper scheme is run by Barclays Bank which charges only £3 to issue a money order in either sterling or American dollars. Lloyds Bank also charges £3 for American dollar transfers up to $1,000. These are American Express International Money Orders.

For very small amounts you could risk sending cash and registering the letter, but this is not advisable. In any case, the person at the other end will then have to pay a fee to convert the sterling to his own currency.

Taking money abroad

Again, this costs money – you are paying for security and convenience. See pp. 228–30 for details.

PLASTIC CARDS

There was a time when owning a plastic card was a status symbol. Now there are so many you need a separate wallet to keep them all in. And what have the credit card companies done to maintain the cachet, or rather wealth, distinction? They have invented 'gold' cards. These are charge cards rather than credit cards, but to qualify for one you must have an income of at least £20,000 a year.

The run of the mill, everyday credit card is quite good enough for people who want to pay by plastic.

Credit cards

There are two main international credit card systems: Visa and Mastercard. Both are widely accepted in most parts of the world, but in some countries one is more popular than the other.

Among the UK banks, Barclays, Yorkshire Bank, Co-op Bank, Bank of Scotland, Allied Irish Bank and TSB belong to the Visa organisation while Midland, Lloyds, National Westminster, Royal Bank of Scotland, Clydesdale, Bank of Ireland, Northern and Ulster Banks have joined Mastercard. Lloyds has also joined Visa but only to issue a debit card.

The credit card company will give you a limit of how much credit you are allowed to run up in a month. If you do not think this is enough, you can try asking for more or you could have both cards. **You do not need to have an account with the bank that gives you the card.**

Once a month, you will receive a statement detailing what you have spent with your card, how much is outstanding and what is the minimum amount that you must pay off each month. You will have to pay a minimum each month: either £5 or 5 per cent, whichever is the greater. You are given a date, usually two weeks hence, by which you must have paid at least the minimum on the bill. If you pay the whole bill, you will incur no charge for interest. So in total, you can have about six weeks' free credit from the time you buy the goods until the date you have to pay for them.

If you pay off part of the bill only, you will pay interest on the outstanding amount from the day the money is due.

The danger with these cards is for those who are completely irresponsible when it comes to spending. If you are the sort of person who will use the card because it is there, then it is probably best not to put yourself in the way of temptation. You can easily fall deeply into debt very quickly by using a credit card.

But there are advantages. You can save bank charges by using a credit card: you need write out only one cheque a month instead of separate cheques for each purchase. You carry less cash around with you. You can use the card in a cash dispenser, although you will pay interest on the money immediately.

Security

For £6 a year you can lodge details of all your plastic cards with one source. Then, if you lose them, you need only contact one number to inform all the others.

Charge cards

Another variety of plastic is the charge card. There is no limit to the amount you can spend using one of these, but you must settle the whole bill every month.

There are no interest charges because you do not have any period of credit. But there is an annual charge and also a joining fee. American Express charges £12.50 to join and £27.50 a year. Diners Club costs £20 to join and £27.50 a year.

Charge cards started out as a convenient way of paying for goods without using cash. Now they also provide cash facilities, free life insurance, and various other services.

TECHNOLOGICAL CHANGES
Home banking
Advanced technology, which can transform the way you run a bank account, has existed for some years now. But the banks, quite rightly, were wary of introducing it too early. Many customers were still coming to terms with cash machines.

But now, gradually, new technological banking is being used. Whether from a bank or a building society, it is called 'home banking'.

There are two very different systems available. But both allow you to contact your bank account, from early morning to late at night, from home.

One system works through a television set, the other via a telephone.

Home banking by television works through the Prestel system. It was first offered by the Nottingham Building Society jointly with Bank of Scotland. Now, Bank of Scotland has its own home banking service available to customers.

Provided you subscribe to Prestel, you can call up your bank account on the television screen. Then you can check your balance, pay bills, order statements, check the state of your standing orders whenever you want.

To bank at home by telephone, you need either a special pulse telephone (the numbers make different sounds as you dial them) or a telephone pad which sits over the mouthpiece. These are available from the companies offering the service.

First off the mark with this was TSB (England and Wales), closely followed by Nationwide Anglia Building Society. After dialling the designated number, the pulse tone passes signals down the telephone line. By dialling code numbers, you can ask for an up-to-date balance or a statement and pay bills.

The answer comes back to you through a genuine human voice which has been pre-recorded for every eventuality. The computer picks the correct information for the voice to give.

Authorisation terminals
These are beginning to appear in shops, though mainly in large department stores near town centres at first. They can almost completely eliminate fraud once the loss of a card has been notified.

When you pay for an item at the check out, your cheque guarantee card or credit card is run through an instrument that looks like a telephone with a slit along the top. While the assistant is wrapping your goods, a message is passed electronically to a central computer which reads the information on your card and then authorises, or refuses, acceptance. This takes a few seconds.

EFTPoS

Shopping in the future will not be by cash or cheque. It will be by EFTPoS. This ugly acronym stands for Electronic Funds Transfer at Point of Sale, popularly called 'cashless shopping'. It means that the money can be deducted from your bank account the instant you make a purchase. In practice, the banks will probably allow a one or two day delay because of customer resistance to paying quite so promptly.

This is the exact opposite of using a credit card, where you do not have to pay anything for at least six weeks. The EFTPoS piece of plastic is accordingly called a 'debit card'.

The attraction of EFTPoS is that it cuts down on fraud. The up-to-the-minute balance of your account is stored in the electronic stripe on the back of a plastic card. The card is passed through an authorisation terminal which, within seconds, tells the cashier whether or not you can pay for the goods. If you can, the money is automatically deducted from your account and credited to the shop's while the goods are still being wrapped. The only paper involved is the receipt from the cash till.

There are several EFTPoS trials going on around the country, especially in petrol stations. But a first step towards a nationwide EFTPoS scheme was launched by Barclays Bank. Called Connect, the eventual plan is for a full scale EFTPoS. But, meanwhile, Connect works just like a credit card (you have to sign a paper voucher) although your account is debited the next working day.

EFTPoS will take hold around the country slowly. But it is inevitably on the way.

FRAUD

The banks' overwhelming worry is the growing problem of fraud. One reason for their reluctance to raise the limit on cheque guarantee cards beyond £50 is because this would increase the amount of fraud.

They are constantly looking for ways of cutting down the opportunities for fraud and this is the reason for the holograms on plastic cards.

SAFETY

Any money deposited with a British bank is largely secure from loss. The Bank of England has set up a protection scheme, run by the Deposit Protection Fund, to which the banks contribute. If any bank or licensed deposit taker (someone registered with the Department of Trade and Industry) collapses, customers are guaranteed 75 per cent of the first £20,000 they have in a UK sterling deposit account. Investments are also protected under the Financial Services Act. The first £30,000 is paid in full and 90 per cent of the next £20,000.

CHAPTER · 3

SAVINGS

As an investor, you are a highly sought-after customer. This is an increasingly sophisticated and competitive market with professional companies eager to part you from your money. So, the more you know about investment decisions, the better able you are to judge the quality of any advice you are given.

Investor protection

New legislation came into force in 1988 designed to protect investors from crooks and rogues who have, in the past, swindled savers out of their money. It is called the Financial Services Act.

All institutions that have anything to do with the public and investments, whether selling or advising, must now be registered. It is a criminal offence not to be properly authorised. This applies to:

☐ insurance companies
☐ investment advisers and insurance salesmen
☐ unit trust groups
☐ banks and building societies
☐ the Stock Exchange and stockbrokers
☐ pension fund managers
☐ futures and commodity dealers
☐ accountants and solicitors who give investment advice

Each has been given strict rules designed to ensure they are competent to carry out their work, are solvent and honest. They must take care to understand their customers' needs and always recommend the best investment for each client. The amount of commission that salesmen receive is being controlled.

Limited compensation schemes now exist for most types of investment (but still be extra careful if you buy an offshore investment) and ombudsmen exist in most areas to arbitrate in disputes.

The watchdogs

FIMBRA: Financial Intermediaries, Managers and Brokers Regulatory Organisation

LAUTRO: Life Assurance and Unit Trust Regulatory Organisation

IMRO: Investment Managers Regulatory Organisation

TSA: The Securities Association (the Stock Exchange)

AFBD: Association of Futures Brokers and Dealers

SIB: Securities and Investments Board, the overall watchdog

Choosing an investment

Before you can even decide what sort of investment you want, you need to understand a few basic principles. Briefly, these are:

- [ ] can you afford to lose some or all of the money in the hope of gaining a higher than average return?
- [ ] can the money be put away and forgotten about, or might you need to get it back quickly?
- [ ] do you pay tax and, if so, at what rate?
- [ ] do you need a regular income from the investment?
- [ ] are you saving regularly or occasionally?

Now ask yourself the following questions:

- [ ] do I want to take a risk with my money? or — yes/no
- [ ] do I want to know that the capital is safe? — yes/no
- [ ] do I want to be able to withdraw the money quickly? or — yes/no
- [ ] do I want to tie it up for a longer period? — yes/no
- [ ] do I pay tax? — yes/no
- [ ] do I pay tax at a higher rate? — yes/no
- [ ] do I want to receive interest monthly? — yes/no
      half yearly? — yes/no
      annually? — yes/no
- [ ] do I want the capital to grow and receive less in dividends? or — yes/no
- [ ] do I want to receive more income? — yes/no
- [ ] do I have a lump sum to invest? or — yes/no
- [ ] do I want to save a set amount regularly? — yes/no

As you learn more about each of the savings schemes explained below, you will see how an understanding of these basic principles of savings helps you come to a decision.

Your tax position

It is important to get this point straight first because the amount of tax you pay can turn a good investment for a taxpayer into a bad one for the non-taxpayer.

If you pay no tax at all, you should first look for savings that pay the interest to you gross (that is, without deducting tax). Next, you should consider savings where, even if the interest is paid net (after the tax has been deducted), you can reclaim it from the Inland Revenue. Only National Savings and interest paid offshore is now paid gross.

If you pay a high rate of tax (that is, more than the basic 25 per cent rate), then you should look first at tax-free or tax-exempt savings such as National Savings certificates. These are worth even more to you than to a basic rate taxpayer. PEPs (Personal Equity Plans) are tax free if you hold them long enough, but the value can fall if share prices go down.

If you do not pay tax, you should think twice before putting money into a building society or bank account. They have a special arrangement with the Inland Revenue whereby they pay a 'composite' rate of tax on behalf of investors. At around 23 per cent, this rate is lower than basic rate income tax.

This tax cannot be reclaimed from the taxman, even if you are not a taxpayer. If you pay tax at basic rate there is no more to pay, but if you are a higher rate taxpayer you will have to pay the extra above basic rate.

However, you can still reclaim tax paid on your behalf from shares and unit trusts.

Charges

Another question to remember when you are looking for a savings slot is: will there be a fee or charge for putting my money here? For example, if you buy shares in the stock market, you will have to pay commission and stamp duty. But there is no cost for opening a building society account.

Risk

There are two forms of risk you take with investments: one is that your money may lose value; the other is that someone may run off with it.

You can generally assume that the higher the rate of interest, the greater risk you are taking that your money could lose value. The risk spectrum ranges from the totally safe National Savings to the highly speculative commodity dealing. Stock market investments fall in the middle. Banks and building societies are at the safer end.

Safety

The security of your money is an important factor and the whole basis of the Financial Services Act. Some groups have organised a fund to bale out any of their members that get into trouble.

Building society savings are protected by a scheme that will pay at least 90 per cent back if a society collapses. But this is guaranteed only up to a maximum of £20,000 original investment per person.

In the past, a larger society has always stepped in to take over the troubled society so savers did not lose.

The banks also have a Deposit Protection Fund which will pay out 75 per cent of the first £20,000 in a UK account if any bank or licensed deposit taker (that is someone licensed with the Bank of England) collapses.

Insurance polices are covered by the Policyholders' Protection Act which states that, if an insurance company fails, policyholders will receive at least 90 per cent of the money due to them. See p. 131 for more details.

In addition, banks, building societies and insurance companies have appointed ombudsmen to hear customers' complaints.

CHILDREN'S SAVINGS

If children want to save, then the criteria they use to pick one investment rather than another are no different from the ones adults use, remembering that most do not pay tax. There are various special schemes aimed at attracting children's pocket money which include clubs, colourful magazines, drawing books, piggy banks and other bits and pieces that appeal to the marketing people from time to time. But the important factor to look at when choosing an investment for a child is the rate of interest paid: if the interest is less than with a conventional account, you could be paying dearly for, say, a set of colouring pencils.

Building societies, for example, are a poor place for children's money, unless the children are wealthy enough to pay tax. However, several of them, working on the principle of 'catch them young and keep them and their mortgage for life', actively encourage children's savings.

SAVING FOR RETIREMENT

The sooner you start saving for retirement, of course, the more money you will have. You should begin planning your retirement finances as soon as you can bear to think about it.

What pensioners mostly need is extra regular income: an investment which pays interest every month is more valuable than one paying out every six months. Indeed, anyone seeking an income from their savings rather than capital growth should pick a scheme that pays interest more frequently. If you take the interest out to spend, you have the money earlier. And if you leave it on deposit, the interest itself starts earning interest sooner.

The interest rates on all the following savings schemes show the position at April 1988. They will in time change.

NATIONAL SAVINGS

These are all schemes run by the Government which uses the money, together with the taxes you pay, for its spending.

National Savings certificates
They are sold in units of £25 and are meant to be kept for five years. You can cash them in sooner but will get less interest if you do.

The National Savings certificates on sale at the time of publication are the 33rd Issue. The interest on these will never change; when the Government wants to alter the rate, it will issue a new certificate.

interest rate	after 1 year 5·5%, in 2 years 5·75%, in 3 years 6%, in 4 years 6·5%
	Average rate over five years: 7%
	A £100 certificate is worth £140.26 after five years
interest paid	when certificates are cashed in
tax	free of all income and capital gains tax
minimum investment	£25 (each unit costs £25)
maximum investment	£1000
charges	nil
safety	secure
how to invest	at a post office or bank
money tied up	five years to receive full benefit
cashing in	ask at post office for application form and pre-paid envelope addressed to: Director, Savings Certificate and SAYE Office, Durham DH99 1NS. It will take about eight working days
general extension rate	you do not have to cash in the certificates after five years. They will continue to earn interest at the general extension rate applying at the time. In May 1988 it was 5.01% tax free.

4th Issue index-linked certificates

These replaced the original granny bonds, 2nd and 3rd Issue, index-linked certificates when inflation shrank to very low figures making the index-linking unattractive. The 4th Issue still gives protection against rising prices but because inflation is now down to about 4 per cent, this is boosted with a guaranteed rate of interest as well.

interest rate	the certificates grow at the same speed as inflation, plus 4·04% on average over five years. After 1 year the interest is 3%; 2 years 3·25%; 3 years 3·5%; 4 years 4·5%; 5 years 6%. After five years the certificates will still earn interest
interest paid	when certificates are cashed in
tax	tax free
minimum investment	£25 (each unit costs £25)
maximum investment	£5000 (in addition to any other National Savings certificates)
charges	nil

safety	secure
how to invest	at post offices or most banks
money tied up	one year to receive any index linking or interest
cashing in	same as ordinary certificates

Retirement, 2nd and 3rd Issue, index-linked savings certificates
Any of these that you hold will continue to be index-linked and earn bonuses and supplements according to the original terms. Supplements are paid in August.

Income bonds
This is for tying up large sums of money for long periods to receive an income each month.

interest rate	9%, but can change
interest paid	either straight into a bank account or sent to you through the post on the 5th of every month
tax	paid gross but taxable
minimum investment	£2000 (sold in multiples of £1000)
maximum investment	£100,000
charges	nil
safety	secure
how to invest	at post offices or from: Director of Savings, Bonds & Stock Office, Blackpool, Lancs FY3 9YP
money tied up	at least one year
cashing in	after six months, and with three months' notice without loss of interest; otherwise there are penalties. In the first year you receive half the rate of interest, after one year and with three months' notice, there is no loss of interest. You can withdraw only in multiples of £1000

Indexed income bonds
These have been withdrawn but existing bonds continue to give a monthly income which is guaranteed against inflation.

Yearly Plan
This scheme was introduced to replace the index-linked Save as you Earn (SAYE). It gives a rate of interest guaranteed for five years on regular savings.

| interest rate | in saving year 5·25%; certificates earn 7·25% for the next 4 years; average overall rate over 5 years is 7% compound |

tax	tax free
minimum investment	£20 a month
maximum investment	£200 a month
charges	nil
safety	secure
how to invest	at any post office but you can pay by bank standing order only
money tied up	one year but you can leave it at the same rate of interest for five years
cashing in	application forms at post offices or from: Savings Certificates Office, Durham DH99 1NS.

Deposit bonds

These offer a competitive rate of interest if you tie up a large sum of money for a long time.

interest rate	9%, but can change
interest paid	once a year on anniversary of purchase; it is added on to the capital investment
tax	paid gross but is liable to income tax
minimum investment	£100; can be bought in £50 units only
maximum investment	£100,000
charges	nil
safety	secure
how to invest	at post offices or through newspaper advertisements
money tied up	at least one year, otherwise there is a penalty
cashing in	you can withdraw only in multiples of £50; after one year at three months' notice; in first year still three months' notice but you will receive only half the published interest rate, unless repayment is due to the death of bondholder. Apply to your local post office or Deposit Bond Office, National Savings Bank, Glasgow G58 1SB.

Investment account

This is sometimes abbreviated to 'Invac'

interest rate	8.5%
interest paid	same as ordinary account
tax	interest paid gross but taxable
minimum investment	£5
maximum investment	£100,000
charges	nil

safety	secure
how to invest	at post offices
money tied up	one month's notice
cashing in	application form at post offices which is sent to: National Savings Bank, Glasgow G58 1SB.

Ordinary account

interest rate	5% on £500 or more held for one calendar year. 2·5% on smaller sums and until the start of the calendar year. For example, if you invested £600 on 9 January 1988, you would receive the lower rate until 1 January 1989
interest paid	once a year on 31 December
tax	first £70 of interest is tax free. Interest is paid gross and taxable after £70
minimum investment	£1
maximum investment	£10,000
charges	nil
safety	secure
how to invest	at post offices
money tied up	up to £100 on demand; up to £50 at any post office without sending pass book away. With a regular customer account, you can cash up to £250 a day at one nominated office
cashing in	at post offices or from National Savings Bank, Glasgow G58 1SB. Will take a few days.

Premium bonds

These are a gamble, not an investment. A prize draw is held every month, with a smaller weekly draw each Saturday. The winning numbers are selected by ERNIE, the Electronic Random Number Indicator Equipment. The amount of money paid out in prizes is equivalent to 6.5% of all the money invested in premium bonds. Winners are notified by post.

interest rate	nil
tax	prizes are tax free
minimum purchase	£10
maximum purchase	£10,000
charges	nil
safety	the capital is guaranteed to be returned
how to buy	at post offices and banks
money tied up	about eight working days to get it back

| cashing in | repayment forms from post offices or banks should be sent to: Bonds & Stock Office, Lytham St Annes, Lancs FY0 1YN |

SAYE share option issue series C

This contract is available only for anyone aged over 16 and entitled to buy shares under a share option scheme. A share option scheme is organised by your employer but must be approved by the Inland Revenue. If you leave your job, you can continue the SAYE contract.

interest rate	none as such but bonuses equal to 12 and 24 monthly instalments are paid after five years, worth 7·21%, and seven years, worth 7·55%
interest paid	when contract is cashed
tax	tax free
minimum investment	£10 a month, deducted from pay
maximum investment	£100
charges	nil
safety	secure
how to invest	ask your employer
money tied up	at least five years. If you fail to keep up the payments, interest is paid on a cancelled contract at 5%
cashing in	ask your employer

Save as you Earn (SAYE)

These are no longer available but contributions under existing contracts will continue until 1989. Building society SAYE schemes are still available, see p. 41.

GIROBANK

Deposit account

This works the same way as a deposit account with any high street bank, but you must have a current account with Girobank before you can open a deposit account. You will find Girobank at post office branches.

interest rate	2·5%
interest paid	every six months
tax	interest paid net and tax not reclaimable
minimum investment	25p
maximum investment	none
charges	nil
safety	secure
how to invest	from Girobank current account using transfer slips in cheque book

| money tied up | no notice period, but loss of seven days' interest |
| cashing in | at post offices, via current account |

High interest deposit account
For this you do not need a Girobank current account and there are no penalties for withdrawal.

interest rates	£1000–£3999: 4·5%
	£4000–£9999: 5·5%
	£10,000+: 6%
interest paid	annually
tax	paid net and not reclaimable
minimum investment	£1000
maximum investment	none
charges	nil
safety	secure
how to invest	by post to Girobank in Liverpool
money tied up	no notice period but postal delay
cashing in	by post

BANKS

The precise terms and conditions of accounts will vary from bank to bank but the broad outlines remain the same. Non-taxpaying investors will not be able to reclaim the tax paid on their behalf.

Deposit account

interest rate	variable: 2·5%
interest paid	every six months, sometimes quarterly or monthly
tax	interest paid net and tax not reclaimable
minimum investment	£1
maximum investment	none
charges	nil
safety	depositors' protection scheme
how to invest	at any branch of a high street bank
money tied up	seven days
cashing in	seven days' notice at branch

Investment account
This will pay a higher rate of interest than a deposit account but your money is tied up for a longer period of time: the longer the period, the higher the interest.

interest rates	1 month: 5·75%
	3 months: 6%
	6 months: 6·25%

interest paid	half yearly or monthly
tax	interest paid net and tax not reclaimable
minimum investment	from £50 to £5000
maximum investment	usually none, sometimes £25,000
charges	nil
safety	depositors' protection scheme
how to invest	at any bank branch
money tied up	one, three or six months, as agreed
cashing in	at agreed notice period or with loss of interest

Higher rate deposit accounts

interest rates	£1000–£9999: 5·75% £10,000+: 5·8%
interest paid	half yearly or quarterly
tax	interest paid net and tax not reclaimable
minimum investment	£1000
maximum investment	none
charges	nil
safety	depositors' protection scheme
how to invest	at any bank branch
money tied up	no notice required
cashing in	no penalties

High interest cheque account

These are almost interest-paying current accounts but they do not quite have the flexibility of a current account. The account includes a cheque book and sometimes a credit card, cash card and overdraft facility. Some permit only large cheque withdrawals, often a minimum of £250.

interest rate	around 5·75%
interest paid	monthly or quarterly
tax	interest paid net and tax not reclaimable
minimum investment	varies between nil and £2500
maximum investment	none
charges	varies, sometimes none
safety	depositors' protection scheme
how to invest	at your bank or from advertisements
money tied up	no
cashing in	you write cheques but often need to leave a certain minimum balance

Save and borrow accounts

These are half and half accounts where you invest a fixed amount each month and can borrow up to 30 times that figure. See p. 14.

BUILDING SOCIETIES

Increasing competition between societies has resulted in a wide variation in the accounts they provide. Ask several building societies with branches near you what they have to offer.

Share account

interest rate	4%
interest paid	half yearly
tax	paid for you at basic rate
minimum investment	£1
maximum investment	no set limit
charges	nil
safety	investors' protection scheme
how to invest	at any building society branch, or by post or bank transfer
money tied up	instant withdrawals usually allowed of several hundred pounds; a few days for larger sums
cashing in	at any branch, or by post

Tiered account

Most building societies now pay higher rates of interest on larger sums within one savings account.

interest rate	5·75% to 7%
interest paid	half yearly or monthly
tax	paid for you at basic rate
minimum investment	£500 for lowest rate of interest; £25,000 for highest
maximum investment	varies according to society
charges	nil
safety	investors' protection scheme
how to invest	at any building society branch
money tied up	instant withdrawals allowed but sometimes with penalty
cashing in	money immediately available

High interest account

These offer higher interest rates in exchange for longer periods of notice.

interest	2·5% above basic; more for larger sums
interest paid	half yearly or monthly
tax	paid for you at basic rate
minimum investment	varies
maximum investment	no set limit
charges	nil
safety	investors' protection scheme

how to invest	at any branch or by post
money tied up	typically 90 days' notice to withdraw or immediate access with loss of interest on the amount withdrawn
cashing in	at any branch, or by post

Guaranteed premium account
By tying your money up for a long time you receive a guaranteed differential over the basic share rate of interest.

interest	7·5%; guaranteed 3·5% above share rate
interest paid	annually, or monthly with lower interest
tax	tax paid
minimum investment	varies £1000 to £10,000
maximum investment	none
charges	nil
safety	investors' protection scheme
how to invest	at any branch
money tied up	usually 90 days; sometimes one year
cashing in	at any branch

Cheque accounts
A few building societies offer these. Some are full current accounts including overdraft and standing orders; others deposit accounts with cheque book. The rate of interest is low but compare this with a bank account which pays no interest at all.

Save as you Earn (SAYE)
The terms are the same at all building societies but you can join only one scheme. You make monthly payments for five years and can leave the money for a further two years for an additional bonus.

interest rate	after five years, a bonus worth 14 months' savings (equal to 8·3%). After seven years, a bonus worth another 14 months' savings (equal to 8·6%)
tax	tax free
minimum investment	£1 a month
maximum investment	£20 a month
charges	nil
safety	investors' protection scheme
how to invest	at any branch or by post
money tied up	you can stop payments at any time. In the first year, you will receive no interest at all, but after that 6% on the amount you have paid in. 8% at investor's death
cashing in	at any branch, or by post

STOCK MARKET

Almost a quarter of the population now owns shares. This is a sharp increase since the Government started its privatisation programme with the British Telecom sell off in 1984.

The Stock Exchange suffered its own upheaval in October 1986, which was dubbed the 'Big Bang'. The divisions between stockbroker and stockjobber were broken down and there was no longer a fixed scale of commission rates.

Small investors were promised cheaper dealing charges but, in the event, this did not happen because minimum charges are now much higher. However, share buying and selling is being made more accessible to the new band of shareholders with the banks opening computerised dealing and a few building societies starting stockbroking services.

A year after Big Bang, many new shareholders and unit trust holders learned a lesson they will never forget. On that 'Black Monday' share prices crashed. The warning that prices can go down as well as up was reinforced in, for some people, a disastrous way.

Buying shares is a risky business and you should only invest spare money you will not need urgently. Your return on shares comes in two ways: income from dividends which a healthy company pays twice a year, and (hopefully) from an increase in the value of the shares, a capital gain.

Stockbroker services

You can pick varying degrees of service, depending on how much you want to get involved yourself in your portfolio of shares.

☐ dealing only: you tell the broker what to buy and sell, and when
☐ dealing and advice: the broker will make recommendations. This is more expensive
☐ discretionary portfolio management: you hand over your money and the broker makes all the decisions for you. This system suits the broker best
☐ non-discretionary portfolio management: for those who take an interest, the broker suggests what to buy and sell but discusses it with you first. Very expensive and only for large sums

Banks
Banks have their traditional service for wealthy customers but in addition they are starting to offer a simplified service for small shareholders.

Building societies
Some now offer a sharedealing service, straight buying and selling, in conjunction with a stockbroker. The society acts as intermediary but the customer can get advice direct from the stockbroker involved.

Share shops
Shares can now be bought in the high street along with the three-piece suite. Department stores such as Selfridges and Debenhams have turned part of their space into share shops.

Ordinary shares

dividend	depends on the success of the company
dividend paid	half yearly
tax	basic rate tax is deducted before you receive the dividend but can be reclaimed if you are not a taxpayer. If you pay higher rate tax, you will have to pay more. Capital gains tax is payable on the profit
minimum investment	around £1000 in each company to be worth while but it is better to spread several thousand pounds over a few different companies
maximum investment	none
charges	since Big Bang in October 1986, there has been no fixed commission structure so you need to shop around; expect between 0·5% and 1·65%. For small deals the most important figure is the minimum charge, usually around £20. Sometimes maximum of £100. Plus VAT. Also gap between buying and selling prices; you buy at the higher price. An 80p contract levy on deals over £1000; split 50p to SIB and 30p for the Takeover Panel. Stamp duty of 0·5%, rounded up to nearest 50p to pay on purchases only
safety	high risk
how to invest	through a stockbroker, bank manager or a few building societies
money tied up	you can get your money back within a couple of weeks if you are forced to sell but, of course, at the price ruling at the time
cashing in	will take a couple of weeks

(See also share option schemes p. 37.)

Personal Equity Plans (PEPs)
These first went on sale in January 1987. PEPs are a Government scheme to encourage more investors to take an interest in British companies.

Provided the rules are obeyed, shares bought through a PEP scheme are tax free. You can only buy one PEP a year, either as a lump sum investment or monthly.

Most plan managers make the investment decisions for you; more expensive ones allow you to choose your own shares. Money can only go into UK companies, but up to one quarter of the investment can buy unit trusts, regardless of where they invest.

dividend	same as shares but must be reinvested for tax relief
dividend paid	half yearly
tax	tax free at highest rate payable if not cashed in for one year
minimum investment	£25 a month; £300 a year
maximum investment	£250 a month; £3,000 a year
charges	initial: varies from nil to £50. Annual: around 1% + VAT. Dealing charges range from nil to 1·6%. 0·5% stamp duty
safety	risky like shares
how to invest	directly with plan manager or through investment adviser
money tied up	one calendar year
cashing in	can be charged for withdrawals

Gilts

These are gilt-edged stock issued by the Government to raise money. They are traded on the stock market with names such as Treasury 8 per cent 1992 or Exchequer 10½ per cent 1997.

Each one has a par value of £100 and you are guaranteed to get that back on the date mentioned in the title. But the actual cost will vary from day to day because the value is affected by the rate of interest, which is called the 'coupon'. This can be as low as 3 per cent or as high as 15 per cent.

There are two elements to the return from an investment in gilts: the interest rate and the difference in price between what you pay for the stock and the redemption value, that is the price you get at the end.

As well as the problem of choosing which gilt to buy, it is also important to get the timing right for the best chance of increasing your money. Professionals exercise their brainpower all day long worrying about this, but broadly the aim is to **buy gilts just before interest rates go down and to sell them just before interest rates rise.**

dividend	variable
dividend paid	half yearly
tax	income tax to pay but there is no capital gains tax.

	If you buy through the post office or TSB, the dividend is paid gross; if you buy through a stockbroker it is paid net
minimum investment	£250 to be worth while
maximum investment	none
charges	commission charges to pay for the small investor but they are lower if you buy through a post office. There the charge is £1 for investments up to £250, then £1 plus 50p for every extra £125. Selling costs are £1 for every £100 to £250 realised; below £100 the cost is 10p for every £10; over £250 it is £1 plus 50p for every additional £125. There is no stamp duty to pay and charges include VAT
safety	the nominal value is guaranteed at the date of maturity but the value of the investment can go up or down before the redemption date
how to invest	through a stockbroker or bank; a limited but broad selection is available on the National Savings stock register at the post office
money tied up	a few days to get back
cashing in	will take about a week from the same source as you bought

Index-linked gilts

These have a lower coupon than ordinary gilts, usually 2 or 2½ per cent, but at the redemption date you receive the nominal value plus an amount linked to the retail prices index which makes up for what inflation has taken away. It is the capital itself which is index-linked.

UNIT TRUSTS

Unit trusts spread the risk of investing in the stock market. Your money is added to everyone else's in the same fund and is managed by a professional fund manager. These are sold by specialist unit trust companies, insurance companies and banks.

There is still a risk because the value of units do go down as well as up, just as the price of shares on the stock market fluctuates.

There are too many unit trusts to choose from – over 1000 – ranging from all-purpose general funds to the highly specialised. There are even now brokers who specialise in unit trust advice.

For a beginner, the best advice is to go for a general fund, on the basis that the wider the fund manager can spread his investments, the smaller the risk.

One way of picking a fund is to look at the performance tables which were published in specialist magazines for previous years. But remember that, while a fund may come out top of the league one year, it may not do as well the next.

Unit trusts are essentially a medium- to long-term investment. There are charges involved in buying and selling, just as there are with stocks and shares, and your units need to rise 6% just to cover the costs.

Money in any fund is divided into small units of equal value. The prices are quoted on Saturdays in *The Guardian* but two different figures are given: one is the 'offer' price and the other the 'bid'. The offer price is what you will have to pay to buy the units; the bid price is lower and is what the company will pay to buy them back. The difference between the two, around 6%, is the amount which covers administration costs. Unit trust managers can choose how they price their units, provided the customer knows. They can:

☐ sell units at the next calculated price, which can be the following day
☐ sell at the previous price valuation, as they always used to
☐ use a mixture of both

This is far more confusing for the customer to know which price he will pay, or receive if he is selling.

As well as investing a lump sum in a unit trust, you can start a monthly savings plan; the minimum is £10 a month.

dividend	the dividend you will receive depends on how high a dividend the unit trust receives from the companies it has invested in
capital profit	the gain from an investment in unit trusts depends on how the price of the units has risen or fallen since you bought them
dividend paid	usually half yearly; the money can be paid to you or used to buy more units
tax	deducted but can be reclaimed; capital gains tax also to pay
minimum investment	at least £500 to be worth while
maximum investment	none
charges	initial charge 5%; annual charge 0·75% to 1%
safety	trust fund arrangement protects your money against fraud but the value can go up or down
how to invest	contact a particular unit trust direct or ask your bank manager, stockbroker, an insurance broker, or financial adviser
money tied up	immediate withdrawal possible but you

want to choose your timing to take best
advantage of the price

cashing in   same as investing

INVESTMENT TRUSTS

These are similar to unit trusts but there are certain important differences. You invest in the shares of an investment company whose business is buying and selling shares.

The value of your investment is not directly linked to the value of the investments that the company owns, as it would be with unit trusts, and generally the market price of the shares is worth less than this portfolio. This is why investment trust shares are often said to be traded at a 'discount'.

You can only buy an investment trust through a stockbroker, unless you have a regular monthly savings plan. These you can start direct with the company.

dividend	varies
dividend paid	half yearly
tax	basic rate is deducted before you receive the dividend but it is reclaimable; higher rate taxpayers will have to pay more
minimum investment	at least £1000 to be worth while
maximum investment	none
charges	same as buying on the stock market
safety	high risk
how to invest	through a stockbroker or bank manager. For more information contact the Association of Investment Trust Companies, address on p. 248
money tied up	couple of weeks
cashing in	couple of weeks

LOCAL AUTHORITY LOANS

Like the Government, local authorities need to raise money and one way is to take loans from the public (the other way is through the rates). Once fixed, the terms will not change during the period of the loan.

Fixed term loans

interest rate	varies daily, but comparable with high street banks; higher rates paid on very large sums (£15,000+)
interest paid	half yearly
tax	basic rate tax deducted and not reclaimable
minimum investment	around £500 to £1000

maximum investment	none
charges	none
safety	secure
how to invest	contact individual local authorities or Local Authority Loans Bureau (address on p. 249). There is a fee of £2.50 if you send a stamped addressed envelope for a list but the information is free if you telephone 01-407 2644
money tied up	for period of loan, one or two years
cashing in	at end of period only

Negotiable yearling bonds
These can be sold before the end of the period of the loan and operate very much in the same way as gilts.

interest rate	agreed each Wednesday for new issues; variable for bonds in issue
interest paid	half yearly
tax	income tax deducted but reclaimable; capital gains tax to pay
minimum investment	£1000
maximum investment	none
charges	stockbrokers' commission if you buy or sell in the market but none if you buy when the bonds are first issued and hold to redemption
safety	as with gilts
how to invest	through a bank or stockbroker
money tied up	no
cashing in	takes a couple of weeks

ETHICAL INVESTMENTS

A new group of funds has been set up to invest only in companies which have no association with the unacceptable elements of life. Indeed, they go further and look for companies with a proven record of benefiting the community and their employees.

They will not invest in companies connected with:

- ☐ South Africa
- ☐ tobacco
- ☐ alcohol
- ☐ armaments
- ☐ gambling
- ☐ nuclear processing
- ☐ fur trade
- ☐ experiments on animals

☐   repressive regimes
☐   bad pollution records

But if you feel strongly on a particular subject, read the small print. For example, some companies will not invest in supermarkets because they sell alcohol and tobacco, but others will. This narrows the fund manager's choice of investment but, so far, their performance is no worse than most.

For more information contact the Ethical Investment Research Information Services (EIRIS), address on p. 248.

FINANCE COMPANIES

These are usually subsidiaries of large UK or foreign banks and are commonly known as money shops. Make sure you know the parentage of any finance company before placing money with it.

Deposit account

interest rate	varies but probably about the same as banks
interest paid	quarterly or half yearly; sometimes only at the end of period
tax	interest paid net and tax not reclaimable
minimum investment	up to £50
maximum investment	none
charges	none
safety	first 75% of up to £10,000 guaranteed
how to invest	look for newspaper advertisements or write to Finance Houses Association
money tied up	three or six months
cashing in	at end of period only

ALTERNATIVE INVESTMENT

There is a myriad of artefacts under this heading: investing in gold coins, diamonds, wine, busted bonds, antiques, stamps, paintings, clocks, limited editions, silver, Persian rugs, or anything else you can think of that might increase in value after you have bought it.

These are investments best left to the experts. If you specially want to own, say, finely-printed second-hand books and enjoy seeing them on the shelf, then by all means buy. But if you are acquiring for the sole purpose of investing, then there are far surer ways of increasing the value of your money.

Some alternative investments are more accessible than others.

Gold coins

Gold producing countries have come to appreciate the attraction of selling it in the form of coins and most now mint their own.

In 1987, the UK created a new gold coin, the Britannia, with a face value of £100. It costs around £250 to £275 to buy although the price varies daily with the price of gold bullion. The Britannia is 22ct gold and sold in 1oz, ½oz, ¼oz and ⅒oz sizes. This is a troy ounce which is 10 per cent heavier than an ordinary ounce.

The most popular gold coin world-wide is the Canadian Maple-leaf, which toppled the krugerrand when imports of the South African coin were banned. The old UK coin is the Sovereign, which is still available. America produces the Eagle.

There is VAT to pay on purchases (unless you keep the coins stored offshore) but you cannot reclaim the VAT when you sell.

You buy gold coins through a coin dealer or high street bank.

Commodities

Commodity prices can show spectacular gyrations; so many of the factors affecting the price are beyond anyone's control: bad weather; a bumper crop; a political uprising; fluctuating exchange rates.

Commodities break down into two categories: the metals (such as copper, tin, lead, silver, zinc); and the soft (including coffee, rubber, wool, barley). The commodity markets trade in either physicals or futures: that is you either take delivery of the actual commodity or you buy for delivery at a future date, though in practice you never really take delivery.

You can join a syndicate and buy through a commodity broker but the best way for a small investor to start buying commodities is through commodity funds or specialist trusts: a unit trust, an investment trust, or an offshore commodity trust.

Currencies

The simplest way of investing in foreign currencies is to open a foreign currency deposit account at a bank, although the interest rate is low and charges are high. You can do this only when, as at present, there are no exchange controls.

Or you can put your money into a currency fund which will almost certainly be based offshore. Neither ties your money up for more than a few days.

A managed currency fund operates on the unit trust principle: your money buys units in a fund. The money is aggregated and used to buy and sell currencies. The minimum investment will be at least £1000 and you will have to pay charges at about the same rate as unit trusts charge: 5 per cent initially and about 1 per cent a year.

LIFE INSURANCE

You can take out a life insurance policy which will pay money to your dependants when you die, called term insurance. But you can also take out a different type of policy which is a long-term investment with life insurance included. This is an endowment policy.

There are other life insurance policies which are also used for savings: unit-linked insurance; annuities, which are a kind of pension; and various bonds.

There is no longer tax relief on the premiums for life insurance policies taken out since March 1984.

Endowment policies with-profits

interest rate	comes in the form of bonuses: regular (reversionary) bonuses which are added every year but fluctuate; and terminal bonuses determined when the policy matures. The size of bonus varies from company to company but it is not guaranteed by any of them
tax	income tax or capital gains tax is not generally payable on life insurance policies
minimum investment	£10 a month
maximum investment	none
charges	premium include fees
safety	fairly safe over long period and safer than unit linked
how to invest	contact an insurance company direct or ask an insurance broker to obtain quotations
money tied up	5 to 10 years
cashing in	you can but will get poor value; in the early years of the policy you may get nothing back. See p. 129 for an example of early surrender values

Unit-linked policies

Most of the premium you pay buys units in a fund of investments run by the insurance company.

interest rate	variable
interest paid	when you cash in the policy or die
tax	same as endowment policies
minimum investment	£10 to £50 a month
maximum investment	none
charges	premiums include fixed fee, about 5·5% and annual charge of around 0·75%
safety	riskier than with-profits
how to invest	same as endowment
money tied up	a few years
cashing in	you can but will get poor value if unit prices are low at the time

Annuities

This is a way of receiving extra money in retirement. An annuity is an investment of capital to receive a regular pay out. You can take out an 'immediate' annuity which starts paying straightaway or a 'deferred' annuity which begins at a later date.

How much you receive depends on how old you are when you take out the policy and what type of annuity you buy. There is no going back once you have bought an annuity; if interest rates improve, you are stuck with the rate at which you bought, but if rates fall you stay better off.

interest rate	variable but fixed when you sign the policy
interest paid	in form of pension when you retire continuing until you die
tax	interest content of pension is taxed as earned income; capital content is tax free
minimum investment	up to £1000 lump sum or £10 a month
maximum investment	none
charges	yes
safety	interest rate guaranteed
how to invest	as above
capital tied up	until you die
cashing in	not possible

Guaranteed growth or income bonds

A lump sum or single premium investment offering a guaranteed rate of interest. You invest your money for a fixed period of years and for a fixed rate of return. These bonds are often available for limited periods only.

While the interest on income bonds may be high, the capital does not increase, so will be eaten away by inflation.

interest rate	fixed at the outset, around 8% net
interest paid	annually for income bonds; on maturity for growth bonds
tax	tax paid at basic rate, higher rate taxpayers will have to pay more
minimum investment	£500 to £2500
maximum investment	none
charges	none built-in
safety	interest rate guaranteed
how to invest	as above
money tied up	one to ten years
cashing in	not possible until maturity

Managed funds

This is the insurance company's equivalent of a unit trust but has the ability to invest widely. They include a small element of life insurance.

Single premium bonds
These are constantly fighting for attention which is usually focused on unit trusts. They do not pay out an income and their only selling point is that you can withdraw 5 per cent each year without paying tax, making them more suitable for high rate tax payers.

Property bonds
These investments are less restricted than unit trusts but the principle is similar. Your money is paid to an insurance company which gives you a life insurance policy. The proceeds are invested in commercial property which is revalued monthly. Minimum investment £500 to £1000.

You may have to wait six months to get your money out.

Offshore investments
Some unit trusts and insurance companies have operated in tax havens outside the UK, or 'offshore', for some years. Now building societies are starting to open overseas.

Companies go offshore to avoid tax and this takes them to places such as Jersey, Guernsey, Isle of Man, the Bahamas, Cayman Islands and Luxembourg. Regulations are not as strict in these countries as they are in the UK so investors should check the company's credibility before passing over any money. Offshore companies are being brought into the net of the Financial Services Act but they are dragging way behind and are not authorised at the time of introducing the investor protection rules.

Offshore funds work like unit trusts and are mainly of use to British expatriates who are temporarily not subject to UK tax.

Home income plans
This is a way of raising money from your house when you are elderly. See pp. 111–14 for details.

Friendly societies
These have been under a cloud since they were cut back in the March 1984 Budget. See p. 129.

They are limited to handling only very small sums of money which makes it difficult for them to compete with other types of savings. A few more astute friendly societies are creating new inventive schemes.

Business Expansion Scheme
There is tax relief at your highest rate on investments in an approved Business Expansion Scheme (BES). You can invest between £500 and £40,000 a year in small, new unquoted UK companies.

This is a high risk investment and, for tax relief, you must hold the shares for at least five years. Some companies aggregate your money with others to invest in a spread of BES plans, but watch the charges for this. (See also p. 166.)

HOW YOUR SAVINGS GROW

If you save £20 a month:

	6%	7%	8%	9%	10%	11%	12%
after 12 months	£248	249	250	252	253	254	256
after 2 years	510	516	521	526	531	537	542
after 3 years	789	801	813	825	837	850	862
after 4 years	1084	1106	1128	1151	1174	1198	1222

If you invest a lump sum of £1000

	6%	7%	8%	9%	10%	11%	12%
after 12 months	£1061	1071	1082	1092	1103	1113	1124
after 2 years	1125	1147	1170	1192	1215	1239	1262
after 3 years	1194	1229	1265	1302	1340	1379	1418
after 4 years	1267	1317	1368	1422	1477	1534	1594
after 5 years	1344	1410	1480	1553	1629	1708	1791

CHAPTER · 4

BORROWING

Debt is no longer the dirty word it used to be and, certainly, using someone else's money instead of your own is an acceptable practice today. Indeed, if you are considered a good risk, you are positively encouraged to borrow.

But if you want or, in fact, need to borrow, obviously you want to do so on the best possible terms. Do not be fooled by deliberately misleading advertisements that say: 'only £5 a week to buy this three-piece suite', or '£10,000 no questions asked at 10 per cent per annum'. There is more to it than this and, anyway, this sort of wording is illegal. You need to know far more details before signing any agreement.

You should know:
- [ ] exactly how much you are going to pay each month
- [ ] for how long
- [ ] the terms for paying off the loan sooner than planned
- [ ] what the APR is
- [ ] whether you are allowed to miss one or more payments without penalty

The initials APR stand for annual percentage rate and this figure enables you to compare more precisely the rate you are paying. This is because it must include any hidden charges which the lender adds on. The sort of unseen extras that might be sneaked in are an arrangement fee for setting up the loan; the frequent calculation of interest; or the cost of insurance to cover you if you become unable to repay the loan.

Whenever you are applying for credit, you have the right to ask for a quotation. This will give you all the details of the terms of the agreement.

A 'flat' rate loan at 10 per cent can work out far more expensive than a 'true' rate of 10½ per cent. 'Flat' rate is the basic rate; 'true' rate means the same as APR.

So, remember always to look at the true rate of interest, or APR, rather than the flat rate. All lenders must by law show the APR whenever they mention interest rate figures.

By law, until you are 18 years old, you are not legally liable for your debts. So, in practice, you are unlikely to be given credit until you reach that age.

WHERE TO BORROW

There are various places you can go to ask for a loan and you should approach the cheapest and most appropriate one for you.

The questions to decide first are:
- [ ] how much you want to borrow
- [ ] how quickly do you want to pay it back
- [ ] how much you can afford to repay

If you want to borrow a large sum, the best buy is an insurance policy loan or a bank or building society loan.

For smaller amounts linked to buying a specific item, you can sometimes buy using a shop's own credit scheme or compare prices in a mail order catalogue. If you want the loan for a short time only, use a credit card or ask for an overdraft.

The best deal is an interest-free loan which some large stores offer from time to time. But check the price of the item first: you might still be able to buy it cheaper for cash elsewhere.

The places you will see offering loans are:
- [ ] a bank
- [ ] a building society
- [ ] a money shop
- [ ] money broker
- [ ] money lender

or you can borrow money against an insurance policy.

You can buy on credit with a credit card, on mail order, hire purchase, provident checks and using stores' own credit schemes.

Just how much you can, or want, to borrow depends on the circumstances. If you desperately want a motor bike and do not mind spending less money in the pub, then you will borrow as much as you need. But there is a point at which the lender will say NO you simply cannot afford this.

This is not a show of concern for your welfare, only with the likelihood of getting his money back.

With some loans you can claim tax relief: this occasion is mainly when you borrow money to buy a home. There is a limit to the amount on which you can claim tax relief and this is £30,000 including all the loans you have for the purpose.

For more details about home loans see Chapter 5: Buying Your Home.

BANK LOANS

The bank is the obvious place to start if you need a little extra money. The bank manager has several schemes to offer but it is his duty to make the best deal for the bank that he can. And what is a good deal for him is not necessarily the best for you.

Overdraft

The cheapest way of borrowing from a bank is by arranging an overdraft. It is also very flexible. There is no set interest rate at any bank – the manager makes up his mind about exactly how much to charge depending on how highly he values your custom. You can negotiate this but the rate will be somewhere between 3 and 5 per cent over bank base rate. Base rate itself is a flat annual rate, not an APR.

The beauty of an overdraft is that **you pay interest charges only when your ordinary bank account is in the red**. So, each time you pay in a cheque or receive your monthly salary, you swing back into credit for a time and do not pay interest. But you will have to pay cheque account charges while you are overdrawn.

Bank managers do not take kindly, however, if you help yourself to this facility. It is not 'your' money that you are taking but the 'bank's'. It is a courtesy, and a more likely way of succeeding in future, if you ask the manager first.

The request could be either for a specific amount over a limited period, or a regular agreement for you to spend more money than you have in the account. It is entirely up to the manager what he allows you to do. National Westminster Bank, followed by others, has created what it calls the Pink Credit Zone. This is a pre-arranged overdraft which is permanently available.

But, if you want to borrow money for a longer term, he will point you to a personal loan.

Personal loan

If you want to buy consumer goods, the bank manager will prefer you to take out a personal loan rather than an overdraft.

His argument for this is that with a personal loan you will know exactly where you stand each month and just how much money you have to repay.

The loan will probably be spread over two years and it will cost you more than an overdraft.

BUILDING SOCIETY LOANS

Building societies are no longer restricted to lending money only for buying or repairing houses. Just like banks, they can make personal loans for any purpose such as buying a car, going on holiday or paying for a hobby.

The maximum they can lend is £10,000, although in practice they usually set a limit of £5000 to £7500. You can borrow small sums down to £500.

The interest rates are very similar to those of the banks, although a few societies give a 2 per cent discount to long-standing customers.

With societies that have a cheque account, you can negotiate an overdraft. Unlike banks, building societies do not charge customers for cheques and standing orders, even when they are overdrawn.

As building societies become more experienced in this form of lending, they will branch out into new schemes, such as revolving credit.

Revolving credit

Many banks run schemes which offer continuous credit. You pay an agreed sum of money each month into a special account and in return you can borrow up to 30 times the monthly figure. No questions are asked about how you want to spend the money.

The money is paid into a separate bank account with a separate cheque book but you use your usual cheque guarantee card. Interest is charged at around 5 per cent over base rate when the account is in the red but you receive interest at a lower rate if you have built up a credit balance. You will pay a charge each time you write out a cheque.

Budget account

Only a few banks offer a budget account and they operate in different ways. Basically, you calculate how much you will spend in the coming year on all your foreseeable bills, add on the charge for running the account, divide by 12 and pay this amount each month into a special bank account with a separate cheque book.

In theory, you will be all square by the end of the year but, if not, you settle the difference. See p. 14.

Small business loans

For information see p. 166.

Impressing the bank manager

Really, all he cares about is that you will repay the loan when you say you will. Any other consideration is secondary.

The bank will use credit scoring (see p. 64) to assess your request; this gives less opportunity for impressing the manager.

It does not matter what you want the money for, as long as the purpose is legal. So, when deciding whether or not to let you have the loan the bank manager will be looking for a good track record.

Perhaps you have borrowed before and repaid a loan. Or you may have been saving regularly with the bank for some time. These are both very good points in your favour.

If you do not have any such proof of your reliability, having a monthly salary cheque paid into your current account is a good sign.

But, even without this, you can still convince a bank manager of your creditworthiness. Does your appearance matter? This will depend entirely on the bank manager. Some will expect you to look clean and tidy when you sit down on the imitation-leather visitor's chair.

Others, and probably the majority, **would rather see you in your normal work clothes, even if you have just come off a building site.** They are not misled by someone who has rushed home to change, hoping to impress with an uncharacteristically smart appearance.

Security

If the bank manager does not know you already when you approach him, he may ask for security for a loan. You may have thought it essential anyway, before asking for a loan, that you have something such as an insurance policy to offer the bank manager as a guarantee against the loan. But this is not so.

Banks do not like having to resort to selling a customer's personal belongings if you default on a debt. They would much rather make sure that the customer is creditworthy in the first place.

So, security becomes a very small consideration, unless you wanted an unusually large loan, when the bank might insist on your taking out a second mortgage on your home.

Never hesitate to ask your bank manager for a loan: he will always listen to a proposition. But, the better you have prepared your case for meeting repayments and organising your finances, the more likely he is to accede.

MONEY SHOPS

Not everyone wants to use a bank to raise a loan. Recognising this fact, some finance companies have set up shops in the high street to lend money and provide financial services for the individual in less forbidding surroundings.

These have become known as 'money shops'. Their aim is to be readily accessible to anyone wanting to borrow money and, in particular, to those who might be nervous about walking into one of the high street banks.

The names you will see in the street are subsidiaries of large organisations, sometimes foreign ones. The well-established money shops can be divided into two groups: those owned by a finance company and those owned by a bank. The names you are most likely to come across are: Avco; Beneficial Trust; Chartered Trust; Citibank; Forward Trust; HFC; and Western Trust and Savings.

Very often the parent is an American company. Money shops are better established in the United States and American banks are keen to export their expertise over here.

The loans available from money shops are very similar to those offered by the high street banks but the interest rates will be higher. There is a choice of unsecured personal loans, secured personal loans (usually a second mortgage) and revolving credit accounts which can include a cheque book and a cheque guarantee card.

The interest rate charged will vary from place to place but do watch the APR.

There will probably be a minimum amount you can borrow, say £1000, and a maximum. For very large loans you can negotiate the terms. Some money shops will also offer revolving credit schemes similar to those run by the big banks.

So, why should you borrow from a money shop when you can obtain cheaper loans from a bank? One advantage is that they are open all day Saturday and normal office hours during the week. Then, money shops specialise in dealing with individual customers only; they have no other business.

Many customers of money shops already have a bank account but choose to spread their borrowing further afield.

MONEY LENDERS

Someone who is having difficulty borrowing money may well consider going to a money lender. These people often place small advertisements in local newspapers and work within a limited geographical area.

The true interest rate will be high because he assumes the recognised lenders have already turned you down. The only reason that this would have happened is because they consider you a bad risk.

Think twice or three times before borrowing from a money lender because the interest rate you will be charged reflects the risk they are taking.

MONEY BROKERS

A money broker may be able to negotiate a loan for you when you yourself have failed. Unlike a money lender, he will not be lending you his own money, but he will charge you commission for his work.

The commission will be included in the APR figure which will almost certainly be extremely high. If you approach a money broker but decide in the end not to take the loan, you can still be charged a fee of up to £3.

LIFE INSURANCE POLICY

A less well-known way of borrowing is through an existing life insurance policy. The amount you can borrow will be a percentage of the surrender value of the policy and, of course, you will pay interest on the loan.

You may be able to borrow up to 90 per cent of the cash-in value of an endowment or whole life policy. You are unlikely to be able to borrow against a unit-linked policy.

This kind of borrowing is often used for emergency top-up funds but the loan can run for the life of the policy. You pay back only the interest while you are borrowing the money, as the capital sum will be deducted from the amount repaid to you when the policy matures.

The rate of interest you pay will vary from company to company. But, because there are no extra charges and the interest is payable half yearly, the APR will not be very much higher than the flat rate; there will be less than ½ per cent difference.

This makes borrowing against a life insurance policy a cheap option and an even better deal because you are repaying only interest out of your income, and none of the capital. The capital is reclaimed from the proceeds when the policy matures.

CREDIT SCHEMES

As well as borrowing money to buy goods, another way you can possess them immediately is to shop on credit. You pay for the goods in instalments over a period of months or years.

Credit Cards

There are two kinds of credit cards: those run by the banks or building societies and credit cards run by individual stores.

Bank credit cards

For small borrowings, credit cards are the easiest form and can, if used correctly, be free of interest charges. The credit cards in this country fall into two camps: the Mastercard run as Access by Midland, Lloyds, National Westminster, Royal Bank of Scotland, and Bank of Ireland. The other is the Visa card from Barclays (Barclaycard), the TSB (Trustcard), Girobank, Leeds Building Society, Yorkshire Bank, Bank of Scotland, Allied Irish and the Co-op Bank.

The interest rate is quoted monthly and the APR works out like this:

monthly rate %	APR %
1·5	19·56
1·75	23·14
2	26·82
2·25	30·62

There is an interest-free period before the first payment is due so, by paying off the whole bill, there is no charge at all. On average you will get about six weeks' free credit after buying the goods.

The amount you are allowed to borrow will depend on how much you can negotiate with the credit card company. If you really want to borrow up to the hilt, you could have both an Access and a Visa card. The individual limits range from £250 to over £1500 for most customers though the very rich are allowed to borrow tens of thousands of pounds. If you pay for goods or services by credit card and the goods are faulty or the service failed, the credit card company is jointly liable with the trader if the cost is between £100 and £30,000.

Stores' credit cards

The disadvantage of using a particular store's own card is that you are restricted to buying in that chain of shops. The shopkeepers love this. They claim that shoppers benefit by hearing about special promotions and they welcome the chance of tying customers to their stores.

The terms are more expensive than a bank's personal loan but about the same as Access or Barclaycard's APR. However, with many you do not have the advantage of a period of free credit.

Shops' revolving credit

This operates in a similar way to bank schemes. You pay a fixed amount each month and, in return, you can buy goods to the value of 20 or 30 times the monthly sum. As you pay off the debt you can buy more items and the retailer hopes that you will keep topping up your loan with new purchases.

There are also straightforward charge account loans and hire purchase or extended credit accounts.

OTHER WAYS TO BORROW
Hire purchase

If a store does not provide its own credit facilities, you can apply to a hire purchase company for a loan though it is more usual for the retailer selling the goods to arrange the HP loan for you.

The trader will be paid commission by the finance company for any loan signed up; garages often offer HP agreements. But you should make sure you know exactly how much the money is costing you: the terms of HP deals can range from being a reasonable way of borrowing to being extremely expensive.

Any goods you buy on HP do not legally become yours until you have finished paying for them. As the name suggests, you 'hire' the goods while you are repaying the loan.

You will have to pay a deposit and then make regular monthly repayments which include the interest charge. To be covered by law, the amount you borrow must be below £15,000.

If you do not keep up the repayments, the item can be repossessed because, legally, it still belongs to the HP company. But, once you have paid more than one-third of the full HP price, it has to obtain a court order to do so.

Mail order

This is a very well-advertised area of buying on credit. No interest is charged on purchases and repayments are spread over 20, 38 or 50 weeks. For expensive goods, you can pay over 100 weeks (or 150 weeks for televisions and videos) but in this case you will pay interest at about 25 per cent APR.

The prices charged by the catalogue companies can be higher than you would find in the shops but you receive the goods before you have to pay for them.

The advantage of buying by mail order is that you have the opportunity to choose goods in your own home which are then delivered to your front door. There is no delivery charge. Mail order agents are paid commission, even on their own purchases. The rate is about 10 per cent if they take the commission in cash or 12½ per cent if they take the value in goods. This cuts down the cost of the goods they buy. Also, when hire purchase restrictions are in force and credit is difficult to obtain, it is still easy to buy on mail order. Mail order repayments are sometimes made weekly though the trend is towards monthly settlement.

Trading checks

For those who can manage only weekly repayments, trading checks are available. This is a service aimed at people who can budget on a weekly timescale only. Agents call at your house on Thursday or Friday evenings, whichever is pay day, and collect the contribution.

In return, customers receive either a check or a voucher which they can spend in any shop accepting that particular company's scheme.

Checks are issued for small amounts of money, typically £20 and £50 and the money is repayable over 23 weeks. Trading vouchers are issued in specific amounts to buy an individual item at a named shop. The maximum is £1000 repayable over two years and the APR is about 50 per cent.

It is also possible to borrow sums of up to £1000 in cash from check traders. This is an expensive way of borrowing because of the high cost of collecting repayments.

The most expensive of all is a short-term loan. Often customers borrow over 13 weeks to pay the gas or electricity bill. **The APR for this sort of loan is over 100 per cent.**

Check trading is an expensive form of borrowing because of the cost of employing an agent to call every week; other lenders simply receive your cheque through the post or by banker's standing order. It is aimed at people who do not have bank accounts and who are unable to budget other than weekly.

Credit unions

These are groups of individuals who set up and organise their own savings and borrowing schemes. To form a credit union, you must have a common link, such as the area in which you live, your place of work, or some other association.

The weekly savings are pooled in a common fund, out of which members can borrow. The rate of interest is fixed at 1 per cent a month, an APR of 12·68 per cent, which means that monthly repayments work out at £6.50 for every £100 that you borrow for one year.

At the end of the credit union's year, 20 per cent of any surplus goes into reserves and the remainder is distributed to savers in proportion to their savings. The maximum that unions are allowed to distribute is 8 per cent but in practice the amount varies between 4½ and 6½ per cent.

The most that you can save in a credit union is £2000 and this would entitle you to the maximum borrowings of £4000. You can use the loan for whatever purpose you wish, and it is used most frequently for buying household goods.

There are two associations which help people set up credit unions: the Association of British Credit Unions and the National Federation of Credit Unions. See pp. 248 and 249 for addresses.

YOUR RIGHTS
Credit scoring

This is a widespread method of assessing someone's ability to repay a loan. Retailers, banks, credit cards or anyone else involved in lending are likely to use it.

Credit scoring takes the human element out of judging loan requests. You will fill out a questionnaire, just as you would anyway, but the questions are weighted. Depending on your answers, each question is awarded a certain number of points. At the end, the totals are added together: you pass if they are above a certain figure and fail if they are below another. If you fall between the two you may be given another chance – that means someone will look into your case.

It is not possible to get the better of credit scoring. It is more complicated than guessing which is obviously the 'best' way to answer the questions. Each company will have its own credit scoring system specially devised for that particular type of business.

If your request for credit is turned down, you can ask for a second chance but you have no right of appeal.

Credit reference agency

These are independent companies who keep files on individuals' credit-worthiness. When you approach someone for a loan they will probably refer your file to a credit reference agency even though they also use credit scoring.

But this system is not infallible and, if the information about you is incorrect, you are unlikely to find out. However, if someone has used an agency they must, if you ask, tell you.

You then have the right, for a fee of £1, to see your file and, if you find incorrect information, you can amend it. You are entitled to know what information a credit reference agency holds about you even if you have never applied for credit. See p. 250 for addresses.

Data Protection Act

Since November 1987, you have the right to look at any information held on a computer about you. This includes all credit and bank records. But it will cost £10 to see your file.

Consumer Credit Act

Borrowers' rights are protected by law under the Consumer Credit Act. This covers hire purchase agreements, credit card purchases, bank loans and loans arranged through an intermediary. But only loans between £100 and £30,000 come within the terms of this Act.

Now the Consumer Credit Act is fully in force, shoppers have a slight breathing space after signing an application in which to change their minds. The contract will not become legally binding until the lender has approved your application, which will probably be a few days after your first approach. Also, if you sign the form in your own home after a face to face interview, you will have a 'cooling off' period during which you will be able to change your mind about a loan, even if you have signed a document.

Except for a mortgage and a commitment made entirely by post or telephone, you will be able to back out of a deal within five days of signing an agreement and receiving the lender's copy which he has also signed.

Problems repaying

If you have any difficulty repaying a loan, you should tell the lender immediately. If it is a bank loan, it is in the bank's best interest as well as your own to help you through a difficult patch and the manager may be willing to negotiate a new, slower way of repaying the debt.

If you have bought the goods on credit, then all the company can do to get its money back is to sue you. But, if it is an HP agreement, the HP company can repossess the goods because, legally, they belong to him until you have paid for them completely.

If you have paid more than one-third of the total price, then the HP company will have to obtain a court order to repossess. If you have repaid less than one-third, he does not, though this still does not mean that he can enter your home without your permission.

CHAPTER 5

BUYING YOUR HOME

The process of buying a house is appalling: there are financial and legal hurdles to be overcome and you are unlikely to reach the finishing line without at least one stumble.

However, you can save yourself mishaps by going about the deal the right way and by being prepared for anything going wrong.

WHERE TO START

First, the two big decisions: find out how much you can afford and where you want to live. The choice of area may be determined by your work, or other commitments. But then again, you may have no restraints of any kind on where you live. Start by deciding as precisely as you can the area where you want to buy.

Whatever and however you are buying, do not rush into the process. There is rarely any need to make a hasty decision and you are far more likely to end up with the home of your dreams if you have thought through every aspect of choosing a house or flat with care.

Even if house prices appear to be rising every day, you will be better off taking a considered view. After all, the average person stays six years in a house before moving and you could be there for 20 years: a long time to live with a mistake for the sake of believing you will save a few hundred pounds at the beginning.

HOW MUCH CAN YOU AFFORD TO PAY?

Once you have an idea of house prices in the area of your choice, you can start to define the type of house you are looking for. There is always a gap between what you want and what you can afford, invariably you must scale down the first to meet the second.

You will have to take out a mortgage to raise the money and, as a rough guide to how much you will be able to borrow, multiply your gross earnings by 2·5. If you are buying jointly with someone else, the second salary can be taken into account. This applies whether it is husband and wife buying, or two friends.

At times when money is easily available, you can hope to borrow more than this. When money is tight, you may have to look longer to find it.

You should be able to borrow 85 to 95 per cent of the purchase price. On occasions when the banks and building societies have plenty of money to lend, you may be able to negotiate a 100 per cent mortgage. But you cannot rely on this happening because, as soon as their funds dwindle, this is the first facility to disappear.

One reason why building societies are usually reluctant to lend you all the money for the house is that you need show no commitment to the deal. If you have not put a penny of your own money into the transaction, they argue, then you are more likely to default on the repayments because you have nothing of your own to lose. If you have put down a 10 per cent deposit you are likely to think twice before jeopardising that money.

Another reason is that, when building societies are short of funds, it is a way of forcing you to invest with them first.

You will have to pay a 10 per cent deposit on the day you exchange contracts. Be extremely careful who you pay this money to. It is safe to hand the deposit to a solicitor, or an estate agent if he is a member of one of the professional associations. But never pay deposits to anyone else or you may not get your money back if the deal falls through before you complete.

If you do not have enough saved up for the deposit, try asking a generous relative, or the bank manager. You may be able to borrow it, but it will be expensive money. Alternatively, ask if you can pay a deposit of only 5 per cent instead.

Is it wise to commit yourself to every penny you have in the world to buy a house? To a degree, this depends on your temperament. Some people are quite happy to forgo holidays and clothes to buy a house while for others this would be too great a sacrifice.

But do remember that the mortgage repayments are only one element in the cost of buying a house. Before you can move in you may have to pay a valuation fee, a solicitor, removal firm, stamp duty and land registry fee.

Once you have settled in, there will be rates, redecorations, gas and electricity bills. You will soon discover how expensive houses are to maintain in good order. See Chapter 1 for details of how to budget.

THE COST OF BORROWING

Monthly repayments on a £30,000 loan with Mortgage Interest Relief at Source (MIRAS) at 25%

Mortgage rate %	20-year loan £	25-year loan £	30-year loan £
9	231.60	210.10	196.50
9·5	238.80	217.50	204.60
10	245.40	224.40	211.80

Mortgage rate %	20-year loan £	25-year loan £	30-year loan £
10·5	252.90	232.20	220.20
11	259.50	239.40	227.40
11·5	267.30	247.50	236.10
12	273.90	254.70	243.60
12·5	282.00	261.00	252.30
13	288.90	270.30	259.80
13·5	296.70	278.70	268.80
14	303.90	286.20	276.60

TAX RELIEF

The compensation for paying out large sums of money to buy a house is the tax relief you receive on the interest payments, up to a £30,000 loan. At present, for every pound you pay in interest charges, you receive tax relief at the highest tax rate you pay, which for most people is the basic rate of 25 per cent. Tax relief used to apply to the individual borrowing the money, therefore two unmarried people could both claim tax relief on £30,000. From August 1988 the relief applies to the house, so only one limit is allowed.

There are two occasions on which you can get tax relief on mortgage interest repayments and also avoid capital gains tax on more than one property:

☐   when moving
☐   on marrying or co-habiting

You can claim tax relief on two total mortgages, up to £30,000 each, when you **move house** and you have trouble selling the first. But you must be genuinely trying to sell and realise that the concession lasts for only 12 months from the date you move out. If you still have problems selling the house after a year, and can persuade the tax inspector that you are really trying, the time limit can be extended. You will not have to pay capital gains tax on either property for two years after you move out.

Then, if you **get married** and both of you have a house to sell, you can both claim tax relief on three homes up to a total of £90,000. Again, this concession lasts for one year and the capital gains tax concession for two years.

Since April 1983, tax relief at basic rate has automatically been deducted from the majority of repayments made to building societies. This is called Mortgage Interest Relief at Source (MIRAS).

Those with larger than £30,000 mortgages can still choose to receive tax relief on the first £30,000 through their PAYE. Higher rate tax-payers have only basic rate relief deducted by the lender; they have to negotiate with the taxman for the balance.

Gazumping

You may be unlucky and discover that, even if you have had an offer accepted by the vendor (seller), someone else comes along and makes a higher offer which is accepted. This practice is called gazumping, and it happens particularly when house prices are rising quickly.

There is nothing legally to stop anyone gazumping and even if contracts have been exchanged you cannot reclaim any expenses you have incurred. You can hope only that your vendor is someone with more integrity. The practice cannot happen in Scotland because of the tender system of house buying there.

WHERE TO FIND THE MONEY

Building societies and banks vie with each other to lend mortgages. They are now joined by new companies whose sole business is making home loans by a fast, telephone operation.

A number of insurance companies now offer mortgages direct to customers, or through brokers.

Be prepared to put in some solid groundwork at this point. There is no need to accept the first offer of a mortgage you receive; you can thank the AB Building Society very much but then go and see what the XY Building Society can offer and compare the terms. It depends on how easily available money is at the time.

There is less scope for picking and choosing when mortgages are harder to find, but you need never feel overly grateful for the loan. No one is doing you a favour. Banks and building societies are in the business of lending and you, the customer, are essential to this. Unfortunately, too many large institutions have lost sight of the fact and treat the customer almost as if they are doing him a favour instead of providing a service.

If you already have a building society savings account, then that society is the best place to ask for the loan first. You stand a much better chance of obtaining a mortgage from one that already holds your money. In fact, if you have enough savings you would do well to spread them around with several societies to improve your options.

Guaranteed mortgages

Some building societies and banks run schemes whereby, if you save a minimum amount of money for a period of usually two years, they guarantee to give you a mortgage when you want one. The amount they will lend is related to the sum you have saved.

Anyone who knows that they will be saving for a fixed time with the sole intention of buying a house could put at least some of their cash in one of these schemes, or register under the Government Homeloan scheme (see p. 70). But always check the rate of interest you are offered on your savings; it could be unacceptably lower than you would get elsewhere.

Make sure you ask the building society precisely what rate of interest it will charge you for the mortgage. The whole business is so competitive now that you might find a cheaper rate with a particularly aggressive society.

First-time buyers

First-time buyers might not think so at the time, but they are in a highly favoured position. Most lenders court the first-time buyer: one reason for this is that once they have you, you are more likely to go back to them for your next mortgage (and always remember that *they* make money out of *you*).

Builders, particularly those building estates, sometimes run promotions for first-time buyers, especially if the houses are not selling too well. They may offer to arrange a 100 per cent mortgage, or perhaps give you free kitchen equipment, or pay your conveyancing fees.

Some of the larger building firms have sales offices which will take the whole burden of buying off your shoulders. All you need to do is sign your name and the builder looks after the mortgage and the legal work. If you are not a first-time buyer, the builder may offer to buy your existing house from you. If he does, make sure he gives you the full market price, otherwise it is no bargain.

But, above all, remember that you get what you pay for and, while 'special offers' may seem attractive, the goods may have attractive packaging and little else. You will have paid for these extras in the price of the house but these elements, perhaps a fitted kitchen, a cooker or a refrigerator, will not rise in value as your house price increases. In fact, they become worthless and so the overall value of your house does not improve as much as you may expect.

Homeloan scheme

The Government has a scheme for first-time buyers called the Homeloan scheme. If you save at least £600 over two years with a building society or some other acceptable institution, you will get an interest-free loan of £600 and a tax-free bonus up to a maximum of £110.

To qualify, you must fill out a form HPA1 from the building society notifying it that you are joining this scheme. Also, the house you are buying must cost less than a fairly low maximum.

SHARED OWNERSHIP

A plan to help first-time buyers with insufficient money to own a house is 'shared ownership'. These schemes are run by some local councils, new town development corporations and housing associations.

To find out if there is a shared ownership scheme in your area, ask at your town hall, or if you live in a new town, write to the development corporation or contact the Housing Corporation, address on p. 249.

How it works

Shared ownership means that you own a portion of your house and rent the remainder. The scheme is designed for those who cannot afford to buy a house outright in the first place. Later, you have the opportunity to buy the rest of the house in tranches of, say, 10 per cent.

In the beginning you pay for a proportion of your house. This is commonly 50 per cent but can be any agreed amount, say 25 or 75 per cent. You take out a lease on the remaining proportion from the landlord which is the housing association or local authority.

You pay rent on the leased portion, just as you would if you were in a straightforward rented house. The rent can, as anywhere, rise over the years.

As the value of your house goes up, so the value of your share increases. Then, at any time you wish, you can either buy a further share of your house or buy all the remainder in one go. You will pay the market price operating at the time.

FOR MORE INFORMATION

There are many places where you can find information about buying a house. All the building societies will have their own printed leaflets while The Building Societies Association has various useful free booklets and the Royal Institution of Chartered Surveyors and the National House Building Council give free advice. Addresses on pp. 248–50.

WHEN YOU MIGHT HAVE DIFFICULTIES

A brand new house on an estate is a straightforward mortgage proposition. However, if this is not what you have in mind, there are some houses that can be difficult to mortgage.

For instance, if you have an urge to buy a derelict windmill standing on the edge of a cliff for conversion, you might have some difficulty finding someone foolish enough to lend money on it. The building society is not bothered that your square-edged furniture will not fit; but they do worry about being able to get their money back if you default.

Some societies will not lend on sub-standard older property and this has contributed to the decline of residential areas in many inner cities. Now the fashion is to revitalise these areas so you stand a better chance of being able to borrow on a run-down Victorian terraced house. Extremely old property in bad order is still hard to mortgage.

Similarly, if the house has a preservation order on it, this could cause you problems when it comes to finding a mortgage. Also, if you want to buy a flat with a short lease, or a house with a sitting tenant in part of it, you will have difficulty getting a mortgage.

WHAT TYPE OF MORTGAGE?

With the preliminaries out of the way, the next decision is: what sort of mortgage do I need? The basic choice is between a repayment and an endowment. Which is best for you depends on your circumstances.

Here is what to look for:

Repayment

This is the most straightforward kind of mortgage. You borrow so many thousand pounds at the going mortgage rate over a set number of years; each month you are repaying part of the capital you have borrowed and some of the interest.

You will probably repay the loan over 20 to 25 years for your first house. But there is no automatic life insurance cover to pay off the loan if you die early. If you have dependants who would suffer financially you can arrange this separately.

Since the introduction of Mortgage Interest Relief at Source (MIRAS), tax relief is granted at source through lower repayments to the building society. This is mostly done using a constant repayment system which means that your repayments stay the same (assuming there is no change in the interest rate) throughout the life of the loan.

The alternative method is increasing net repayments. By this method you will repay in the same pattern as under the old system when you received tax relief through your PAYE payments. Tax relief is allowed on the interest element of the payments only and, because in the early years you are repaying more interest than capital, you benefit from larger tax relief.

Increasing net repayments allow you to pay less in the early years of the mortgage. With constant repayments you will pay the same all the way through.

Endowment

Under this system you take out a life insurance policy which will mature on the same day as the mortgage is due for repayment and for exactly the right amount to meet the bill. If you die before the term is up, the mortgage will automatically be paid off.

Each month you pay the interest on the loan to the building society or bank and the premiums on the insurance policy to the insurance company. There is more than one kind of endowment mortgage. You can take out a low cost, a with-profits or a without-profits. If you have taken out a with-profits policy you will receive an additional cash lump sum at the end as well. One disadvantage of endowment mortgages is that, when interest rates rise, you do not have the option of extending the length of the loan as you do with a repayment mortgage; you must pay more.

Another problem can arise if you want to pay off the loan early. Endowment policies, like other insurance policies, have a poor early surrender value and you can lose heavily.

However, you can choose to keep the policy going, even though you no longer have a mortgage. And when you move house, you can transfer the same policy to your new home.

If you took out an endowment mortgage before the March 1984 Budget, you will be getting tax relief on the premiums you pay. This advantage was abolished in that Budget.

Low cost endowment mortgage

These were introduced when endowment mortgages were unpopular because of their expense. They work on the principle that, when the with-profits policy finally matures, there will be more than enough money to repay the loan.

So, you take out a policy for less than you will eventually need because, when the policy matures, it will have grown large enough with the profits added on to repay the debt. And, naturally, you are meanwhile paying smaller premiums because the amount insured is lower.

If, in the end, there is more than enough money, you will receive the bonuses as well. But, if there is not enough, then you will have to find the outstanding balance.

With-profits endowment mortgage

The premiums are higher for a with-profits policy, but at the end you will receive, hopefully, a large sum of money; exactly how much depends on how well your insurance company has invested.

If you have the money to spare, this is one way of saving but, if you are down to your last halfpennies, it will not be worth the struggle as you are trying to save at the same time as repaying the mortgage.

It may sound like a small fortune when you are promised £80,000 or whatever in bonuses, but, by the time the policy matures in 20 or 25 years, this will not be such a grand sum of money.

Without-profits endowment mortgage

The premiums for this policy are cheaper because, in theory, the policy will mature with exactly enough money to pay off the loan, leaving no excess to pay you a lump sum. They are less popular than with-profits policies.

Pension mortgages

These are becoming increasingly popular now new legislation allows more people to have their own pension. There is still highly attractive tax relief allowed on pensions even though it has been abolished for life insurance. The principle is roughly similar to endowment mortgages with the second element of repayments going towards a pension instead of life insurance.

At retirement the lump sum paid with the pension is used to repay the mortgage.

The mortgage comes in two parts, like an endowment loan. One repayment goes to the bank or building society; the other to an insurance company in the form of a pension policy. The advantage is the extra tax relief you receive at your highest rate on the premiums you pay towards the pension element. The contributions accumulate free of tax and at the end you get a tax-free lump sum.

When the pension policy matures, it pays off the lump sum outstanding on your loan and, it is to be hoped, has some money left over to pay you a pension. The drawback, obviously, is that the pension you get will be less than it would if you had not paid off the mortgage. So, be sure you have sufficient additional pension arrangements to provide for your old age.

Unit-linked mortgages

This works like a unit-linked life insurance policy. Your money is tied in with a fund of units which will go up and down with share prices. It is a riskier way of repaying the mortgage and, initially, building societies did not offer them. Now they do.

If the stock market rises dramatically, you might be able to pay off the mortgage early. But if it does badly, you might not have enough money to repay the mortgage when it is due.

The fund manager will be keeping an eye on your money and if, when you are getting close to repaying the mortgage, he thinks there will be too little in the fund, will ask you to pay more in premiums.

Fixed rate mortgages

These are available from time to time but you are taking a gamble about which way interest rates will move. If you believe rates are going up, then a fixed rate mortgage is a good buy. But you could find yourself stuck on a higher rate when everyone else is paying less. One thing you can be sure of, the bank or building society offering them will be confident that they do not lose out.

Most likely you would only be locked in to a fixed rate mortgage for three years or five at the most. Some only fix the rate for one year. Then you go on to a variable rate or a newly decided fixed rate.

Equity mortgage

Equity mortgages have been created to overcome the high cost of housing. It is a form of shared ownership in partnership with a bank or building society.

You buy 100 per cent of your new home but only pay interest on, say, 70 per cent. You pay no interest at all on the money you have borrowed for the remaining 30 per cent. However, when you sell the house, the lender who granted the equity mortgage and has an interest in the equity, takes 30 per cent of the increased value of the house. You have the option to take on full ownership if you can afford it, possibly after five years.

Topping-up a loan

Even with a 10 per cent deposit saved up and a loan from the building society, you may still be short of the total amount you need to buy your house. These last few hundred pounds are going to be the most difficult, and the most expensive, to raise.

But you can do it. Start with the family; a rich relative may be able to help with a short-term problem. Then, ask your building society or bank manager for a loan or, failing that, if your mortgage is a repayment kind, ask an insurance company for an endowment policy against which to borrow the remainder.

If you already have an endowment, you may be able to take out another. If you wish, you can take out an insurance policy for more than you exactly need to buy the house, the excess will be a bonus for you.

Joint mortgages

A husband and wife taking out a mortgage together should always register the property in both their names. If they do not, and the husband (or wife if it is in her name) dies, although the spouse should automatically inherit the home, there may be doubt.

If you are unmarried but living together, however permanently, the woman can lose her right to the house if she does not have a financial stake in it. So, in this situation it is crucial that she legally owns half the house.

Today, it is quite common for people, whether unmarried couples or two or three friends, to buy jointly. This is still a good way for people to launch themselves on the house market, or to buy a more expensive property than they could afford by themselves even though tax relief is now restricted to £30,000 maximum.

The most important factor is that everyone involved is aware of, and agreeable to, the conditions. These will usually say that, if one partner wants to sell, the other will have the opportunity to buy that share, or else the property will be put up for sale on the open market.

It is important for the two of you to agree the terms of occupation beforehand and draw up a proper legal document to provide for any later changes.

Difficulties

Even with a high level of unemployment very few people fail to meet their mortgage repayments. Payments to the mortgage lender take priority over any other commitment in most people's budgeting.

Anyone who finds himself in difficulty with mortgage payments should go and see the building society (or bank) manager straightaway. They will nearly always be understanding. If you are unlucky enough to have an unhelpful manager, go straight to the head office.

If necessary, the building society, or bank, can make arrangements for you to pay only the interest and not the capital part of what you owe for a time. You will catch up with the repayments later.

The manager would far rather do this than take repossession proceedings if you totally fail to make repayments.

If you are receiving income support, you cannot have the capital paid but that is the part you can ask the lender to postpone.

AIDS

Men wanting to buy a house together now find it more difficult to take out an endowment loan since insurance companies tightened up with AIDS-related questions. This does not affect repayment loans.

Paying off the mortgage early

You can pay off the mortgage earlier than you have agreed if you wish and you should not have to pay any penalty or extra money for doing so. At most there will be a small administration charge, say £15.

If you wish, you can pay off lump sums every now and then to reduce the overall cost and amount of interest you will pay in the long run.

WHAT TO LOOK FOR IN THE HOUSE YOU BUY

How do you go about choosing exactly the right house for you to buy? Especially with a first home, it is difficult to know just what will suit you.

People go about buying houses in a ridiculous fashion. You spend a couple of hours poring over the estate agent's handout, or you simply read a newspaper advertisement, which gives you only a general idea of what the house is really like; then you spend maybe half an hour looking over a house, to which you are about to commit every penny you have in the world.

If you were buying a new car, you would at the very least go for a drive in it. But you cannot live in a house for a few weeks to make sure it suits you before deciding whether or not to buy.

To help make up your mind ask yourself these questions:
- [ ] is it freehold or leasehold?
- [ ] if it is leasehold, will there still be a reasonably long lease left for you to sell in a few years' time and will it be mortgagable?
- [ ] are there any restrictions in the lease that might be an irritation?
- [ ] is it new or second hand? new houses tend to be further away from town centres but there is no risk of being caught in a chain of sellers.
- [ ] does the house have enough room for your future use?
- [ ] is there a garden and is it large enough? or too large?
- [ ] is there a garage large enough for your car?

☐ does the sun come into the house? if it is a gloomy house, the direction of the sun is one thing you cannot change.

☐ do you have to share a driveway with a neighbour?

☐ is there room to build an extension should you need to?

☐ are the boundaries clearly defined?

☐ will the house be expensive to heat?

☐ how much are the rates?

☐ does the house have main drainage?

☐ are there likely to be any unusual costs involved with this particular house, such as the upkeep of a thatched roof?

☐ does it need rewiring or replumbing?

☐ can you, and visitors, park your car easily?

☐ does a neighbour's tree overhang, and overshadow, your property?

☐ is the street very busy or noisy?

☐ is there water nearby that could be a hazard to your children?

☐ are there other children around for yours to play with?

☐ what are the neighbours like? as far as you can tell, are they likely to be compatible?

☐ are there schools nearby?

☐ are the shops conveniently close?

☐ is there a bus stop or railway station close by?

☐ will you be able to find work in the area?

☐ can you commute fairly easily?

☐ is it close to a factory which might throw out noxious fumes?

☐ is there a noisy playground nearby?

☐ is the view likely to change?

☐ the house may have eccentricities that appeal to you, but will it be difficult to sell?

☐ is the area safe for your animals? and what about the neighbours' animals?

☐ does the house feel comfortable?

☐ are there any building works or road building planned for the area?

☐ if it is a flat, who is responsible for the maintenance of the structure of the building?

Do-it-yourself conveyancing

If you sold one house for £30,000 and bought another for exactly the same amount, the move could cost you £2000. You can save a great deal of that money by doing the legal work yourself. It is quite feasible to do your own conveyancing. Solicitors reckon it is about eight hours' work.

Conveyancing simply means transferring a property from one ownership to another. And there are just two basic premises that are important: if you are selling, you want to be sure you get the money; if you are buying, you want to be sure you can move in.

There are two types of conveyancing: one for registered land and another for unregistered land. To find out which you have, contact your local land registry office.

If you do decide to have a go at conveyancing yourself, buy a good guidebook. You can buy the forms you need for about £5.

Licensed conveyancers

Solicitors no longer have a monopoly on conveyancing. A new but still small category of licensed conveyancers are now in business who do not need legal training although they must be authorised.

They usually offer a cheaper service than solicitors, although these are cutting their prices to compete. But ask if there will be any extras not quoted in the basic fee before going ahead. And make sure they are registered with the Council for Licensed Conveyancers, and a member of the trade association, National Association of Conveyancers. Addresses on pp. 248 and 249.

THE SOLICITOR

A solicitor will charge you up to 1 per cent of the purchase price for conveyancing if you are buying and a further 1 per cent if you are selling as well.

Because of the new competition solicitors are facing, costs have fallen by about one-third in the past couple of years.

There is a minimum charge of around £150.

For this, he will:
- [ ] draw up a draft contract
- [ ] act as stakeholder for the deposit (he keeps any interest that accrues on the money)
- [ ] send a list of questions for the seller to answer
- [ ] conduct local authority searches
- [ ] conduct bankruptcy searches
- [ ] check that the property is registered
- [ ] check the lease if there is one
- [ ] can act for the building society as well and draw up the mortgage deed
- [ ] make sure any stamp duty is paid
- [ ] make sure the money arrives on completion day

Building society's solicitor

The solicitor who acts for the building society will charge according to a guideline scale of fees. But, whatever it is, you are the one who pays.

Your own solicitor can act for the building society as well, in which case the fee is lower.

Example fees, to which VAT must be added:

Mortgage	Fee
£10,000	£78.75
£15,000	£93.75
£25,000	£108.75
£30,000	£112.50
£35,000	£114.38
above £35,000	add 75p for each £5000

Searches
The solicitor writes to the local authority to ask if a motorway or any other nasty is planned in the vicinity. This takes many weeks and can hold up the sale. If this is happening to you, telephone the local authority yourself, explain the problem and they may give your application priority.

Choosing a solicitor
☐ ask friends, neighbours and colleagues for recommendations
☐ ask your building society or bank manager for suggestions
☐ the Law Society keeps a list of solicitors in each locality
☐ Citizens Advice Bureaux have lists
☐ ask for an estimate of the bill; there is no set scale of charges for conveyancing. Remember you will have to pay VAT on top.

OTHER COSTS YOU WILL HAVE TO FACE
There is growing competition between banks, building societies and insurance companies to sell houses and grant mortgages. The traditional concept of home loans is beginning to change. It should make house buying cheaper.

Stamp duty
On any house you buy costing more than £30,000, you will have to pay a tax called stamp duty. The rate is 1 per cent of the price of a house over £30,000.

You pay stamp duty only on the price you pay for the house itself; if the money includes carpets and curtains, or any other fitments, you do not pay duty on those.

Land registry fee
When property changes hands in some parts of the country, mainly urban areas, it is recorded on a land registry.

You will have to pay a fee whether the house you are buying is registered or not. But the cost of each is different.

There is no VAT to add:

Purchase price	First registration	Subsequent registrations
£	£	£
0–15,000	20	20
15,001–20,000	25	25
20,001–25,000	30	30
25,001–30,000	35	40
30,001–35,000	40	50
35,001–40,000	50	60
40,001–45,000	60	70
45,001–50,000	70	80
50,001–60,000	80	90
60,001–70,000	90	100
70,001–80,000	100	125
80,001–90,000	110	150
90,001–100,000	120	175
100,001–150,000	140	200
150,001–200,000	160	225

THE SURVEYOR

Whether or not you employ your own surveyor to look over the house, you will have to pay the building society's valuer. He inspects the house you are buying to make sure it is adequate security for the building society. This is called a valuation inspection.

It is not his worry if you are paying twice as much as he thinks the house is worth, though his report will show what he considers a fair market value.

This is a rough guide to what the building society's valuation report will cost. You will need to add on VAT.

Purchase price	Fee
£	£
20,000 to 25,000	45
25,000 to 30,000	50
30,000 to 40,000	55
40,000 to 50,000	60
50,000 to 60,000	65
60,000 to 70,000	70
70,000 to 80,000	75
80,000 to 90,000	85

It is not safe to rely on a valuation inspection because this tells you very little. You can pay for your own separate surveyor to provide you with a full structural survey and this will cost about £250.

Building societies have relaxed their rules on their own valuation reports. They now allow you to see a copy of their valuer's report (previously they would not, even though you were the one who had to pay for it). Some societies will now give you the choice of a valuation survey or, more expensive, a structural survey which you can keep. This saves duplication of effort.

Many societies offer 'half and half' surveys which are combined valuation and structural surveys. The Royal Institution of Chartered Surveyors has a prepared form which provides a reasonably-priced survey and valuation for both house and flat buyers. This is called the 'report and valuation scheme' and gives a concise report on the state of the property you are buying and a valuation.

Do you need a separate survey?

If you are buying a brand new house, it will be covered by the National House Building Council's ten-year guarantee. However, there would have to be a major structural fault for you to be able to claim anything after the first two years.

During those two years, the builder has to put right any defects; after that it is the NHBC's responsibility but only for serious faults.

With older property it is advisable to pay for a survey. Then, if the house falls down from dry rot the day you move in, and the surveyor had failed to notice it, you could sue the surveyor for negligence. But in less severe cases this would not be worth while. A good surveyor should pick up both existing problems and potential ones to warn you about. He will give you an idea of how much it is going to cost to put right.

Do not expect a clean bill of health from a surveyor. You are paying him to find out what is wrong and you want to know the worst. It is not his job to tell you the good points about the house. You may be horrified to hear of rot and woodworm and leaking roofs but these defects are quite common in older properties.

And, whatever you do, **do not ask the estate agent who is selling you the house to survey it for you.** His responsibility is to the person paying him to sell the house, not to you.

If you are having a full survey, the surveyor will give an opinion on the price you are paying; inspect the surface areas; and lift the floorboards if they are loose. But he will not look at anything that is fixed, covered, unexposed or inaccessible; he will look only at exposed woodwork.

If you ask (and pay extra) he will undertake a drains test.

His report is confidential to you: it will not be shown to the vendor. The report should include comments on:

- [ ] roof structure (as far as he can see it)
- [ ] gutters
- [ ] pipes
- [ ] damp-proof course
- [ ] walls
- [ ] brickwork
- [ ] pointing
- [ ] rendering
- [ ] dampness
- [ ] water tanks
- [ ] insulation
- [ ] partitions
- [ ] floorboards where he can see them
- [ ] plaster work
- [ ] windows
- [ ] doors
- [ ] fittings
- [ ] chimneys
- [ ] fireplaces
- [ ] ventilation
- [ ] plumbing
- [ ] gas and electric central heating

Choosing a surveyor

- [ ] ask your building society if its surveyor can do the work
- [ ] ring the Information Centre at the Royal Institution of Chartered Surveyors (address on p. 250) for names of qualified surveyors in your area
- [ ] ask your solicitor or bank manager to recommend one
- [ ] ask for an estimate of the fee – there is no set scale
- [ ] ask if the surveyor carries indemnity insurance

BUILDINGS INSURANCE

The bank or building society will arrange this for you from a limited list of insurance companies. Or you can make your own arrangements. There will be an additional fee of about £20 if you choose a company not on their list.

Increasingly, banks and building societies are bringing out their own brand house and contents insurance policies. Just like Sainsbury's cornflakes, they are made by a well known company for the building society to put its own name on. Some of the banks have their own insurance company.

Very often, these policies are good value because the institution can use its muscle to negotiate favourable terms. And then, if you have a claim, you can leave the bank or building society to do all the negotiating with the insurance company. See also pp. 121–2.

MAKING AN OFFER

1. If the house is being sold through an estate agent, make the offer through him. This saves the embarrassment of bargaining.
2. Decide in your own mind exactly how much you are prepared to offer.
3. Offer less than this. If you are not sure how much, 10 per cent is a reasonable starting point.
4. If the offer is rejected, the seller may indicate what he will accept. Otherwise, make a slightly higher offer.
5. The point comes when you must either agree a price or forget the whole thing.
6. Ask whether carpets, curtains and any other accessories are included in the price.
7. It is advisable to get an inventory of exactly what will be left behind, whether it is included in the price or you are buying separately.
8. Once the price is agreed, instruct a surveyor.
9. If your offer is accepted, ask the vendor if he will take the house off the market for a few weeks at least, to avoid your being gazumped. A vendor is under no obligation to do so, but it will show goodwill on his part. It is particularly worth while when the vendor has instructed two agents to act for him; the one who has not made the provisional sale will be tempted to find an alternative buyer, at a higher price, to earn his fee.

If you are not dealing through an estate agent, the same basic rules apply, but be sure, when you are making any offer, whether written or verbal, that you say it is 'subject to contract'.

You may be asked by the estate agent to put down a small deposit at this stage to 'show good faith'. This will be returned if the deal does not go through. There is no need to pay this deposit, unless the agent threatens you will lose the house to someone else and you believe him. This practice is not allowed in Scotland.

This deposit is held by the estate agent as 'stakeholder' and he will put it on deposit somewhere to earn interest. If the deal falls through and your money is returned, you will not be given the interest: the estate agent keeps it.

When contracts are exchanged, you will have to pay the vendor a deposit of 10 per cent of the purchase price. This sum should be held by his solicitor as stakeholder.

BUYING A FLAT

There are different and extra problems to bear in mind if you are buying a flat. It is essential to be aware of these.

Leasehold

Invariably, any flat you buy will be leasehold: you buy a lease which has a certain number of years left to expire and at the end of that period your right to live in the property also runs out.

By law, if this happens you must be given the opportunity to take out another lease, but this will involve spending a large sum of money, almost equivalent to the freehold price, all over again. In some cases, the right to a new lease might be opposed by the freeholder, or it might be offered subject to new conditions.

Look carefully at the length of lease left to run. Generally, building societies will not give you a mortgage if the lease has less than 20 years to run after you have paid off the mortgage. So, to get a 25-year mortgage, the lease must have at least 45 years left to run.

You might think that a 60-year lease is quite long enough when you buy. But think what will happen when you come to sell. Will any prospective buyers be able to get a mortgage then?

Even leases of only three years are marketable – but at a price. The price by then will be very deeply discounted and open to cash buyers only. As with any other cash deal, the buyer will expect to knock you down.

Sometimes houses are sold leasehold rather than freehold, in which case the same terms apply. But, usually, you will buy the freehold of a house, which means that it is yours forever.

There are some freehold flats around, but be wary of these and do not buy one without detailed advice.

Ground rent

You will have to pay this to the landlord. This could be a small sum, say £5 a year, or it may be more, around £500. You pay it to the landlord so that he retains his right to the freehold.

Service charges

The biggest bugbear of a leasehold property is the service charge. You must be sure that you understand exactly what you are getting for your money.

It could be very little or it could include cleaning communal areas, hot water and porterage. You may find you have to pay extra every time the outside needs repainting. Or the service charge may include a provision for a 'sinking fund' which builds up to meet the large exceptional bills.

As all flats in a block pay an equal service charge, depending on the size of your flat, the expense works out fairly. The person in the basement contributes to a new roof and the person on the top floor pays towards flood damage down below; the person on the ground floor contributes to the maintenance of the lift.

You have no control over the service charges, which can rise every year, and you will have to pay the bill. Make sure you know who is responsible for paying for what.

Insurance

The building should be insured by the freeholder. See pp. 115–21. You need to insure your personal possessions separately.

BUYING A COUNCIL HOUSE

If you are a council tenant, you have the right to buy the house you live in. If you do, you will be able to do so at a discount to the market price. This is up to 60 per cent for a house and 70 per cent for a flat.

Anyone who has been a council tenant for three years has the right to buy and the discount increases depending on how long you have lived in the house. But you have to repay part of the discount if you resell within three years of buying.

The first thing to do is to ask the landlord, that is the local authority or housing association, for a Right to Buy claim and read the Department of the Environment's Housing Booklet form.

If you live in a house you can buy the freehold; if it is a flat you can buy a lease. You can borrow money towards the cost of buying from a building society, the same way as you would if you were buying any other house.

MOBILE HOMES

'Mobile homes' is a misnomer. The one thing they do not do is move, although by definition they must be capable of being moved. But, if you own a mobile home or caravan and rent the pitch from a landlord, you are protected by improved legislation, which gives greater security and safety.

To start with, anyone living in a mobile home must have a written agreement with the owner of the site. In this, the owner must tell the resident:

☐ the name and address of the site owner
☐ the name and address of the resident
☐ the date the agreement begins
☐ a description of the pitch
☐ how permanent his interest in the land is
☐ the terms of the agreement

He must also give details of the pitch fees and any other charges.

A resident is entitled to stay on the site as long as he wants, unless the written agreement specifies that the owner's planning permission will run out. A resident can end the agreement by giving four weeks' notice to the landlord, but the site owner has to apply to a court to remove a resident. Even then he can do so only if:

☐ the mobile home is not the main residence of the occupier
☐ the condition of the mobile home is detrimental to the site
☐ the resident has refused to comply with the terms of the agreement

You can sell a mobile home that you own and pass the agreement on to the new occupier, but the site owner can claim a commission, up to a maximum of 10 per cent of the price. But, if you transfer the home to a member of your family, no commission is payable.

If a resident dies, the widow, widower, or any member of the family who was living there at the time of death can inherit. People living together but who are unmarried count as husband and wife.

The site owner must have a licence and must obey the rules about the number of homes on a site, the landscaping, fire precautions, and health and safety.

Anyone who rents a mobile home is not covered by the Mobile Homes Act 1983, but will have the same protection as other tenants under the Rent Acts. The Mobile Homes Act does not apply to people who use the caravan for holidays only.

THE COST OF SELLING A £30,000 HOUSE IN THE UK

	£		£
Estate agent's fee	600	plus VAT	690
Solicitor's fee	260	plus VAT	322
			£1012

The average selling cost will be between 3 and 4 per cent of the price of the house.

THE COST OF BUYING A £30,000 HOUSE WITH A £20,000 MORTGAGE

	£		£
Mortgage arrangement fee (only to a bank)	75	plus VAT	86.25
Solicitor's bill	260	plus VAT	322.00
Land registry fee	40	no VAT	40.00
Surveyor	200	plus VAT	230.00
Building society's surveyor	45	plus VAT	51.75
Building society's solicitor	112.50	plus VAT	129.37
Mortgage indemnity insurance	80	no VAT	80.00
Building insurance premium	50	no VAT	50.00
			£989.37

The average buying cost will range from 2·5 per cent to nearly 4 per cent of the price of the house.

BUYING A HOUSE IN SCOTLAND

The Scottish system of buying a house is quite different from the English and Welsh. If you want to buy a house in Scotland, you put in a tender and, once this has been accepted, then both you as the buyer and the seller are legally bound to go ahead with the deal. You know that the house is yours so you cannot be gazumped or let down at the last minute.

The process starts off the same way: you see a house advertised that you think you might like, you arrange to view it and, if you decide you are interested, you instruct a surveyor to check it over.

At this stage, if ten people are interested in buying the same property, there will be ten surveyors' reports. Meanwhile, you instruct a solicitor who satisfies himself that you will have the funds to buy the place should your offer be successful.

At the same time, the building society sends its own surveyor round. If, after seeing the surveyor's report you want to buy the house, you write down how much you are willing to pay and hand this to your solicitor.

The vendor's solicitor then announces the closing date on which all offers will be opened and the vendor chooses which offer he or she finds most acceptable. This is usually the highest but, if that one is hedged about with unacceptable conditions, the vendor may choose another.

At this point the two sides agree the completion date, usually two months' hence, which in Scotland is called the entry date, and both sides are committed to going ahead with the transaction.

However, the practice in Scotland is slipping a little. For example, you can agree with someone privately that you will accept a certain offer.

And there is no legal reason why the Scottish system should not be used in England and Wales. You need only to find a solicitor and estate agent to co-operate.

Libor linked loans are starting to make an appearance, even from a few building societies. Libor stands for London Inter Bank Offered Rate and is the rate of interest which banks charge each other.

The interest rate will be between 1 per cent and 1.5 per cent above Libor, varying according to the lender. A Libor loan has a variable interest rate, the opposite of the usual mortgage.

The interest rate you pay for the loan changes each month, or quarter, as Libor moves, either up or down. Payments will be adjusted once a year.

CHAPTER · 6

HOW TO SELL A HOUSE

Selling an £80,000 house could cost you £2000 in estate agent's and solicitor's fees. Or you could do the whole job yourself. You will find yourself involved in much of the work anyway.

When you are selling and buying a house at the same time, you have to perform a balancing act requiring delicate timing. To complete both transactions on the same day so that (a) you have the money to buy your new house and (b) are not homeless, will seem impossible, especially if you have been caught up in a long chain of buyers and sellers all trying to stay on the same tightrope.

But, once you have decided to move, you will want to know if you should try to sell the old house first, or commit yourself to buying a new one and then start selling? This chicken and egg question really depends on the house market at the time, and on the sheer chance of finding the right house and the right buyer.

You can go about selling in two ways. You can simply put the whole matter into the hands of an estate agent (or several), or you can sell your house yourself.

ESTATE AGENTS

You do not need an estate agent to sell a house for you, but you may not have the time to do the job yourself. What the estate agent offers is a list of names of people looking for a house like yours. He will advise you on the price you should be asking but if you do a little research on local prices yourself, you will get a pretty good idea of the value.

He may show prospective buyers round the house for you or he may just arrange the appointment and leave you to take them round. He should also conduct the embarrassing haggling over price, though often you will find it more efficient to talk directly with the buyer yourself.

Estate agents charge around 2 per cent (plus VAT) of the selling price. The range is from 1½ to 3 per cent varying around the country. You might pay 1½ per cent plus the cost of advertising in the North and 3 per cent for an expensive property in London. **The fee is negotiable and you can bargain with an agent before giving him the contract.**

An estate agent should:
- [ ] put a market value on the house; you can ask a number of different agents to do this without committing yourself
- [ ] provide particulars and photographs of the property
- [ ] keep tracks on all offers that are made
- [ ] make enquiries about the buyer's finances, for example, to find out if he has a mortgage arranged
- [ ] offer advice on the buyer's survey report and renegotiate price
- [ ] show prospective buyers around if the vendor is at work during the day
- [ ] can help arrange mortgage if necessary
- [ ] advise on repairs that may be necessary before the property is sold

If you give the estate agent 'sole agency', he will charge you a lower commission. Sole agency means that he is the only person who can sell your house for you. But make sure you do not give him 'sole selling rights'. With sole agency, if in the end you sold the house to a friend without going through the estate agent, he has lost his fee. But if he has sole selling rights, he could claim the fee even if you sold the house to your mother.

Often he will ask for sole agency for a limited period of time. The fee will then be about ½ per cent lower. After about six weeks, he subcontracts the particulars to other local agents who will receive an even lower fee from him if they sell it for you. These secondary agents will not be terribly enthusiastic about putting much effort into selling your house.

He may charge you for advertising in local newspapers, but you should be told that this will happen before agreeing terms. If the fee is high to start with, you should challenge any extra payments, or shop around.

There are private house selling agencies springing up around the country. You pay a fixed fee (about £100) to the company which puts details of your house, provided by you, on to a computer. The details are matched up with potential buyers and the two of you sort out the deal. Your house details stay on the file, at no extra cost, until your house is sold. You will find the agencies advertising in local newspapers.

SELLING THE HOUSE YOURSELF
If you want to sell the house yourself, first you can put up a notice board outside inviting buyers to look around. But be careful who you allow to come in if you are alone in the house. Then, put a postcard in the local newsagent's window which is a minimal cost. Finally, put an advertisement in the local newspaper. You may need to advertise for several weeks and the cost of this will mount up.

If you are not sure what price tag to put on your house, look around the local estate agents to see what they are asking for similar properties and check the local newspaper. You can soon get a feel for local prices and, if you are having difficulty selling the house, you can always reduce the asking price.

Making your house attractive

Silly as it seems, prospective buyers are vastly impressed by a neat and tidy house. In winter make sure the house is comfortably warm and in summer, fresh and airy. By putting a lot of hard work into maintaining an unnatural tidiness (and bribing the children to do the same) you can give the appearance of living in an easy to run, effortless house.

If the house and garden are full of mess and rubbish, a buyer will think this is a very difficult house to look after. An American tip is to place a vanilla pod or coffee beans under the grill just before the viewers arrive. They will smell a delicious aroma of home cooking but see no sign of dirty pans and dishes. Their subconscious will tell them that this is a happy, contented, down to earth home requiring no effort. Anyway, that is the theory.

The extras

You may be tempted to install double glazing or central heating to add to the value of your house. These extra refinements will not necessarily increase the value of your home, though they might make it easier to sell if the market is slow. But, if you are just on the point of moving, it is a bit late to start home improvements — even worse is to have the house in a mess while people are looking around.

Remember the importance of first impressions: it could be worth painting the front door a bright cheerful colour to entice viewers inside.

Your responsibilities

You do not have to volunteer any information to prospective buyers. You may be moving out because the next-door-neighbours have noisy parties every night, but you do not have to say so, unless asked.

You must answer truthfully any questions you are asked, for example about the state of the roof, the condition of the drains or whatever. You can be a little less categoric about the neighbours and to the straight question 'why are you moving?' you will, honestly, be able to give several answers. **The less said the better.**

Bargaining

You will be lucky if someone offers you exactly the price you are asking unless you have priced the property too low. Buyers naturally want to pay as little as possible. From the outset, have a figure in mind that you know you will accept and below which you will not go. Then you can go ahead and bargain confidently.

Fixtures and fittings

There are grey areas here and you should not leave any doubt about what you are taking and what you are leaving behind. Prepare a typed list and see that your solicitor includes it in the contract. If you intend leaving the carpets and curtains behind, this is a good selling point. Or if you do not mention them in the first place, you can use them as a bargaining point later.

When you have reached a final agreement with a buyer, write down exactly what you intend to take with you. Among the items that could be in doubt are shelves, wall lights, and shower curtains. You can negotiate separately about selling items such as window blinds, which are usually more nuisance than they are worth to take with you.

In any communications you have with the buyer, always state that the deal is 'subject to contract'. This is very important. Otherwise, you can find yourself committed to handing over the house on terms that do not suit you. But 'subject to contract' means that neither side is committed to anything until you sign the contract.

DIY conveyancing

It is easier to do your own conveyancing when you are selling a house than if you are buying. Even so, it is still time consuming and involves many paper transactions, see p. 77.

If you were to begin your own conveyancing and then found that an unexpected complication made it too difficult, you could still pass the work over to a solicitor at that stage.

Licensed conveyancers

There are a number of these around the country: they will do the conveyancing for you possibly at a lower price than solicitors charge, see p. 78.

THE CONTRACT

Once you and the buyer have agreed the finer points, you can draw up a contract. If you are using a solicitor he will do this for you. When you, the seller, have signed the contract and sent a copy to the buyer's solicitor, then you are bound to go ahead with the transaction on the completion day stated in the contract. This is usually one month after the date of exchange.

If either side is not willing to move on completion day, he is liable to pay compensation. If the buyer is delaying, he will have to pay interest on the amount owed, the rate for which will be stated in the contract. If the seller is delaying, the buyer is in a weaker position; he cannot claim any interest, he can serve a 'notice to complete' only and if this has no effect, he can go to court.

At exchange of contracts, the buyer will pay a 10 per cent deposit which is usually held by the seller's solicitor as 'stakeholder'.

There are two standard forms of contract: one is 'national conditions of sale' and the other is the Law Society's conditions of sale. You can buy these from Oyez Publishing or the Law Society. They are known as draft contracts and you can make amendments to them to suit your circumstances.

BRIDGING LOANS

You may have to commit yourself to paying for a new house before you have received the money from the old. In this case, you can ask your bank manager for a 'bridging loan'. These are expensive, about 5 per cent above base rate, so you will want to have a clear idea of how long you are likely to need the money for. The bank manager is unlikely to grant a bridging loan for an indefinite period, anyway.

Increasingly, lenders are offering special bridging arrangements if you borrow from them. And you will get tax relief on the repayments for 12 months while you sell. See p. 68.

HOW TO SELL A HOUSE WITH AN ESTATE AGENT

1. Ask neighbours for their opinion of local estate agents.
2. Check that the agent is a member of the Royal Institution of Chartered Surveyors or Incorporated Society of Valuers and Auctioneers or National Association of Estate Agents.
3. Ask three agents to value your house before agreeing to give one the business. Remember that the agent recommending the highest price is not necessarily the best or the most reliable.
4. You can give one agent 'sole agency' in which case the fee will be lower.
5. Otherwise, you can give multiple agency to as many as you want, but check the terms carefully otherwise you might have to pay a fee to more than one of them.
6. Negotiate the fee. You can argue, but expect to pay 1½ to 2½ per cent or even 3 per cent in Central London. The agent has a statutory duty to agree his charges with you when you first instruct him to sell.
7. Check whether the agent will charge you for any newspaper advertisements.
8. Check that, if you manage to sell privately, you are not still liable to pay his fee.
9. You can agree to have the estate agent's 'For Sale' board outside your house, but you do not have to if you prefer not. It is mostly giving him free advertising.

THE STAGES OF SELLING A HOUSE WITHOUT AN ESTATE AGENT

1. Look round locally to get an idea of the price you should ask.
2. Erect a sign outside the house saying it is for sale.

3. Place a card in the newsagent's window.
4. Advertise in the local paper.
5. Make the house look clean and tidy.
6. List the items you will leave behind.
7. Make sure potential buyers can contact you easily.

when you have a buyer
1. Agree the price 'subject to contract'.
2. Agree any items you are selling separately.
3. Agree what you are leaving behind.
4. Tell your solicitor (if you are using one).
5. Otherwise, buy a guide to DIY conveyancing.

MOVING HOUSE
There is very little difference in cost between moving 500 yards and 500 miles.

Hiring a removal firm
The choice is between paying someone to do it for you and doing it yourself. If you go the whole hog and pay a removal firm to pack everything for you and then unpack at the other end, it will cost several hundred pounds for an average size family.

If you are moving because of your job, you may be able to persuade the company to foot the bill, in which case you may as well make it as easy for yourself as you can.

Whatever you do, ask for at least three quotations – they will vary enormously. The dearest could be three times the cheapest, but do not assume that the cheapest is necessarily the best.

The price you pay depends on which day of the week you want to move (Fridays and Saturdays are more expensive); whether it is a one- or two-day job; the time of year (peak holiday period is more expensive); how keen the remover is to have your business.

To choose a removal firm, ask anyone you know who has moved recently who they used and what they thought; check if the firm is a member of an association, which will have a code of practice; do not use a specialist firm (unless you need to) because they will be more expensive.

But if you do not fit into the average mould, find a specialist firm which can cope with your requirements: you may be moving overseas; or have valuable antiques; or you may be moving to a high block of flats.

Most complaints about removers arise because the van is late, followed by complaints about breakages leading to arguments over insurance. Another cause of complaint is unexpected expenses often arising because the customer has forgotten to mention that there are parking meter restrictions in the road, or that the lift is too small to take the furniture, so the removal men have to carry everything by the stairs. The removal firm will be able to give you a leaflet of helpful hints.

Make sure you know whether the quotation includes insurance. You should have remembered to transfer your house contents insurance to the new address on the precise day and you may find that your insurance policy will cover you for the transfer as well. If not, make sure that you are covered one way or the other, either by the removal firm or on your own policy.

If you are not moving very many possessions, you can hire a van and packing crates and do it all yourself. Look for advertisements in the local paper. It will be a very tiring day and you will need help from as many strong friends as you can find.

Before you move – details to remember

This is a busy time and there are many things to do.

- ☐ arrange for the electricity board to read the meter on the day you move out
- ☐ do the same with the gas board
- ☐ make sure this has been done in the house you are moving to
- ☐ inform the electricity and gas boards in the new area that you are now responsible for the bills
- ☐ arrange to have any gas appliances disconnected and reconnected when you arrive in the new house
- ☐ ask for a final bill for the telephone
- ☐ ask your buyer if he wants the telephone left on or disconnected and tell British Telecom
- ☐ inform British Telecom in the area you are moving to that you will be taking over the existing telephone making sure the outgoing owner also contacts them; or arrange to have a telephone installed
- ☐ hire a removal firm, or van and packing cases if you are doing it yourself
- ☐ tell the local authority that you are moving out and will no longer be responsible for the rates. They will arrange any rebate due to you. If you use a solicitor, he will do this
- ☐ tell the local authority when you are moving in
- ☐ if you want your letters redirected, ask the post office for a redirection form. This will cost £2.50 for one month, £5.75 for three months, £14 for a year
- ☐ have your name put on the new electoral roll
- ☐ inform everyone who needs to know of your new address

As well as friends and neighbours, remember to include: bank/building society savings accounts/driving licence centre/television licence/television rental/video recorder rental/credit card company/any HP or credit agreements/all insurance policies: house, life, car/doctor/dentist/club memberships/subscriptions to magazines and charities/road fund licence/cancel the milk and newspapers.

As soon as you arrive in the new house, check that everything is as you expected it to be: that nothing has been taken which should have been left behind. Lastly, hope for a fine day.

CHAPTER · 7

RENTING ACCOMMODATION

Private rented accommodation is nowadays very difficult to find. House owners today are very reluctant to rent out flats because they fear it is impossible to be rid of bad tenants. This is not strictly true, but it is nonetheless difficult to evict unwanted tenants. New housing legislation, in the process of becoming law, should improve the situation.

There are different categories of tenancies and your rights differ according to which you belong to: full or restricted protection.

You will have full protection if the tenancy started after 14 August 1974 and the landlord does not live in the same house. If you were a tenant before that date, the position is more complicated but basically, if the landlord does not live in the same flat or house and does not provide any services such as changing the sheets, cleaning the flat or house, or providing meals, you have full protection.

So, restricted protection applies mainly to tenants who have a resident landlord. Your rent can be registered by the rent tribunal but you will have little security.

If you have full protection, you could be in either a regulated or shorthold tenancy. A regulated tenancy's rent has been registered by the rent officer and is totally secure from eviction except in a few, very specific circumstances.

A shorthold tenancy is one that you know from the outset has a limited life of between one and five years. In London the rent must have been registered by the rent officer at the outset. This is not necessary outside London. For the fixed period of the tenancy, you have total security unless you are in breach of the covenant of the lease but none after that, as long as you were given proper notice. Before granting the tenancy the landlord must give proper (or valid) notice that the tenancy is to be a protected shorthold tenancy.

Whatever sort of tenancy you have you should be sure that it comes within the Rent Acts. **You could be just a licensee which means you have very little security.**

Licences mainly apply to rented rooms such as student hostels, but some unscrupulous landlords have tried to draw up contracts which leave the tenant a licensee and not a regulated tenant.

Fair rent

A tenant with full protection can apply to the rent officer to determine the amount of rent the landlord can charge. Once a fair rent has been registered, this is the most the tenant need pay.

Of course, it may be that this is in fact higher than the tenant was paying previously. The only occasions when you will have to pay more than the fixed rent are if the rates go up, or if you have a variable service charge.

If the rent officer does say that you should pay a higher rent, you do not have to pay it all at once. You pay half of the increase straightaway and the remainder 12 months later.

When fixing a fair rent, the rent officer takes into account the position of the property, its age, size and state of repair. He does not take notice of any changes in the condition of the property (for better or worse) nor of the financial status of either landlord or tenant.

Neither does he put a scarcity value on the rent, however few properties there are to rent in the area. This can make a 'fair' rent seem very low in some situations.

If you move into a flat that has a registered fair rent, it will apply to you just as it did to the previous tenant. However, the Government has indicated that fair rents may be abolished.

Reasonable rent

A tenant with restricted protection can apply to the rent assessment committee for a 'reasonable rent': once this is agreed, that will be the maximum the landlord can charge.

Eviction

A landlord must obtain a court order before evicting anyone, whatever sort of tenancy it is. In certain situations tenants can be evicted.

You may be evicted if:
- [ ] you fall very far behind paying the rent
- [ ] the landlord now needs the space for himself and would be in a worse position than you without it
- [ ] you are a nuisance to the neighbours
- [ ] you use the flat for illegal or immoral purposes
- [ ] you damage the property
- [ ] you sublet the property without the landlord's permission
- [ ] the landlord finds you alternative and comparable accommodation
- [ ] you rented the flat as an employee and no longer work for the company
- [ ] the landlord wants possession because the flat is in a redevelopment scheme

You will certainly be evicted if:
- ☐ the landlord told you before you moved in that he had lived in the accommodation himself and will need it back
- ☐ the landlord wants to retire to your accommodation
- ☐ you signed a shorthold tenancy agreement which has ended
- ☐ the property is a holiday home and you have no more than an eight-month agreement

A tenant with restricted protection cannot be evicted if he has a contract unless he breaks the terms of the contract (and then he can still be evicted only with a court order).

Even after the contract has ended, he can stay there until a court orders him to leave.

Family's right of tenure

When a tenant dies, his family can continue living in the rented house. His wife can take over the tenancy and, on her death, she can pass it on to a child. But the tenancy can be passed on only twice.

Deposits

The old practice of charging 'key' money, that is asking you to pay a lump sum before you move in, is now illegal. If you feel you have been forced to pay this, you can claim it back by applying to the local authority.

However, reasonable deposits are permissible with furnished or unfurnished lettings. The deposit must not be greater than one-sixth of the annual rent. The deposit will be returned to you when you move out. You can also be asked to buy the fixtures and fittings in a flat. But this must be an appropriate sum for the items involved; if you think you have paid more than the fixtures and fittings are really worth, claim the excess back again through the local authority.

Advance rent

You can be asked to pay rent in advance when you first move in. You do not need to pay more than two months' rent in advance.

Rent book

Only tenants who pay rent weekly need a rent book but it is a good idea to ask for one anyway so you have a record of your payments.

The rent book will tell you your rights, the amount of rent to pay, and give the name and address of the landlord.

Service charges

These can be disturbingly high so it is important to understand your position. If you are protected by the Rent Act, a charge for services will probably be included in your rent. This must be explained in your contract.

Unless your contract specifically allows it, no increase in the cost of services can be passed on to you. However, if you are living in a flat with a long lease, then the service charge can rise from year to year because you pay the actual cost of the services.

If your contract does permit increases, you have a right to know how the charge has been calculated before you pay the bill and the landlord must tell you how the charges have been arrived at.

If you think the charges are too high, or you have been charged for a service you did not receive, you should complain to the landlord or managing agent. If you cannot come to an agreement you can take the landlord to court.

One way out of this dispute is to pay the amount you think is fair and then leave it to the landlord to sue you for the balance. You may have to pay some of the money for service charges in advance if the contract has stipulated this.

For any large-scale expense the landlord must consult the tenants first; but this applies only to work and not to services. He must obtain at least two estimates and you, the tenant, can obtain a separate estimate, too, if you wish. However, this does not apply to small blocks of four flats or less.

Under the Housing Bill, a local authority must provide anyone buying a council flat with an estimate of service charges for the next five years.

Gas and electricity meters

A landlord can charge more than it costs him for reselling gas and electricity to you through a meter. But there is a maximum price he can charge and also a maximum charge for renting the meter.

But, be careful. Meters are sometimes faulty and you may be paying for more energy than you use. See p. 110.

Housing associations

More and more housing associations are being set up around the country as groups of people get together to buy and restore houses or to build new ones. If the Government accepts the association's scheme, it will receive help with the building costs through grants from the Housing Corporation.

The housing association charges the tenants a rent which is assessed and controlled as a fair rent by the rent officer, just like any other protected tenant. Housing Association tenants have security of tenure under the Housing Act 1980 rather than the Rent Act.

Co-ownership schemes

These are similar to housing associations but the members buy the property rather than rent it. Co-ownership schemes can apply to the Housing Corporation for grants. After five years, the members will receive a share of any profit when they sell out of the scheme.

Repairs

Generally, as a private or housing association tenant, your landlord is responsible for carrying out any necessary repairs. He is also required to provide standard amenities such as hot and cold water and a bath or shower.

However, check the terms of your agreement. Particularly with older tenancies or leases longer than seven years, the responsibility for repairs may be different.

As a tenant you can carry out some improvements yourself and get a grant towards the cost of work. But you will have to pay the balance of the cost yourself, you cannot claim it back from the landlord if you received the grant. It is more advisable to try and persuade the landlord to undertake the work and claim the grant for himself.

And remember that the rent officer will ignore the value of any work which the tenant has paid for when calculating a fair rent.

Council housing

Most rented accommodation is now council housing. The amount of rent you have to pay is fixed by the local authority and you cannot argue against paying it.

Moreover, the local authority can raise the rent whenever it wants, the only stipulation being that the amount demanded is 'reasonable'.

When a council tenant dies, the tenancy can be passed on to the husband or wife, or to any member of the family who has been living there for 12 months and regards it as their main home. The tenancy can be passed on once again.

Most council tenants have a secure tenancy which means that they can be evicted only if they have seriously broken the terms of their lease, and then only by court order.

Tenants now have the right to buy their council home. See p. 85.

THE NEW LAW

Planned legislation will substantially change the position for almost anyone living in rented accommodation over the next few years.

Council tenants will be offered the chance to opt out of council control through a scheme which has become known as Pick-a-Landlord. They can transfer the tenancy of their home to a housing association, a housing trust, or a co-operative they may set up themselves. If they choose to do this the council is no longer the owner of their home and they become an **Assured Tenant**.

Assured tenants, who will make up the bulk of renters in future years, agree the rent with their landlord for a given period. The rent will thus be the market value of the accommodation rather than a fair rent. Once agreed, it cannot be varied throughout the term of the agreement. If a tenant leaves before the end of the period, the agreement can be renegotiated with a new tenant but the landlord cannot remove someone just because he wants to increase the price. New laws on harassment aim to prevent bad landlords from 'winkling' tenants out of their homes so they can let it for a higher price, but only time will tell whether these are effective weapons.

Shorthold Tenancies, designed to stimulate renting in the private sector, are intended to increase the mobility of labour in areas where housing is in short supply. It is a way of encouraging anyone with a spare room to let it for a specified period, safe in the knowledge that they will get the accommodation back at the end of the period without the expense of resorting to the courts.

RENTING OUT A PROPERTY

If you are renting out part of your home or a separate property you will have to go to court to evict a tenant who is not paying the rent.

When the tenancy comes to an end, you are entitled to have possession of your property again. But, if the tenant does not move out, you cannot force him out. You will have to go to court for an eviction order; you do not have the right to break into the house or to harass the tenant in the hope of persuading him to move.

If you are providing bed and breakfast, or other services, and you live in the house yourself, the tenant will have restricted protection only. But you will still need a court order to make him leave.

A landlord has the same right to apply for a fair rent as the tenant. And, again, once this has been registered then no one can reapply for an amendment for two years.

New laws should make renting out easier. See Shorthold tenancies above.

Sitting tenants

Like council tenants, if you are a sitting tenant you may have the right to buy your home. If you are renting privately you may be able to persuade your landlord to sell the house to you.

In that case, you go about buying the house in which you are living in just the same way as you would buy any other property.

If you buy a house that already has a sitting tenant in it, you will be bound to honour the agreement. You will be able to buy the house cheaper than you would if you had vacant possession but you may have a little difficulty finding a mortgage.

MAIN POINTS OF THE HOUSING AND PLANNING ACT
which came into effect from January 1987

☐ increased Right to Buy discounts to 60 per cent for houses and 70 per cent for flats. Council houses can now be sold at discounts of 42 to 60 per cent and flats from 44 to 70 per cent

- [ ] council tenants who buy their homes will have to repay part of their discount if they resell within three years instead of five
- [ ] local authorities must give an estimate of the service charges which a purchaser can expect for five years after buying a property
- [ ] if a landlord disposes of his interest in a tenanted house or flat, the Right to Buy and the right to a mortgage remain
- [ ] the Act introduced new grounds for repossession of dwellings let under secure tenancies:

  a) a landlord wishing to obtain possession of dwellings on the grounds that they are included within a redevelopment scheme must serve a notice on each secure tenant giving the main features of the scheme and stating his intention to gain possession

  b) tenants must make representations to the landlord within 28 days

  c) after the landlord has considered the representations, he must apply to the Secretary of State for the Environment for approval of the scheme
- [ ] tenant co-operatives can apply for grants for housing management and training
- [ ] tenants of a flat bought under Right to Buy may be eligible for the right to a loan from a landlord or the Housing Corporation for repairs payable during the first ten years of the lease. Loans are secured by a mortgage on the flat; if a housing association is the landlord, tenants may be eligible for a loan for service charges during the first ten years of the lease
- [ ] if a council or other public sector landlord disposes of a house or flat to a private landlord, secure tenants will be protected. Tenants will also retain their Right to Buy
- [ ] local authorities can pass on housing management functions to housing co-operatives or housing associations

IN YOUR HOME

Moving into your house will have taken much time, trouble and fretting. Unfortunately, the problems and expenses do not end once you have closed the front door. Many are just beginning.

To start with, you will find the largest, perpetual bill to face is for the rates. Under the income support rules, if you are on a low income you may be able to get help with the rates bill and, if you are in rented accommodation, perhaps a rent rebate as well.

The Government has plans to abolish rates and introduce a community charge or poll tax.

RATES

These are a tax that you pay to your local authority for providing local services such as: the dustmen; sewers; street cleaning; libraries; parks; fire service; schools; social services.

Your bill is calculated according to the size and quality of your property and its surroundings, including the garage and any outbuildings. It does not take into consideration how many people use the services.

When you buy a house, you will be told the 'rateable value' of the house and the 'rate in the pound' that the local authority is charging. To work out your rates bill, you multiply one figure by the other.

For example, if the rateable value of your house is £200 and the local authority charges a rate in the pound of £1.10, then your rates bill for the year is £220.

Even if you are renting property you will pay rates, though they may be included in your rent.

If you improve your house, maybe by adding an extension or a bathroom, you should inform the local rating authority because this could affect your rates bill. If you had to ask for planning permission, the local authority will in any case be aware of your building work.

You will have to pay any higher rates due either from the date the work is completed, or 1 April whichever is earlier. Rates are supposed to be reassessed every five years but there has not been a revaluation since 1973. And the problems this has caused are behind the plans to abolish the rating system and go over to poll tax. See overleaf.

The rates bill falls due in April each year and that is when your local authority will tell you exactly how much you have to pay for the coming year.

The money is due in advance for the whole year though you can ask to spread the cost. You can pay in two half-yearly lump sums if you wish or, by far the best way, pay in monthly instalments spread over ten months of the year. See p. 12.

Rate reduction

If you think the rates you are paying are too high, you can ask for a reassessment. You may feel, for example, that the late night noise from the gambling den next door warrants a lower bill.

Ask at your local valuation office (you will find its address in the telephone directory under 'Inland Revenue', or you can ask at the town hall) for a form 'proposal for the alteration of the valuation list'.

Complete this and try to persuade your neighbours to join in the fight. There is added strength in a united complaint. The appeal will be heard at a valuation court which you or your adviser will be required to attend to state your case for a reduction in rates.

After weighing the evidence, the court will give a ruling on what it considers fair. However, you do not have to settle for this if you are still dissatisfied; your next step is an appeal to the Lands Tribunal but you will probably need a surveyor or solicitor to help you and you will have to pay their costs unless these are awarded against the valuation office.

If a house is standing empty you do not have to pay rates to start with but the local authority can, after three months, start charging rates at the normal level.

Poll tax

In April 1990 in England and Wales, and a year earlier in Scotland, the domestic rates system which has existed in one form or another since 1601, will be replaced by the poll tax, officially called the community charge.

Under the new system, virtually everyone over the age of 18 must pay a share of the cost of running their local council, including people who claim income support who will have to pay at least 20 per cent of the charge.

The amount you will have to pay is made up of the cost of providing all local services – police, education, refuse, roads, firemen, etc – after taking account of grants that will come from the Government to the local authority.

You must register to pay your poll tax or face a fine. You may also be fined up to £400 if you do not put your name on the voting register, which is why it is called a poll tax. Everyone will pay the same amount in poll tax unless they are receiving benefits. The idea is that the charge will reflect the efficiency of local councils.

At its simplest, a household with two adults will pay broadly the same as it does now but, for a variety of reasons, there will be a very mixed bag of gainers and losers depending on where you live.

HOUSING BENEFIT

A new housing benefit scheme took effect from April 1988, largely because the previous one was completely unworkable.

Those in most need will be able to get their rent paid in full but everyone will have to contribute something towards their rates – at least 20p in the pound.

To be eligible, you must have less than £3000 in capital. There is no entitlement for anyone with more than £8000 and a sliding scale in between.

Water rates will be allowed for when working out the income support level and everyone will be responsible for paying their own water rates.

There are three main changes to the new rules:
1. The rules for assessing housing benefit will be the same as those for assessing income support (see pp. 151–2).
2. People on the same income level, whether in work or not, will get the same help.
3. There is a simpler system for adjusting benefit as earnings rise.

WATER RATES

You pay water rates in half-yearly, or sometimes monthly, sums to the local water board. It is not possible to get a rebate for water. You are paying for the supply of water and sewerage collection, treatment and disposal.

The bill is calculated by multiplying the rateable value of your house by the water authority's charge. There is one charge for water and a smaller one for sewerage treatment, plus a standing charge for both.

You will pay a higher water rate than your neighbour if you have a swimming pool. You may have to pay more if you have a garden hose or sprinkler to water the plants or wash the car but most authorities do not charge extra.

Water meters

Water is on the Government's list of planned privatisations. But this will not be such a straightforward and unchallenged proposition as British Telecom or British Gas. However, one element which is clear is that water metering will eventually form part of our daily lives.

Already some parts of the country have water meters. And anyone who uses only a small amount of water can ask to have it metered.

HOME IMPROVEMENTS

People are improving their houses in preference to moving more than ever before, even though there is now no tax relief on money borrowed for home improvements.

You can expand your living space in various ways: by adding rooms over the garage, or in the loft or by extending out into the garden. You will need planning permission from the local authority for any major changes you make. But, unless there are special local authority regulations you do not need permission for small extensions. So you can go ahead, unless you are raising the height of the roof or bringing the front of the house forward or increasing the overall size of a terraced house by more than 50 cubic metres or one-tenth of the cubic capacity, whichever is the greater. Other than terraced, houses can be enlarged by 70 cubic metres or 15 per cent of the cubic capacity, whichever is the greater, without permission.

Home improvement grants

You can obtain a grant from your local authority to help towards the cost of repairing an old house, providing a bathroom and, in some instances, installing proper kitchen facilities. If the house is in a very bad state, you may be able to get most of the money, but usually the maximum is 50 per cent. Councils are very short of money now.

This is not a loan – the local authority is giving you the money to improve the condition of your house, although there may be certain conditions about reselling.

To obtain a grant, you must follow the procedure demanded by the local authority. You cannot have the work done first and then ask for a grant towards the cost. The local authority must come along and inspect the property in its original state before giving you the go-ahead. You will need to produce several quotations from local builders.

There are three different types of grants to apply for: repair grants; improvement grants; and intermediate grants. The grants are discretionary, you are not entitled to the money by right, and different authorities have varying attitudes towards handing them out.

Householders can obtain improvement grants for insulating the loft, pipes and water tanks. The elderly and severely disabled on low incomes are entitled to larger grants for this.

Intermediate grants are for installing standard amenities, such as hot and cold running water, an indoor toilet and bath. Repair grants are for substantial and structural repairs to pre-1919 houses, and will cover reroofing, repointing, and installation of a damp-proof course.

You cannot get a grant for rewiring a house alone but if you are having a larger job done, then rewiring will be included as part of it. It is worth asking your local authority if a grant is available for any job you have in mind.

To qualify for a grant you must own the house in question, though in some instances tenants can be allowed grants as long as the landlord approves the work being done. The rateable value of the property must not exceed £400 in Greater London or £225 elsewhere until the poll tax takes effect.

Is it worth it?

You will gain the extra space of course, but will an extension add to the value of your house? Small improvements such as loft insulation and double glazing can make the house easier to sell, but you cannot necessarily add on £500 to the asking price to recover your outlay.

An extra bedroom or second bathroom will certainly increase the value of your house, possibly by more than it cost you to install. A shower, in particular, is a good selling point.

But the costs of substantial alterations are high. A good quality extension will cost about £475 a square metre to build and a loft conversion about £375 a square metre. Since July 1984, VAT at the rate of 15 per cent has become payable on all building extensions and home improvements.

Decorating

Whenever you buy a second-hand house, the chances of your liking the decorations already there, even if they are brand new, are a hundred to one against. But even if you are happy with your predecessor's colour schemes, you will at some stage have to redecorate.

Decorating is expensive, particularly if you pay someone else to do the work. But it is false economy to buy cheap materials. You have only the hassle of repeating the job the following year if the paint blisters or the wallpaper disintegrates.

SECURITY

You should be extremely aware of the necessity of keeping your house secure, particularly if you live in a city centre.

You should have secure locks on all your outside doors and also locks on the windows. If you have rooms where access from the outside is easy you can fix iron grilles over the windows.

Whether or not to install a burglar alarm is a more difficult decision. By having a little box on the outside wall you are telling the world that you think you have something inside worth stealing. And then these alarms tend to be over sensitive; they are often set off because of a fault rather than a burglar, and this has the same effect as crying wolf. A noisy (not necessarily large) dog might be a better deterrent.

Remember that if a burglar is determined to break in, he will succeed. So, your main concern is to dissuade him from even trying. If a light is on in the house, he will think twice about breaking in, so a time switch can be useful.

When you go away on holiday, obviously remember to cancel the milk and the newspapers but also ask a neighbour to call in from time to time to move the curtains around and switch the lights on and off. Then, do not leave anything valuable where it can be seen from the road. That is flaunting temptation.

And once you have fixed security gadgets, do remember to use them.

Otherwise they are a complete waste of money. To keep unwanted callers outside, fit a chain to the front door and a spy hole so you can see who is knocking. Again, remember to use the door chain.

You can ask the crime prevention officer at your local police station to come round and advise you; they are happy to do so.

If anyone calling himself an official turns up unexpectedly, ask to see his identity card. If you have any doubts at all, ask him to come back in half an hour while you telephone the authority he claims to represent to make sure he is genuine.

Do not be embarrassed about doing this. If he is genuine, he will understand. If he is not, he will not come back. And do not ever, ever, let anyone come into your house if you do not know who they are.

False pretences

If a dealer offers to look over any old 'junk' you may be interested in selling, tell him to come back in a week's time. Meanwhile, get an idea of the real value of the items from another source and when he returns, keep an eye on him the whole time he is in the house. Even better, arrange to have someone else in the house with you.

HEATING COSTS

Always remember that hot air rises, so the air you are paying so expensively to heat is simply floating up and out through the roof. But there are quite a few steps you can take to help keep your heating costs down and it is worth investing in most of them.

Insulation

The first thing you should do is to insulate the loft. It will cost about £100 to insulate an average three-bedroomed semi yourself.

You may be able to obtain a grant to help with the cost of materials. See p. 106.

Pipes and tank lagging

Like loft insulation, this is an elementary (and inexpensive) job which should be done immediately if your pipes and hot water tank are not already lagged.

Cavity wall insulation

This is expensive. A three-bedroomed semi costs about £300 to insulate using foam or £400 with mineral fibre. So it will take longer to recoup the outlay in saved heating bills.

Double glazing

How much you will save on your heating bills by installing double glazing is debatable. It is obviously cheaper to do the job yourself if you are able but it will still take many years to recoup the expense. Completely replacing one small window will cost about £250.

Double glazing can shut out noise if you live in a busy area and can deter burglars because it takes longer to break two panes of glass.

Above all, do make sure that you can open the windows quickly in case a fire breaks out. It is easy to become trapped inside a secure house.

Temperature

To cut costs, try turning down the central heating thermostat a degree or two. Very likely, you will not notice the difference but if you turn down the heat by 4°F (2°C) you can save 10 per cent on your electricity bill.

You can install separate thermostats in each room. This way you are not heating a little-used room unnecessarily. In any rooms that are unused turn the radiator off altogether.

Separate heaters

It may not be worth the cost of installing central heating. If you are out a great deal or have several rooms you do not use, it will be far cheaper to heat only those rooms as and when you need.

With electric fires, you can use a time clock which automatically turns on the fire and heats the room before you get up in the morning or arrive home at night.

Costs

The price will vary according to where you live. Not only do fuel prices differ around the country but in the colder parts of the country you will spend substantially more on heating bills than you would on the milder south coast.

Both the gas and electricity boards claim to provide the cheapest form of heating with figures to back up their argument. True comparisons are very difficult.

Many factors will affect how much you pay:

- □ size and age of house
- □ number of people living there
- □ which part of the country you live in
- □ quality of insulation
- □ type and age of boiler
- □ how warm you like to be
- □ whether you take more baths than showers
- □ an annual central heating service contract

Electricity costs

Here is how much use one unit of electricity gives:

3 KWH radiant heat	20 minutes
2 KWH fan heater	30 minutes

cooker	meals for one person for one day
kettle	12 pints of water
colour television	6 hours
black and white television	9 hours
iron	2 hours
fridge	one day
tumble drier	30 minutes
hair drier	3 hours
vacuum cleaner	2–4 hours
electric blanket	7 evenings (**under**); 2 full nights (**over**)
spin drier	4 hours

One unit of electricity is equal to one kilowatt or 1000 watts, running for one hour. So, if you buy an electrical appliance marked 250 watts, you know you can use it continuously for four hours and you will burn one unit of electricity.

This is how much you will be using:

dishwasher	1–1½ units per load
freezer	1½–2 units per cubic foot a week
automatic washing machine	9 units to wash clothes of a family of four for a week
twin tub washing machine	6 units to wash clothes of a family of four for a week
bath	4–5 units if tank lagged
shower	2–2½ units

One unit of electricity heats three gallons of hot water from 10°C (50°F) to 60°C (140°F). A bath uses 25 gallons of water; a shower uses half the amount of water and moreover at a lower temperature.

Gas and electricity meters

Sometimes these meters are faulty and you may be paying for more energy than you are actually using. You can have a meter checked by asking the gas or electricity boards.

The gas board will charge around £16 to £21, depending on where you live, if the meter turns out to be working properly. However, if you are right and the meter is faulty, beyond a 2 per cent tolerance either way, you will not pay anything.

Different electricity boards have different policies about charging: some charge nothing, whatever the outcome. Others will demand, say £15, if the meter turns out to be accurate. They charge mainly to deter time wasters.

In the first instance, the electricity board will come and look at your meter to see if there is anything obviously wrong. If you are not satisfied, they will conduct a timing test and, failing that, a check meter test.

If you still do not accept their findings, you can ask for the Government meter examiner to take the meter away. The examiner at the Department of Energy will strip the meter and check it thoroughly. His findings are final and legally binding.

The Electricity Consumers' Council has produced leaflets that indicate many reasons for a higher bill than you expected.

They suggest:

- [ ] you check that the meter reading is right
- [ ] the price has gone up
- [ ] the last bill was paid late and that amount has been included in this bill
- [ ] the last bill was based on an estimate which was too low
- [ ] the bill includes other charges such as HP payments
- [ ] the weather was very cold
- [ ] there was someone at home ill
- [ ] there were more people at home than usual
- [ ] a new baby
- [ ] a new heating system
- [ ] new equipment such as a freezer or tumble drier
- [ ] there have been workmen in the house using electricity
- [ ] the wiring or thermostat may be faulty

EXTENDED GUARANTEES OR SERVICE CONTRACTS

When you buy a new domestic appliance you will almost certainly be asked by the manufacturer if you would like to take out a service contract. They will explain to you just how worth while this is and how much peace of mind it provides. But does it?

Service contracts, or extended guarantees, cost about £60 a year for a washing machine down to a one-off £17 for a vacuum cleaner.

This will probably cover parts and labour for four years beyond the first-year guarantee which you are given anyway. About a quarter of washing machines sold need repairing in the first five years and about half of tumble driers. Fridges and freezers rarely need repairing.

Like any form of insurance, you cannot tell in advance if you are going to get your money's worth out of the policy. If you want to know that you can call a mechanic out at no charge other than the premium, a service contract will be worth while. But if you do not like paying out any additional money and you think you can cope with minor repairs yourself anyway, then save the cost of the insurance.

HOME INCOME PLANS

Elderly home owners may be living in a house, already paid for, worth tens of thousands of pounds and yet not be able to afford simple repair jobs. There are several solutions, but none is ideal.

One option is to sell the house and move to a smaller and cheaper one, thereby releasing some of the capital. Another is to rent out rooms to lodgers. But there are likely to be many excellent reasons why you do not want to do either.

A further choice is a home income plan. The drawback here is that you need to be at least 70 years old before you can take out such a plan.

There are two schemes at present, one run by the Abbey National Building Society in conjunction with Royal Life Insurance Company, and the other by Allied Dunbar.

The insurance company lends you money against the value of your house. You can borrow up to 65 per cent of its current market value with Abbey and 80 per cent with Allied Dunbar. This money is used to buy an annuity which provides you with an income for the rest of your life. The money is paid to you in monthly instalments. When you die, the amount you owe to the insurance company is repaid out of the proceeds of your house, which means that your heirs will receive a smaller inheritance than they otherwise would.

Although the capital is repaid out of your estate when you die, you have to pay interest on the money while you are still alive. Both the Allied Dunbar and the Abbey National plans work on a fixed rate of interest so from the very beginning you know exactly how much you will receive each month.

You are entitled to tax relief on the interest payments if the loan is no more than £30,000 just as you were when you had a mortgage. You may have to pay a small amount of tax on the income from the annuity, but a home income plan could reduce your inheritance tax liability because, when you die, the value of your estate will not be so high.

An additional option is Capital Protection. This scheme is slightly more expensive but it means that if you die shortly after taking out the loan, only part of it has to be repaid. This way, your beneficiaries do not feel that they have lost a large part of their inheritance for no reason.

If you die in the first year, only 25 per cent of the loan is repayable; in the second year it is 50 per cent; and in the third year, you need repay only 75 per cent. After that you have to repay in full.

Home income plans do not suit everyone; the stumbling block is the fact that many people still want to be able to pass on as much as they possibly can to their children.

There are many questions you should ask:
Q.   Must I own the house before taking out a home income plan?
A.   *Yes. However, if the house is not fully paid for, you can take money out of the annuity to pay off the mortgage up to 10 per cent of the loan.*
Q.   Must I really be 70 years old?
A.   *Yes. And if you are a married couple, your joint ages have to be at least 150. This is because the insurance companies cannot provide a worthwhile income until you reach this age.*
Q.   How much can I borrow?

A. *Up to 65 per cent of the value of your house when you start the plan with Abbey National; 80 per cent with Allied Dunbar, with a maximum of £30,000.*

Q. Can I borrow more later when the value of my house increases?

A. *Yes. You go about it the same way as the original plan.*

Q. Will I receive the same amount each month?

A. *Yes. Allied Dunbar and Abbey National plans have a fixed rate of interest.*

Q. Can I cancel the home income plan after taking one out should I want to regain 100 per cent of my house?

A. *You can repay the loan at any time. And, even if you do, you will continue to receive money from the annuity. You cannot stop the annuity.*

Q. Does the scheme operate for a leasehold flat?

A. *Yes. But you might not be able to borrow as much.*

Q. Could my heirs pay off the loan themselves when I die rather than sell the house?

A. *Yes. All the insurance company wants is its money back.*

Q. Can I move house if I have a home income plan?

A. *Yes. The loan is repaid from the proceeds of the sale. You will nevertheless continue to receive the annuity. If you wish you can then take out another loan on the new house.*

Q. I receive income support. Will this be affected by money from a home income plan?

A. *Yes. You will almost certainly lose the income support. Your entitlement to a rate rebate might also be affected.*

Q. How can I get the most money from a home income plan?

A. *Only by waiting until you are even older. But you might as well go ahead as soon as you can because you are unlikely to make up the money you lose by waiting one or two years.*

Q. How do I receive the money?

A. *It is paid directly into your bank account or building society account.*

Q. Can I take a lump sum at the beginning?

A. *Yes, in some circumstances and up to a maximum of 10 per cent of the loan. But this will reduce the amount you then receive each month.*

Q. When do I repay the loan?

A. *When you die.*

Q. How will this affect my inheritance tax liability?

A. *The value of your estate will be reduced by the amount of the loan so this could reduce your inheritance tax bill.*

Q. What about my income tax?

A. *If you pay tax at the basic rate, you will receive tax relief through MIRAS as you do on a mortgage. If you are a higher rate taxpayer, you will have higher rate tax relief as well, but you will have to pay extra tax on part of the annuity.*

Q. Will it cost me anything to set up?

A. *Yes. You will have to pay a surveyor's fee for valuing the house and a solicitor. The Abbey National and Allied Dunbar help out with these expenses.*
Q. What happens if I have to sell my house and go into a home?
A. *The debt is repaid out of the proceeds of the sale. But you will continue to receive the annuity until you die.*

Here is an example:
A woman aged 75 paying basic rate tax owns a house worth £30,000. She borrows 65 per cent of this, which is £19,500. This buys an annuity worth £3149 a year. But, on the interest element of the annuity, she had to pay tax at 25 per cent amounting to £336 a year. This left her with a net annuity of £2813 a year.

Now, she has to pay interest on the loan. If this is 10 per cent a year, on the loan of £19,500 the bill is £1950. Tax relief on these payments is £487 leaving a net bill of £1463.

So, by deducting the tax bill from the annuity income, she is £1350 a year better off.

The figures for a married couple who are both aged 75 look like this:

Value of house	£30,000
Loan (65% of value of house)	£19,500

This £19,500 is multiplied by an annuity rate (given by the insurance company).

Gross annual annuity	£2705
of which interest is	£1245
tax on interest at 25%	£311
Net annual annuity	£2394

Interest is payable on the loan of £19,500:

Interest at 10%	£1950
Tax relief on interest at 25%	£499
Interest net of tax	£1451

By deducting the net interest of £1451 from the net annuity of £2394 the couple are left with an extra £943 to spend. This might not sound a great deal of money. But the alternative is to have nothing and you will receive this amount every year for the rest of your life. There are other schemes around, called home reversion plans, where you actually hand over all or a part share of your house in exchange for an income or a highly discounted cash sum. Think very carefully before committing yourself to one of these.

CHAPTER · 9

INSURANCE

It is an unnecessary expense to be over-insured; it is dangerous to be under-insured: you should aim for the happy medium. Insurance breaks down into two broad categories: insurance which offers recompense if your belongings are damaged or lost; and assurance which pays money to your dependants when you die.

You can insure almost anything in the world: your legs; your garden party against rain; a supertanker; a dog. The aim is to pay for no more insurance than you need and to be certain that you are clear about what the policy offers you.

Most disagreements between insurance companies and policyholders occur because of misunderstandings about the scope of the policy. Rule one is to make sure you are getting what you want before you sign the proposal form.

For information about motor, holiday and self-employed insurance see pp. 221, 231 and 171.

YOUR HOUSE
You need two kinds of insurance policy if you own a house; one for the building and one for the contents, although some insurance companies will combine the two in one policy.

HOUSE CONTENTS INSURANCE
You will need this whether you own a house or live in rented accommodation. The stolen goods are recovered in only one-third of all burglaries and the crime is growing faster than the detection. It is foolhardy not to have insurance to replace the cost of your possessions.

With contents insurance policies there is a choice in the type of insurance you can take out. You can either have an 'indemnity' policy, which values your goods in their second-hand state, or more commonly now, a 'new for old' policy, which pays you the price the item costs today. Both of these can be index-linked.

Index-linking

Most policies today are automatically index-linked. That is, the amount you are covered for (and thereby the premium you pay), is increased by the insurance company every year in line with an index related to the consumer durable section of the retail prices index. However, if you think you are paying too much, tell the company. They may agree to leave you on last year's figure.

Remember that you may have increased the amount you have at risk one year, perhaps if you bought a new suite of furniture or a video recorder for example. Each time you renew the policy, think about what you are covering.

All risks cover

This is 'almost everything you could possibly think of' cover. It will be an extension to your household policy and it will cost more but, in return, your insurance policy will cover you for many more situations. It is extremely frustrating to suffer a disaster, claim against your insurance policy and then be told: 'very sorry, your policy excludes this eventuality'.

Any ordinary policy will cover you for the risks specifically named in the policy; 'all risks' covers you for everything, including accidental damage, except for the situations stated to be excluded. For example, the all risks would cover the loss of a stone from a piece of jewellery even if you are out in the street; losing your camera; or it will provide a replacement if you drop a vase and smash it. An ordinary policy will not.

For a rough guide to the cost, the typical rate of an annual premium in a country area is around £1.75 for £100 of cover under an indemnity policy. London and other inner city areas will be more expensive than this, nearer £3 for £100 of full cover.

How to do it

To start, you should make a list of everything in your house that you will have to replace; you will be startled at just how much this adds up to. Walk round the house and list, room by room, everything you own. If you want to be totally covered, do not forget the suitcases stored in the attic, food in the kitchen, toys in the children's bedroom, pictures on the walls and the lawn mower in the garage. See p. 118 for a check list.

You will also be able to claim for any cash you might lose, probably up to a limit of £250. Mirrors and fixed glass that form part of the furniture are covered for accidental damage. If a heavy visitor sits carelessly on a glass-topped coffee table, you can recover the cost of the broken glass, if not the friendship.

You will wonder whether to include some items under 'contents' or 'buildings' insurance; shelves are the obvious example. The simplest guide is to regard anything you would take with you if you moved as coming under 'contents'; anything permanently fixed as 'buildings'.

Of course, you might not necessarily lose or damage something while you are at home. Most policies will provide an extension, giving limited cover for possessions you have with you while you are away from home or while you are in the process of moving house. But they will not automatically cover you when you are not at home. Again, the vital point is to find out exactly what your policy covers and ask for it to be changed if it does not meet your requirements.

A typical policy will exclude damage to cars, pets and documents. In the case of multiple occupancy theft of certain items, if the burglars have not forced an entry, will be excluded. Damage from war, sonic booms and contamination by radioactivity are excluded because, should the worst happen and you are still around to claim, the Government will take responsibility for paying out.

The policy will cover the same catastrophes as a buildings policy when your movable possessions are hit: storm; fire; flood; falling aeroplanes; lightning; escape of water; careering cows. The indemnity policy will make allowance for wear and tear, which is deducted before settling a claim. A new for old policy will pay out the current purchase price if something is destroyed or stolen, as long as the total sum assured matches current prices. If the item is slightly damaged, it may pay for repairs.

You can sometimes find a 'hybrid' policy which gives new for old cover on fairly recent items, such as furniture, carpets, electrical and household appliances and indemnity cover on everything else.

Valuables, such as antiques or jewellery, pose a different problem because the value is more arbitrary and may indeed increase rather than depreciate. It is advisable to obtain an expert valuation for anything you think might be worth £1000 or more. For values under £1000, the insurance company will probably pay up on an individual item, or if the claim for any one item is below 10 per cent of the total sum insured.

But a valuation, whether for an item of gold, silver, fur or diamonds, will become out of date after a couple of years. Remember to update the valuation from time to time. The first valuation will cost about 1 per cent of the valuation figure; you should be able to get a revision for less.

If you live in a rented flat, you will still need to insure your belongings. The landlord will not do it for you. Furthermore, the terms of your tenancy may make you responsible for fixtures and fittings, so find out if you need to insure these as well as your belongings.

Also, it is important to have your contents insured for their full value. If you are under-insured and have to claim, you may find the insurance company operates a practice known as 'averaging'. If the insurance company does not think you are fully insured, it will pay out less than the total amount you are claiming.

On some items you may want accidental damage cover both for when you are at home and when you away. You can cover items, perhaps a camera, spectacles, guitar, by arranging an 'all risks' extension to the policy. Some all risk policies will cover your possessions while you are on holiday abroad.

HOUSE CONTENTS TO INSURE

	cost to replace	second-hand value
LIVING ROOM		
carpet, rugs	_____	_____
curtains, blinds	_____	_____
furniture: chairs	_____	_____
tables	_____	_____
sideboard	_____	_____
books, records, tapes	_____	_____
pictures, wall hangings	_____	_____
television, video recorder	_____	_____
radio, stereo	_____	_____
ornaments and lights	_____	_____
computer	_____	_____
DINING ROOM		
carpet, rugs	_____	_____
curtains, blinds	_____	_____
sideboard	_____	_____
table and chairs	_____	_____
pictures	_____	_____
alcohol	_____	_____
china, glass, cutlery	_____	_____
lights	_____	_____
KITCHEN		
flooring	_____	_____
curtains, blinds	_____	_____
cooker	_____	_____
microwave	_____	_____
fridge	_____	_____
freezer	_____	_____
washing machine/drier	_____	_____
dishwasher	_____	_____
cutlery, crockery, saucepans	_____	_____
kitchen equipment, eg mixer, kettle	_____	_____
tea towels	_____	_____
food and drink	_____	_____
BEDROOMS		
beds	_____	_____
mattresses	_____	_____
carpet, rugs	_____	_____

	cost to replace	second-hand value
curtains, blinds		
chairs		
dressing tables, stools		
chest of drawers		
mirrors		
bed linen		
clothes		
pictures		
jewellery		
children's belongings		

BATHROOM/CLOAKROOMS

flooring		
bathroom cabinet		
toiletries		
towels		
bathroom scales		
mirrors		

HALLWAY AND HALL CUPBOARD

carpet, rugs		
curtains, blinds		
clothing, shoes		
telephone		
telephone table		
cleaning equipment		

LOFT

suitcases		
items being stored		

GARDEN SHED

lawn mower		
garden tools		
bicycle		
ladders		
DIY equipment		

GARAGE

garden furniture		
freezer		
ladders		
items being stored		

The value of the contents of your house could add up like this:

Two-bedroomed terraced house:

	£
living room	3570
bedroom 1	2805
bedroom 2	1480
kitchen	1675
bathroom	185
hall	155
garage	470
	£10,340

Large three-bedroomed semi:

	£
living room	5315
bedroom 1	5610
bedroom 2	2040
bedroom 3	815
kitchen	2145
bathroom	310
hall	490
garage	530
	£17,255

Small three-bedroomed semi:

	£
living room	3570
bedroom 1	3910
bedroom 2	1020
bedroom 3	615
kitchen	1475
bathroom	80
hall	305
garage	410
	£11,385

Four-bedroomed detached house:

	£
living room	5100
dining room	2550
bedroom 1	8050
bedroom 2	2040
bedroom 3	910
bedroom 4	615
kitchen	3060
bathroom	410
hall	705
garage	615
	£24,055

Contents insurance has become very expensive in recent years, particularly in inner city areas. If you are at home all day, it may be worth mentioning the fact to the insurance company as your occupied house is more secure than one left empty.

Some companies give discounts to customers who instal extra-strong security locks or who live in a Neighbourhood Watch area. This is worth asking about.

The company will tell you what type of security they expect – usually a five-bar deadlock and chain – but they will not necessarily come round to check. It is important, though, that you remember to use the bolts once you have them fitted (see pp. 107–8).

Another innovation which has been slow to catch on is a no-claims discount for house contents insurance. Although this is standard with motor insurance, companies do not want to extend it. However, it is available if you shop around.

HOUSEHOLD CONTENTS RATES*

COVER	Central London	Central Manchester	London Suburbs	Country District
Sum insured £10,000	£	£	£	£
New for old	120	95	60	35
Including accidental damage	135	115	85	50
Sum insured £14,000				
New for old	168	133	84	49
Including accidental damage	189	161	119	70
Sum insured £18,000				
New for old	216	171	108	63
Including accidental damage	243	207	153	90

*The precise terms vary between policies; this is an average guide.

BUILDINGS INSURANCE

If you have a mortgage on your home, then the building society or bank will insist that you insure the fabric of the building.

Many of these policies are now index-linked. The cover is increased annually according to a rebuilding cost index which takes account of the rising price of building. It is essential that you make sure your policy covers the full cost of repair.

The Association of British Insurers issues a table of rebuilding costs which gives a rough guide as to how much cover you should have. The scale varies between £34.50 a square foot to rebuild a large semi-detached house built after 1945 in East Anglia and £61.50 for a medium-sized pre-1920 detached house in London. But it is very rare for a whole house to be destroyed and need rebuilding. Nearly all claims are for partial damage only. The figures do not include garages.

Building insurance will cover any damage to the structure of the house, including damage to permanent fixtures and fittings such as a weathervane on the roof. It also takes in the garage and any other outbuildings, sheds or stables. The cover will include a certain amount but not total cover for paths, drives, walls and swimming pools.

As a broad guide, anything that is fixed and which you would leave behind when you move, comes under the buildings policy. This includes kitchen units and loft insulation.

If you are renting, the owner of the building should pay for the building insurance and the lease should make it clear if this is not the case. Make sure you know, because sometimes the tenant is responsible for any internal damage and this might not be covered by your contents policy. If you have bought a leasehold flat, the landlord will insure the buildings and either reclaim a proportion of the premium from you or include it in the service charge.

There are various circumstances when the insurance company may refuse to pay out. For example, if the house or flat is left empty, or with insufficient furniture, for 30 days or more, the policy could become invalid. Or, if you have not maintained your house in a 'reasonable' state of repair, they can decide that the dilapidated condition rather than the storm was responsible for the damage.

If you claim for subsidence or landslip damage, your premiums will be increased; this is spelled out in the policy. Some policies now include provision for 'heave' in the cover – that is an upward movement rather than the collapse of the ground.

If you let out part of your home, you can claim loss of rent if these rooms become uninhabitable. But the insurance company must be aware that you are renting and the cause of the damage must be an insured risk. You can claim the cost of having to rent alternative accommodation for yourself if your own living quarters become uninhabitable.

Other events for which you can claim include accidental damage to underground pipes and cables, glass windows and doors, and bathroom fittings. If you suffer very serious damage, then you can claim for the cost of architects' and surveyors' fees, moving the rubbish and rubble, shoring up a building which is in danger of collapsing, and for any increased costs due to special requirements of the local authority.

But take care if your house has a special construction which might increase a risk – say it has wooden walls or a thatched roof. Any especially vulnerable or non-standard building will cost more in premiums.

Two types of building policy are available: an 'indemnity' and a 'reinstatement' policy. The indemnity policy will cover the cost of restoring the house to its state before the damage.

Today nearly all building insurance policies work on the new for old basis. The reinstatement or new for old policy makes no deduction for wear and tear and, as long as the house has been maintained in good repair, the company will pay out the full amount to restore the house.

If you have been in any way responsible for the accident, say you dropped a burning cigarette which set fire to the carpet, the insurance company will still pay out. Insurance covers you for the cost of damage, it does not apportion blame. That is what is meant by 'indemnity'.

How to claim

If you need to claim on a building insurance policy, you should contact the insurance company as soon as practicable. But if you have to make immediate repairs to prevent further damage, maybe a water pipe burst at the weekend, then emergency work will be paid for by the insurance company without quibble. Make sure you keep a record of the cost of emergency repairs.

PERSONAL LIABILITY INSURANCE

The variety of accidents that can occur are as varied as human nature. For example, someone walking innocently past your house could be struck on the head by a slate falling off the roof.

Many contents and buildings insurance policies automatically include cover for this sort of eventuality, should you be legally liable. If the cover is not there already, you will be able to add liability insurance cover into your policies as an optional extra. In any case, check your policies now.

The insurance pays any compensation you might be liable for if you, or one of your family, accidentally damage someone else's property, or injure them. If the accident involves a car, it will be covered under the car insurance policy. But if your house was the cause (the front wall collapses on a neighbour's feet), then the buildings' policy should cover it.

If an accident happens around the home, say a friend's child trips over a frayed carpet at a party, or if you let your dog run across the road and cause an accident, look at your contents policy to see if it covers you for personal liability insurance.

HEALTH INSURANCE

Because the National Health Service exists in Britain, paying separately to insure your health should be unnecessary. But sickness benefit is no higher than unemployment benefit and many people, particularly the self-employed, would find themselves in desperate straits if they were out of work through illness for a long time.

There are several forms of insurance against hardship following sickness: sick pay insurance, which insurance companies call permanent health insurance; personal accident insurance; and hospital cash insurance. You can also take out insurance to cover the cost of dentists' and opticians' bills.

Permanent health insurance (PHI)

This pays you an income if, through ill health, you are unable to continue working and your earnings stop. Under a permanent health policy, the money is payable for as long as you are off work until you reach the age of 65 for men, or 60 for women. The cost depends on the terms you choose; how much you want to receive; how long you decide to wait before payments start (three, six or twelve months); and whether you want the insurance to stop when you are 60 or 65.

For example, a man aged 35 who wants to receive £100 a week benefit, after a 26-week deferment period, will pay £7.40 a month in premiums until he is 65. Insurance terms for women always work out differently. The same policy for a woman until the age of 60 will cost £6.90 a month.

It is up to you to decide how long a deferment period you want. The decision will depend on how long your employer is prepared to pay you. If the deferment period is only four weeks, the same policy will cost a man £13.80 a month but more for a woman at £17.10.

The terms are different for women because actuarial statistics, on which insurance companies base their premiums, show that women are more susceptible to frequent illness that men. One theory is that, because men die younger, women survive longer to be ill, or take what the insurers euphemistically call 'morbidity time'.

Any permanent health insurance plan will have exclusions, and pregnancy is one. If you are still unable to work three months after the delivery of the baby, then you are 'ill' and can claim on the policy. But otherwise pregnancy is not an illness. Illnesses which are self-inflicted or relate to drink or drugs will also be excluded.

There is no way you can insure yourself against illness for an enormous amount of money, become 'ill', and live in luxury for the rest of your life. If you decide you want health insurance, then the best advice is to take out as much as you can. But there is a limiting factor and the insurance companies will place a maximum figure on the amount they will pay out.

The generally-used formula is this: the amount you receive from the policy or policies, if you have more than one, plus certain state benefits, should add up to no more than three-quarters of your average income over the past year.

The insurance company takes various factors into account when working out how much you will pay; as well as the waiting period and amounts paid out, your age, health record, occupation and sex determine the size of your premium.

Insurance companies do not wish to encourage idlers, so they also define just how ill you must be to claim on the policy. You are likely to come across two definitions: the most restrictive says you must be unable to do any kind of work for which you are 'reasonably' qualified. That means that if you are unable to do your old job, you must try and find another, different one, more suited to your changed abilities. A more relaxed policy will pay out if, because of sickness or injury, you cannot perform your own usual job.

It is important to choose a permanent health insurance policy which is index-linked. After you have taken out the policy, the pay-out will not automatically increase as your earnings go up. It will rise only in line with the terms of the policy. With some policies the amount paid out remains the same through the life of that policy and so inflation, even at low levels, will soon make a nonsense of it.

If you want a policy where the benefit rises by 5 per cent a year, you will have to pay a 15 per cent higher premium; for an extra 7½ per cent each year, the additional cost to the premium is 27½ per cent.

At present, if you are in a job and fall ill but are not covered by a company scheme or insurance policy, the only amount you can claim is Statutory Sickness Pay (see p. 150). If you are self-employed, you get nothing.

There are enormous advantages in joining a group scheme and a group need comprise only three or four people. The reason is that when a company pays the premiums, the employer is able to claim tax relief on the expenditure whereas an individual cannot. If you want to start one in your company, talk to the personnel officer and ask for details from an insurance broker or insurance company.

If the permanent health insurance is paid for by your employer, you have to start paying tax immediately you receive any benefit. But a permanent health policy taken out by an individual has a tax advantage: you do not have to pay tax on any benefit until you have received it for a full tax year; so if the payment begins in May, you can receive the benefit for 23 months before paying any tax – that is, until the following April to April tax year has been completed.

Permanent health cover is a long-term contract which cannot be cancelled by the insurer even if the policyholder's health deteriorates.

Personal accident insurance

This differs from permanent health insurance in that it is a short-term contract and is renewed annually. A personal accident policy will make payments for a specified period if you are unable to work because of an accident. This sort of policy could be of particular interest if you are in a high-risk job, maybe a window cleaner.

The policy will also pay out a lump sum if you die. The policyholder chooses the cover he wants; either for temporary or permanent disablement and pays accordingly.

Hospital cash insurance

This will pay out a set sum of money, say £10 or £20 a day, while you are in hospital. When you come out, even if to convalesce, the money stops.

Private health insurance

The cost of this is now very high. The main reasons people give for wanting health schemes is to have a room to themselves, the ability to choose when they have an operation, to have a choice of specialist and to avoid a queue. If these reasons are sufficiently important to you, you may consider paying for private health treatment.

The three companies which dominate this market are British United Provident Association (BUPA), Private Patients Plan (PPP), and Western Provident Association (WPA).

As an example of the costs, a married man in his thirties with two children living in London can expect to pay around £800 before discount a year, for a full refund of hospital charges and other necessary hospital treatment. Outside London hospitals, the same man would pay about two-thirds of the price.

Because of rising costs, cut-price benefit schemes are cropping up. For example, one policy pays out only if you are unable to get into an NHS hospital after six or 12 weeks; another limits the payout to £10,000; increasingly, there is the option to switch between NHS and private insurance. **Always ask for a discount when you apply: nearly everyone gets it.**

LIFE INSURANCE

There is a saying in the insurance business: 'Life insurance has to be sold', meaning that if salesmen did not persuade you, you would never take out a life policy.

Life insurance started out as a form of insurance called 'protection', which paid out sums of money either on a predetermined date or when you died. In the past decade, however, it has evolved more as a means of saving.

Even though there is no longer the attraction of tax relief on the premiums you pay, insurance companies themselves still enjoy favourable tax treatment which means they can create an attractive investment deal.

Insurance as savings has undergone continual changes over the years as new, inventive types of policy, such as those that are unit linked, were created.

Now, when you are buying life insurance you need to be clear in your mind which sort you want. Do you really want a form of saving, in which case the protection element will be very small? Or do you really need straightforward life cover, which is a lot cheaper?

Insurance as investment

For more about life insurance as a method of saving, see pp. 50–3.

Do you need life insurance?

A very basic question, and one to which the salesmen will answer 'yes'. But really, if you are young, with no commitments or dependants, then you do not. Even as a form of saving you would want something more flexible.

However, it is a good idea once you get married, or if you are supporting an elderly relative. In other words, if anyone would suffer financially by your death, you should take out life insurance.

The definition of life insurance is a contract which will pay out a specified sum of money on the date when a particular event occurs, for example your death or your retirement. To become entitled to a payout, you pay one single premium, or a series of regular ones.

How much will you need?

The more you want, the more it will cost you, of course. And the later in life you join a scheme, the more you will have to pay. You should base your calculations on how much your dependants need without you. And remember that this will increase as time goes by. Also, ask yourself if they will need a lump sum to pay off any particular debts, such as the mortgage, when you die.

How it works

The money that life insurance companies collect in premiums from their policyholders is put into a life fund. Because companies know what they are going to have to pay out, they can make sure that they have sufficient funds. This is the work of the actuary, whose job is to study statistics. He balances the risk of death by assessing a person's age, state of health and job to determine how much premium you must pay.

Insurance companies, sometimes called life offices, offer a range of different policies. These are known as: term; family income; whole life; endowment; unit-linked; and annuity.

Term insurance

This is also known as temporary insurance and is a policy covering a fixed and limited period of time. If the policyholder dies within the period, the dependants get the benefit. If the policyholder survives, then no money is paid out.

This policy can be level term, which means the amount paid out stays the same all the time. Or it can be increasing, when the amount rises from year to year; or decreasing when it falls. Decreasing term insurance is used for mortgage protection policies.

More subdivisions include: convertible temporary insurance (a policy which has the option to convert a policy into something different); and renewable term where, at the end of the term, you can buy the same cover again.

Term insurance can be used to cover you on a journey and is the kind of insurance sold at airports. It is a comparatively cheap, flexible form of insurance but the policyholder is not given any cash when the policy ends.

Family income policy

A family income policy pays the policyholder's dependants an agreed sum at regular intervals for a set period of time, if the policyholder dies within the term of the policy. It is cheap insurance, paid in regular instalments, but you or your dependants receive nothing if you survive the said term.

Whole life insurance

This means that your beneficiaries will collect the money when you die. The policy lasts for the life of the insured. It is more expensive than term insurance, but assuming the policy is kept going, your beneficiaries will always receive the money when you die. They can have either a lump sum or regular payments. Policies come either with- or without-profits (see overleaf).

If you want to discontinue paying towards a policy, the insurance company will give a surrender value, as long as the policy has by this time acquired one.

Surrender values are not guaranteed. When you take out the policy, you are sometimes given a projected value which is an intelligent guess but you may get more, or less, than forecast. This will not be in direct proportion to the number of years' premiums you have paid in. If you cash in a policy very soon after taking it out you will receive nothing. And for the first few years you will receive very little.

Indeed, you may very well get back less than you have paid in premiums. This is because nearly all the costs and expenses of setting up a policy, including commission, have to be met in the early years. This is called front end loading.

Whatever the costs involved in the policy, remember it is the policy-holder who pays them, even if he is not aware of it.

Endowment policy

With an endowment policy, you are certain of getting the money back at an agreed date, say 10, 15 or 20 years hence. If you die before then, the money is paid immediately to your dependants.

An endowment policy is more expensive than term insurance or whole life, but either you or your family are certain of receiving some money. You can time the end of the policy to coincide with a particular, perhaps expensive, event: a future wedding or a round-the-world retirement cruise.

Endowment policies, like whole life policies, can be either with-profits or without. Premiums for with-profits policies are costlier than for with-out-profit policies because you get a higher payout at the end of the policy.

With-profits policies

The basic amount you receive at the end is guaranteed but, in addition, you will receive bonuses, depending on how well the company has performed. These will be 'reversionary', which means they are added at the end of the year, or maybe every three years. In addition there will be a terminal bonus, which is added at the very end of the policy.

Premiums

There are two ways of paying your premiums: either in one lump sum (for a single premium policy) or in regular premiums throughout the life of the policy. These can be paid monthly, quarterly, half yearly or annually.

Unit-linked insurance

A unit-linked insurance policy is one in which most of the premium buys an allocation of units in an investment fund and part of the premium goes towards life insurance cover. The proportions vary according to company – some obtain a higher amount of life cover and less in units; others the opposite. You should decide how much life insurance you want, or whether you want a policy as an investment, and find a scheme accordingly.

Some of the premium also goes in charges and, again, this varies from company to company. You can keep an eye on how well the fund is doing by looking in the *Financial Times* unit prices under Insurances. You can either buy a policy in one lump sum (a single premium bond) or through a regular savings plan.

Annuity

Annuities provide an income in old age. The older you are when the policy starts paying out, the higher the income you then receive. Annuities provide a pension, starting at an agreed age, and they generally pay out for as long as the policyholder lives. The premiums can be paid in one lump sum or in annual instalments before retirement. Because you stand to gain a considerable income from this policy, the premiums are high. See also Home Income Plans p. 111.

Early surrender values

If you cash in a life insurance policy before it has run its full course, you will get a very poor return. The earlier you cash it in, the worse value you will receive. You may not even get back the amount you have paid out in premiums. For example: a man aged 35 next birthday takes out a ten year with-profits endowment policy for £10,000. He pays monthly premiums of £96.30. After two years, he decides to cash in the policy. **The early surrender value is £1,927.** But he has already paid out premiums of £2,311. He is nearly £400 worse off for taking out the policy.

Friendly societies

Tax-exempt friendly societies are doing little business now. In the March 1984 Budget, the size of the policies they could write was cut drastically but they are lobbying to be allowed more scope.

Friendly societies do not have to pay any tax on their investments but they are allowed to invest only in banks, building societies, local authorities, gilts and National Savings.

Tax

Until March 1984, one of the advantages about taking out a life insurance policy was tax relief. On every pound you paid in premiums, the taxman allowed you 15 per cent back. This tax relief has now been abolished but existing policies were not affected.

Money that is paid out under a life insurance policy, either to the policyholder or his heirs if he dies, is free of income tax.

AIDS

Insurance companies are very concerned about the spread of AIDS which could have a big impact on their actuarial tables. They now have a special question on their application forms. The precise wording varies and this might simply ask if you have had a blood test recently.

Single men wanting life insurance will find it more difficult and more expensive as AIDS becomes more widespread.

KEY PERSON INSURANCE

This is for directors and employees whose ability is crucial to the company. See p. 172.

SCHOOL FEES

The cost of sending an 11-year-old child to private school as a boarder is somewhere around £2000 a term. For an idea of the total cost, multiply that by three terms, ten years and two or three children and add on the extra expenses (items such as uniforms, sports equipment, food, travel). To send two children to a modest private school for ten years, if they are non-boarders, will cost about £100,000.

In the past, people often borrowed the money to pay school fees as they arose, and spent the rest of their lives repaying the debt. But when tax relief on interest payments (other than mortgages) was scrapped, there was little attraction in funding school fees that way.

Not so many people today are in a strong enough financial position to pay school fees out of their current income. There are many ways to spread the cost and the overriding advice is to plan as far ahead as possible.

If you are lucky, your child may win a scholarship or grant. But, for the majority, the best way is to take out an insurance scheme: the choice is between capital and income schemes.

Under the capital scheme you pay out a substantial lump sum. Many private schools operate their own capital scheme, in which case the money is known as a 'composition fee'. The fee is paid in advance directly to the school.

The amount you will have to put down depends on how expensive the fees are and also how far in advance you pay. As a rough guide, a lump sum paid when the child starts school to cover all the expected fees could be worth 15 per cent off the bill. But a lump sum deposited four years before the child enters school could knock as much as 40 per cent off the cost. If the parents pay the capital sum, they will not be liable to inheritance tax.

An insurance policy bought in advance can be used to pay school fees. This is an income scheme. You need an insurance policy that is an investment rather than one providing life cover, though this life element means that if you die the sum insured will be paid out and will meet the school fees. Also, if for any reason you do not eventually need the money to pay school fees, you will receive a lump sum anyway.

You should start a policy at least four years before the child starts school. What you do is to take out one policy to mature in each year that the child is at school. So, if your child will be at a fee-paying school for eight years starting in five years' time, you should take out eight life insurance policies now, one of which will mature each year starting five years from today.

LEGAL INSURANCE

Until 1967 this form of insurance was illegal in the United Kingdom. The first policy appeared in 1974 and since then just a handful of companies have entered the market.

There are two forms of legal insurance: legal advice and legal expenses.

Legal advice

This gives 24 hours a day access to a legal adviser 365 days a year. You can ask about any legal problem you have:

- ☐ an argument with your neighbour
- ☐ employment problems
- ☐ personal injury
- ☐ family rows
- ☐ faulty purchases
- ☐ tax problems
- ☐ insurance problems

The advisers are solicitors, barristers and accountants and, in most cases, they will be able to answer on the spot. They will advise your rights and whether the case is worth pursuing in court.

That is the extent of legal advice insurance but it is surprisingly cheap. Some companies and trade unions now offer this as a worker's benefit.

Legal expenses insurance

This form of insurance will cover your costs if you go to court either to bring an action or defend a case. There is usually a maximum of £10,000.

Basic insurance ranges from motoring claims through the whole gamut even, with a few policies, to defending a murder charge unsuccessfully.

However, only one or two companies will pay the cost of matrimonial cases, and disputes over house building are nearly always excluded.

Increasingly, legal protection insurance is sold through brokers who add it to their household or motor policies. For about £5, motorists will have their legal fees paid, for example, if they have an accident with an uninsured driver.

Combined legal advice and legal expenses insurance costs about £70 a year.

PROTECTION

Insurance companies are supervised by the Department of Trade and Industry which can intervene if it is unhappy about the way a company is operating. Insurance policies issued by companies authorised by the DTI are safe-guarded by the Policyholders' Protection Act.

If an insurance company collapses, policyholders will receive up to 90 per cent of the money they were entitled to.

There is one proviso: if the Policyholders' Protection Board thinks you have been promised an 'excessive' amount, they will pay you less. This is to prevent companies deliberately making extravagant promises and going bankrupt on purpose, leaving the Policyholders' Protection scheme to pick up the tab and keep policyholders happy.

Alternatively, the failed insurance company may be kept going either by being taken over by another company, or by other life insurance companies paying a levy towards its salvation. If this happens policyholders may get lower benefits than under the original company, but at least the policy will continue.

INSURANCE SALESPEOPLE

Some of the most far reaching changes in recent legislation affect insurance salespeople. The Financial Services Act has turned their lives inside out. The changes affect even those who only sell the occasional life insurance policy, such as accountants and solicitors, although these professionals can pass business on to an independent broker if they prefer.

The part of the Act which has prompted so much reorganisation is called 'polarisation'.

Polarisation means that insurance salespeople have only two choices: either they can be 'tied' to one insurance company selling only its investment products and become 'company representatives'. Or they can be 'independent' and sell insurance policies from a range of different companies and become 'independent intermediaries'.

But note that this only applies when they are selling investments, which, as well as the obvious shares and unit trusts, include pensions and life insurance when the main purpose is investment. It excludes term insurance, health insurance and building society deposit accounts. And insurance salespeople can do what they like with motor insurance or house contents and buildings policies.

Every one must be authorised under the Financial Services Act and failing to do so is a criminal offence. But the independent salesperson must comply with certain strict rules which are designed to protect investors. Briefly, they must always put their customers' interests before their own and always act in the customers' best interests.

See p. 29 for more details.

Salespeople can operate under a range of titles:

☐   investment adviser

☐   financial consultant

☐   independent intermediary

☐   broker

☐   financial management consultant

The name makes no difference at all. All of them mean basically the same thing: insurance salespeople. And that means they earn their living from commission.

All of them are bound by the same rules of the Financial Services Act and this also controls the amount of commission they can receive.

COMMISSION

Anyone whose income derives only from commission must be susceptible to the temptation that selling product A can earn £200 while product B might earn £500. There have been many ways in which insurance companies have made their policies more attractive to salespeople by bonuses for high volume sales (called over-riders), gifts and other under-the-counter payments.

All that is banned by the Financial Services Act. And, to a degree, the amount of commission paid is now controlled.

This has been achieved by setting up an industry-wide scale of payments. The commissions agreement sets a maximum amount which can be paid and this is:

☐   25 per cent of the premium for basic endowment and whole life policies

☐   35 per cent of the premium for term insurance

☐   30 per cent on permanent health insurance

These percentages are paid on the annual premium for a certain number of years, which varies according to the type of policy. After that renewal commission of 2·5 per cent is paid; for example, if you buy a 15 year endowment policy, the salesperson will earn 25 per cent of the premium you pay for the first two years and then 2·5 per cent for the remaining 13 years.

Although term insurance is excluded from the Financial Services Act, it is included in the commissions agreement.

But there is no compulsion on companies to stick to these rates.

Any that want to pay more to the salespeople can. But, in these circumstances, the salespeople must tell their clients exactly how much they will earn. This is called **hard disclosure**. But if the salespersons' commission is within the agreed scale, they need say nothing to customers. This is known as **soft disclosure**.

By his silence, the customer can assume how much he will earn. Anyone who wants a copy of the commissions agreement to check for themselves can ask for a free copy from LAUTRO, address on p. 249.

The whole system will change again in 1990.

FEE PAYMENT

Not every insurance salesperson works on the commission only basis. Some charge a fee for advice to clients and then pass on the commission they receive to the customer.

If the client decides not to buy any insurance, there is no commission payable obviously. But the adviser gets paid by the client anyway.

WHAT THE SALESPERSON MUST TELL YOU

When you contact an insurance salesperson, he or she must make you aware of certain facts:

☐ whether he or she is a company representative or independent intermediary

☐ if he or she is receiving more than the agreed commission scale

☐ the early surrender value of any policy you buy

The Securities and Investments Board (SIB) has produced a simple guide, together with the Metropolitan and City of London Police Company Fraud Department, advising the public how to handle insurance salespeople. The booklet is called *Self Defence for Investors* and free copies are available from SIB, address on p. 250.

Husbands and wives can take out a joint life policy. This can be a first joint life (or last survivor) policy which means that when one of you dies, the policy pays out to the other. This can be used as a mortgage protection.

Or it can be 'last death' and pay out when the second of you dies, perhaps to provide money to pay inheritance tax.

But you may find it more flexible (and not very much more expensive) to take out two separate policies.

If you had an endowment mortgage, you could make this a joint life one as well, so that when the first of you dies the other receives the money. Indeed, joint life policies need not be restricted to married couples.

What insurance terms mean:

ACTUARY — The person who does the sums to decide how much you pay in premiums.

ALL RISKS — Comprehensive insurance that covers almost anything you can think of.

AVERAGING — If you are not fully covered when you make a claim, the insurance company may pay out a proportion of the total claim only.

COVER — The eventualities the insurance policy provides for.

INDEMNITY — Compensation for loss or injury.

INDEX-LINKED — The cover and premiums go up each year in line with inflation.

LLOYD'S — Lloyd's of London is an organisation through which underwriters act as go-betweens for those seeking insurance and private investors with the money to provide the cover.

NEW FOR OLD — Replacement as new: insurance that pays the current price for an old item.

REINSTATEMENT — Same as new for old.

SURRENDER VALUE — This is how much the policy is worth if you cash it in early.

TERMINAL BONUS — Bonus added at the end of a policy.

THIRD PARTY — The person you injure. The insurance company is the first party, you are the second party and anyone else involved is the third party.

UNDERWRITER — The person who takes the risk of insurance; the one responsible for having the money to pay up.

UNIT LINKED — More volatile results; money invested in units.

WITH-PROFITS — Steady growth relating to how well the insurance company performs.

Life insurance policies

Name	What it covers	Cost
term	payment if you die within a fixed period	cheap
family income	payment if you die within a set period	cheap
whole life	payment whenever you die	more expensive
endowment	payment on a given date or if you die sooner	even more expensive
annuity	regular income starting on certain date until you die	very expensive

Life expectancy

AGE	YEARS TO LIVE			
	MEN		WOMEN	
	years	months	years	months
20	53	4	57	6
25	48	7	52	10
30	43	11	48	1
35	39	3	43	6
40	34	6	38	10
45	30	0	34	3
50	25	7	29	9
55	21	6	25	5
60	17	6	21	2
65	13	11	17	2
70	10	9	13	6
75	8	1	10	5
80	5	11	7	7
85	4	3	5	6
90	3	0	3	10
95	2	2	2	9
99	1	9	2	1

There are two arbitration schemes for insurance companies: the Insurance Ombudsman Bureau and Personal Insurance Arbitration Service. See p. 249 for addresses. They can help you only if your company is a member of one of them; if it is they will look into your complaint. If it is not, you can try the appropriate insurance association which may be able to explain why the company is acting as it is.

THE FAMILY

Life is expensive. It costs money to get married, it costs money to have children and it costs money to bring them up. It costs money to get divorced, and it costs money to die.

Along the way you are entitled to certain help in the form of allowances and benefits and you can help yourself to minimise the costs.

GETTING MARRIED

The cost of weddings is as long as a piece of string. The decision on whether to have a fanfare, trumpets and the cathedral choir, or to slip round the corner to the registry office in a pair of jeans is a totally personal one.

However, there are certain minimum legal costs that you cannot avoid. In this country you can get married legally by a civil or a church ceremony.

Registry office

You have to pay £10 for each notice of marriage, which you must lodge 21 days before the wedding, and £11 for the attendance of a registrar. If you are in a hurry, you can have a superintendent registrar's licence of marriage which costs an extra £28 and enables you to get married the day after you have lodged the notice. A copy of the marriage certificate costs £2.

The choice

The cost of weddings is high, so are there financial advantages in living together rather than getting married? In some instances you are better off; but on other occasions you would do better to get married. The pros and cons break down like this:

WHEN IT'S BETTER TO LIVE TOGETHER:

Living together	Marriage
woman's investment income is taxed as her own	woman's investment income always added to her husband's income*
both of you can claim tax relief and capital gains tax exemption on one property each	allowed tax relief on one property only, pay capital gains tax on second home

can claim single parent's allowance	no extra allowances*

WHEN IT'S BETTER TO BE MARRIED:

Marriage	*Living together*
a woman can claim on her husband's national insurance contributions	she cannot
widow's benefits and pension when husband dies	no widow's benefits
will receive married man's tax allowance which is higher than the single person's*	taxed separately
widow will inherit husband's property	unless he leaves a will, the woman will have to prove right to the estate and may not win
can claim maintenance for herself and child if partner leaves	can claim for child only, anyway more difficult
do not pay inheritance tax or capital gains tax on gifts to each other	liable for capital taxes

* This will change in 1990 when the tax system is reformed

Social Security helpline

Anyone can telephone for advice on social security benefits, on freephone: 0800 666 555.

HAVING A BABY

Apart from the emotional upheaval of having a baby, the change to your earnings can come as a serious shock. If it is your first child and, until now, you have been working full time, then the reduction in income if you give up work will be sharply felt.

The cost of having a baby

To maintain a child for the next 16 years will cost around £60,000 ignoring inflation, and babies start as they mean to carry on. To kit out a new baby can cost more than £1000.

During pregnancy you are entitled to help from the state. It is called Statutory Maternity Pay (SMP) and it replaced the maternity allowance and maternity pay.

STATUTORY MATERNITY PAY

Employers are now responsible for paying their pregnant employees through Statutory Maternity Pay (SMP). Your eligibility, and how much you get, depend on how long you have worked for the company and how much you are paid.

You are entitled to the money whether or not you intend returning to work.

Provided you have worked in the same job for six months and have been paying national insurance contributions you will receive SMP. You will get more if you have worked there for more than two years.

Part time employees have the same rights but must have worked at least eight hours a week for five years to get the full amount.

The top rate works out as 90 per cent of your wages for the first six weeks and then £34.25 for the following 12 weeks. Mothers with a shorter working record will get £34.25 for the entire 18 weeks.

You must inform your employer at least 21 days before you intend to stop work.

But not everyone will qualify. Those who might miss out are the self-employed, or someone who has recently changed jobs. In these cases, you can apply for the new **maternity allowance** from the DHSS. You need to have paid enough national insurance contributions, broadly six months' payments in the past year. Then you will be entitled to £31.30 a week for 18 weeks.

If your baby is born prematurely and you have not had the chance to give your employer the 21 days' notice of stopping work, you will still get 18 weeks' pay.

When to start

With both SMP and maternity allowance, you have some choice about when you take maternity leave. There is a core period of 13 weeks starting six weeks before the baby is due and this is fixed. But the additional five weeks can be taken either before or after the core period, or from a bit of both. However, if you work in any of those weeks, then you cannot receive maternity pay as well.

The earliest that maternity pay can start is 11 weeks before the baby is due. But if you continue working after you are 34 weeks pregnant you will not be able to claim the full 18 weeks pay.

Mothers in special need can apply for a Social Fund **maternity payment.**

Anyone on income support or family credit will be entitled to £85 for each baby (£170 for twins). But if you have savings of more than £500, the amount will be reduced.

If you work for more than one employer, you can claim SMP from each. You can even stagger the time when you take maternity pay. Some employers will pay more than the basic SMP entitlement. But that given is the minimum you will receive.

Maternity payment

Maternity payment replaced the maternity grant. It is a flat rate payment of £85 available from the social fund.

Returning to work

If you have fulfilled the requirements for receiving statutory maternity pay, and also told your employer when claiming the money that you intended to return to work after the birth, then your employer cannot sack you or make you redundant.

You should confirm your intention of returning to work seven weeks after the birth (in fact, this is the date of the expected birth, not the actual birth), and you must also give at least one week's written notice before you return to work. Also, you must return within 29 weeks of the actual birth.

If your employer refuses to take you back because you have had a baby, you can claim unfair dismissal.

The job you return to should be identical, in essence, to the one you left. But, you cannot insist on the self-same job. As long as the conditions are the same, your employer can ask you to take a different job.

You will be entitled to any pay increases that occurred while you were away, but those missing weeks will not count towards length of service for pension rights. However, other benefits such as redundancy pay will be calculated as though you had never been away.

You may be lucky enough to have an employer who agrees to pay you for the whole time you are away, if you say that you will return. But this is not a statutory right.

Child benefit

This is paid at a fixed rate for every child. It is paid regardless of income to the person who is responsible for bringing up the child, which is usually the mother. It is paid every four weeks in arrears.

The amount is £7.25 a week from April 1988 for each child and it is not taxable. 'Child' is defined as anyone under the age of 16, or 19 if they are still in full-time but not higher education.

To claim child benefit, pick up leaflet CH1 and forms CH2 and CH3 from a DHSS office. You should claim as soon as the child is born, but if you claim a little late, you can receive arrears.

One-parent benefit

If you are bringing up a child on your own, you can claim one-parent benefit of £4.90 a week from April 1988. This is a flat-rate sum and not determined by how many children you may have. If you have two children you will still only receive £4.90. It is not taxable. Ask for form CH11 to claim. You can get this in addition to the child benefit as long as you are not living with someone as husband and wife; are temporarily separated (for example in hospital or prison); or are receiving other benefits. You also cannot claim if you already get the child's special allowance or the guardian's allowance.

Child's special allowance

A divorced woman whose ex-husband died after the divorce used to be able to claim this benefit but it was abolished in April 1987. Although the rate for existing claimants has now increased to £8.40 from April 1988, this benefit is no longer available to new applicants.

Guardian's allowance

This payment is for those bringing up children who are orphans or effectively orphans. It is normally paid only if both parents are dead, but it can also be paid in circumstances where the surviving parent cannot be traced, or is in prison for a long sentence, or where the parents were divorced and there is no liability for custody or maintenance. The amount is £8.40 a week from April 1988 and it is not taxable. You should claim on form BG1.

Family credit

This has replaced Family Income Supplement. Low-income working families can claim Family Credit (FC) in addition to child benefit.

Any family where one member works 24 hours a week or more is entitled to FC, the level of which is assessed according to weekly earnings over a five week period.

Lone parents will have the same level of FC as married couples, regardless of whether they are already receiving one-parent benefit.

Families earning less than £51.45 a week will receive the maximum FC of:

- [ ] £32.10 for an adult
- [ ] £6.05 for a child under 11
- [ ] £11.40 for a child aged 11–15
- [ ] £14.70 for a child aged 16–17
- [ ] £21.35 for a child of 18

If a family's income exceeds £51.45, the benefit will taper according to the level of earnings.

Low-income families will no longer be eligible for free milk or vitamins.

Mobility allowance

If you are unable or virtually unable to walk, you can claim the £23.05 a week mobility allowance. There are no contribution conditions but you must be aged between 5 and 65 when you first claim. To apply ask for form NI 121.

Christmas bonus

Pensioners are entitled to a bonus of £10 at Christmas. The bonus is also paid to anyone receiving invalid care allowance, widow's or widowed mother's allowance, or the attendance allowance. It is available for Christmas 1988 but may be abolished in future years.

Attendance allowance

This allowance is for people who need a great deal of care because they are severely disabled, either physically or mentally. No contributions are needed and you can claim on behalf of a child once it reaches the age of two.

There are two rates: the lower rate is £22 a week for someone needing care either during the day or at night; the higher rate of £32.95 is for people who need care both day and night.

SCHOOL FEES

If you want to pay for your child to be educated privately, you should start planning well before the infant is ready to go to school: the sooner you start paying, the less it will cost in the long run. See p. 130 for details.

SINGLE PARENTS

'Single' applies to anyone who is unmarried, widowed, separated or divorced. See p. 141 for details of one-parent benefit.

Maintenance

If you are separated, your husband may have to pay you maintenance and he will certainly have to do so for your children. If you get divorced, then he is liable for the children only, as long as you have enough money of your own.

If the court does not order him to pay you money, you may need to contact your local DHSS office to ask for income support if your income falls within the limits. The DHSS will try to contact him to force payment. See p. 192 for information about maintenance payments.

If you are in a full-time job on a low salary, you may be able to claim family credit, see opposite.

Additional personal allowance

You may also be able to claim an additional personal tax allowance for your children. This is for anyone who has no husband or wife to help bring up children and also includes a married man whose wife is totally incapacitated. The allowance is worth £1490 a year. See p. 186.

DIVORCE

In the year a woman becomes separated or divorced (or, in fact, widowed) she is entitled to claim the single person's allowance in her own right for the full year while her husband continues to receive the married man's allowance. Make sure the tax inspector has given you this.

If you need help in any way, you can contact several organisations which will help. They include: Child Poverty Action Group, Cruse National Widow's Association, National Council for One-Parent Families, Gingerbread, and Families Need Fathers. See pp. 248–9 for addresses.

Modern legislation has now made postal divorces possible and has helped to take some of the pain out of the process, but it will always be an unhappy experience. If you have been married for more than one year and the marriage has broken down irretrievably, you will be able to get a divorce. There are two stages – a decree nisi followed by a decree absolute. The time between the two is usually six weeks and is designed to ensure that each party is aware of what is happening.

Any financial matters or custody to be decided will be resolved between the decree nisi and decree absolute.

Cost

This is unquantifiable and depends on how complicated the case is. If both partners agree, have lived apart for more than two years and are childless, a postal divorce, using no solicitors, will cost £50.

The solicitor's fee for an undefended case could be about £300, but ask for some sort of estimate before you start. You will also have to pay £40 for filing the divorce in the court.

Who pays

If you cannot agree between yourselves how to split the costs, the judge will decide.

Legal aid

Legal aid is no longer allowed for undefended divorces since they can be carried out quite simply. Defended divorces, particularly if they turn into a bitter wrangle, can become very expensive and legal aid may be granted if you are eligible. Very broadly, if you have less than £5000 in disposable capital and a disposable income of less than £5765, you can apply. You may, however, be entitled to 'Legal Advice and Assistance' (the Green Form scheme), which can apply up to decree nisi (the actual processing of the divorce petition). This does not cover you for what is called Ancillary Relief, that is, the financial arrangements or maintenance or custody of any children. See also pp. 245–6.

Children

If there are children involved, the judge will want to be sure that they are adequately provided for. This means agreeing which parent will have custody and who is to pay for the children's upkeep.

Separation

If you do not want to go all the way and get divorced, you can apply for a legal separation. It is advisable to have a properly drawn-up document and to take the advice of a solicitor. Otherwise you may have difficulty changing the maintenance terms of the deed later on.

For instance, if a wife is granted even a nominal sum of maintenance, however small, it is easier to have this amount subsequently increased when she might need it. It would be more difficult for her to start asking for maintenance afterwards.

WIDOWHOOD

To be classified as a widow and claim a widow's allowances, you must have been married to the man when he died: if you were divorced, unless the divorce had still to be made absolute, you will not be his widow.

In the year your husband dies, you can claim the single person's tax allowance for a full year, on top of the married man's allowance that your husband had been claiming up to the time of his death.

Widow's payment

From April 1988, widows will receive a £1000 tax-free lump sum immediately on bereavement instead of a widow's allowance.

Widowed mother's allowance

This is worth £41.15 plus £8.40 for each child if your late husband had made sufficient national insurance contributions (April 1988 figures).

This allowance is taxable but the child's portion is not. The allowance will continue for as long as you qualify and provided you do not remarry.

Widow's pension

Widows over 45 will get a weekly benefit immediately. From 45 to 54, widows will receive an age related pension. This rises from £12.35 at 45 to £38.27 at 54. Women widowed at 55 receive the full pension, which is £41.15 a week.

Your entitlement to the full amount depends on whether your husband made enough national insurance contributions. But, you might be entitled to an additional amount based on your late husband's salary if you were widowed after 5 April 1979. This entitlement will continue for as long as you qualify and provided you do not remarry.

If widowed before 11 April 1988 you keep the benefits you had been receiving.

Death grant

This has been abolished. Those in need can claim money from the Social Fund.

Funerals

These are expensive. If there is no money and no one to pay for the funeral when you die, the local authority must take care of the body. If there is someone who might reasonably be expected to take responsibility for the funeral but does not have enough money, they can claim a grant towards the cost of the death certificate, a plain coffin, transport, flowers, undertaker's fee, and the cost of a simple burial or cremation.

Costs

Although this is a distressing time, if you are having to arrange a funeral, you really should ask for quotations before choosing an undertaker. The excuses for not doing this are that it is 'tasteless' to compare prices when a loved one has just died and 'penny pinching' to quibble about the cost afterwards.

The doctor will be able to give you advice and so will a solicitor. Or you can seek guidance from the National Association of Funeral Directors, address on p. 249. The standard death certificate costs £2 and a special death certificate, which you will need to claim on an insurance policy, costs £2. You will need two doctors' certificates for a cremation and they cost £19.65 each.

For a straightforward burial in a churchyard cemetery, you will pay £19.50 and twice as much if you live outside the area. Additionally gravediggers might cost £50, a minister £20, embalming about £20–£30. The fee in a crematorium can range from £55 to £90. If the body waits in a rest room, this can cost up to £5 a day. You will pay another £15 to have the ashes scattered. The other expenses you will incur are: the cost of a casket, moving the body; hearses and cars; a headstone.

The cheapest, most basic funeral will cost around £200, an average funeral will cost from £300 to £350. No VAT is payable. An elaborate coffin can cost £600 or more.

Widowers

Widows receive more financial assistance than widowers, but the Cruse National Widows Association and the National Association of Widows will give advice and guidance to men as well as women.

CRIMINAL INJURIES COMPENSATION BOARD

If you are injured as a result of a criminal act, you can claim compensation from the Criminal Injuries Compensation Board. This is a Government-funded committee set up to give money to victims of violent crimes.

You can claim from the board if you are injured as the result of a crime, or if you have been trying to prevent a crime, or while trying to apprehend someone you believe has committed a crime.

If you were to die as a result of your injuries, your husband or wife could claim a bereavement award which is fixed at £3500.

It does not matter if you do not know who committed the attack or whether or not the person is prosecuted. You can still claim.

CHAPTER · 11

IN WORK AND OUT OF IT

If your employer sacks you, could you claim unfair dismissal? Your rights at work are protected by law but you need to know what they are.

Your entitlements and conditions of work will be set out in a contract of employment but this is not necessarily a very comprehensive document.

CONTRACT OF EMPLOYMENT

The whole contract does not have to be put in writing but the main terms of employment must be and, naturally, it is clearer for both sides should you come to a dispute to have a written agreement.

The written statement must include these details:
- [ ] the name of both employer and employee
- [ ] job title
- [ ] the date you start working
- [ ] how much you will be paid and how regularly
- [ ] normal hours of work and any compulsory overtime
- [ ] annual holidays and holiday pay
- [ ] details of the pension scheme or statement saying that there is not one
- [ ] what happens if you are ill
- [ ] period of notice on both sides
- [ ] disciplinary rules
- [ ] complaints procedure

In addition, a thoughtful employer will make sure you have the following information:
- [ ] the requirements of the job and to whom you are responsible
- [ ] the circumstances which can lead to suspension or dismissal and disciplinary rules and procedures
- [ ] opportunities for promotion and the necessary training required
- [ ] welfare and social facilities
- [ ] health and safety rules and fire regulations
- [ ] any suggestion schemes

Ideally you should also be told:
☐ whether you may be expected to move house
☐ whether you may be asked to perform different duties at any time
☐ whether this job will place any restrictions on your future work for other employers

Your pay packet

Your employer must give you a payslip with your wages showing exactly what you have earned, how much of this you are actually being paid, and what has been deducted. It makes no difference if you are paid weekly or monthly, by cheque, direct into your bank account or in cash.

Deductions

Before he hands over the money, your employer will deduct:

☐ tax, under the PAYE system
☐ national insurance contributions
☐ company pension contributions
☐ union subscriptions, if you have agreed to their deduction

Payment by cheque or cash

Some workers are still paid in cash but both employers and trade unions are in favour of encouraging everyone to have their wages paid directly into a bank account.

The advantage is mainly that of security – neither you nor your employer is handling large amounts of cash. Also, from your point of view you will find it easier to ask for a bank loan if the manager knows you have a regular pay cheque.

Tax

For more detailed information about tax, see Chapter 14. After deducting all allowances, you are liable to pay tax at the following rates on your salary: (*1988–89 figures*)

£	*tax* %
First 19,300	25
Over 19,300	40

By looking at your PAYE code (see p. 199), which is assessed by the Inland Revenue, your employer knows how much tax to deduct each week or month. You have to pay tax only on the amount that is left after taking away your personal allowance and pension contributions.

Once a year, in April, you will be handed a P60 by your employer which tells you exactly how much money you received and how much you paid in tax for the past financial year. It is important to keep this safely as proof of the tax you have paid.

STATUTORY SICK PAY

When an employee goes sick, his employer may have to pay Statutory Sick Pay (SSP) for up to 28 weeks' sick absence in any one tax year.

You will not be paid SSP until you have been off work for at least four days in a row; then you are in a 'period of incapacity for work' (PIW).

Your national insurance contributions entitle you to SSP and neither you nor your employer can opt out of the scheme.

After 28 weeks, the DHSS may pay **state sickness benefit** which is £31.30 a week or £39.45 if the claimant is over pension age. And later still **invalidity benefit**, comprising a pension of £41.15 and an invalidity allowance.

Exactly how much SSP you are entitled to receive depends on your average pay, including bonuses and overtime. The rate is divided into two bands (April 1988 figures):

if you earn	*you will receive*
£79.50 + a week	£49.20
£41 to £79.50	£34.25

The employer then recovers these payments from the Inland Revenue. You will not be given SSP if your average earnings are below £41 a week.

The change means that the employer is required to take responsibility for paying workers when they are ill and also for deciding that the worker is genuinely off sick.

SSP is taxable. Married women who are still paying the reduced national insurance contributions are entitled to receive SSP although they are still not eligible for sickness benefit.

UNEMPLOYMENT

If you are out of work, you can receive unemployment benefit if you fulfil certain conditions:

☐ you must satisfy the contribution conditions
☐ you must be unemployed and unable to find a job
☐ you must be capable of, and available for, work and free from any other disqualification or disallowance

You can find out more information from leaflet NI 12 on unemployment benefit, obtainable from unemployment benefit offices.

Unemployment benefit is not paid for the first three days of unemployment and then it can be paid for one year excepting Sundays or, more exactly, for 312 days. After that you must work for an employer for at least 13 weeks for a minimum of 16 hours a week to qualify for benefit again. If you are unable to find work, you will have to claim income support. If you have been sacked or made yourself voluntarily redundant, you receive no benefit for the first 26 weeks. And any income support will be reduced by 40 per cent.

Immediately you become unemployed, you should claim at your nearest unemployment benefit office, the address of which you can find at the post office. Benefit will be paid by Girobank cheque which will be posted to you on the day after you sign and claim benefit.

Benefit is usually claimed and paid every two weeks and you can cash the Girobank cheque at the post office of your choice. You can also pay the cheque into your own bank account.

You should also claim income support (then you will automatically receive the associated benefits) because unemployment benefit is fairly low.

How much?
The standard rate of unemployment benefit for those under pension age, from April 1988 is:

personal rate	£32.75
adult dependant	£20.20

If you are over pension age, it is:
personal rate	£41.15
adult dependant	£24.75

If your national insurance contributions record is insufficient, you will get less than this. Apart from the amounts payable for children, the benefit is taxable, though tax is not deducted before you receive it. The tax will be assessed by the Inland Revenue at the end of the tax year.

INCOME SUPPORT
This has replaced supplementary benefit and applies to the same people who claimed supplementary benefit: pensioners; unemployed; single parents; and those unable to work because of illness.

Anyone over 16 whose income is below the set figure can claim. But those who work for 24 hours a week or more, or are in full-time education, do not qualify.

Income support comes in three sections:

☐ basic rate
☐ family responsibilities
☐ special circumstances

Basic rate applies to all claimants. For single people, the amount depends on age: those under 18 receive less than 18–24 year olds. The rate is higher for those over 25. Lone parents over 18 get the 25+ rate; and couples over 18 receive more than couples under 18.

Family responsibilities are an extra amount paid each week for every child, depending on age. There is a flat rate for each family with one child or more, the 'family premium'. And an extra family premium for a blind child or one receiving the mobility or attendance allowance.

Special circumstances premiums are paid to those with extra needs and can be paid in addition to the other payments:

- [ ] pensioners' premium, for those, or with a partner, aged between 60 and 79
- [ ] higher pensioner premium. This is paid instead to pensioners over 80 or those over 60 already receiving a disability premium
- [ ] disability premium is paid automatically to anyone who is blind or receiving long-term incapacity payments
- [ ] higher disability premium is for severely disabled people living alone and receiving attendance allowance at the higher rate
- [ ] lone parents' premium is a fixed amount paid to single parents with at least one child

Any savings you have up to £3000 will be ignored and there is a sliding scale of benefit if you have savings between £3000 and £6000: each £250 of savings will be assumed to provide an income of £1 a week.

Earnings of £5 a week, after paying national insurance contributions and income tax, will also be ignored when calculating the benefit due.

And any couples who have been unemployed for more than two years, disabled people and single parents can earn £15 a week without affecting their benefit.

All previous payments for heating, laundry and diet have been abolished. Anyone in special difficulties can apply for extra money from the social fund.

How to apply for income support

Claims should be made in person or by post to your local DHSS office. Your request is assessed by an adjudication officer. However, if you disagree you can appeal to the Social Security Appeal Tribunal and the Social Security Commissioners.

basic rate for a single person over 25	£33.40
single parent over 18	£33.40
couple over 18 with at least 1 child	£51.45
family responsibilities premium	£6.15
pensioner premium for couple	£16.25
higher pensioner premium for couple	£18.60

SOCIAL FUND

This replaced the lump sum payments made under supplementary benefit, maternity and death grants. Some of the payments are grants, others are loans which have to be repaid.

Loans will be made to anyone with savings under £500 who has a problem with budgeting for expensive one-off items, such as new furniture. Those with more than £500 may still be eligible. Deductions will be made each week from the weekly benefit to repay the loan.

REDUNDANCY
Should you lose your job through redundancy, you are entitled to compensation from your employer. Only in the following circumstances do you not possess an automatic right:

- [ ] when you have worked for less than two years in the job
- [ ] if you have passed retirement age
- [ ] if you work part-time (less than 16 hours a week)
- [ ] if it is a fixed-term contract
- [ ] if you usually work outside the United Kingdom
- [ ] if you are offered a comparable job by the same employer

How much?
You are entitled to a lump sum payment depending on your age and earnings. You must be over 18 and you must have worked at least 16 hours a week for two years, or at least eight hours a week for five years.

The most you will receive by law if your firm has no special scheme is £158 a week and for no more than 20 years even if you have worked for the company for longer than this. This works out at £3160 and it is tax free.

Period of notice for redundancy
Assuming you have no better agreement with your employer, the minimum period of notice you must be given is:

4 weeks' to 2 years' employment	1 week
2 to 12 years' employment	1 week for each year
over 12 years' employment	at least 12 weeks

Proving redundancy
It is important that your employer admits that he is dismissing you because you are redundant. Otherwise, you are not entitled to any compensation.

Sometimes employers sack workers when they are, in effect, redundant to avoid paying out large sums.

If you think this is happening to you, you can appeal to an industrial tribunal (the address is in your local telephone directory, or ask at a Citizens Advice Bureau for help). You should take action immediately as you might forfeit your rights if you wait longer than six months.

Golden handshakes
Your employer may offer you a large lump sum when you are made redundant. These are unofficially called 'golden handshakes'.

The first £30,000 you receive is tax free. Larger amounts are taxed at 40 per cent.

UNFAIR OR WRONGFUL DISMISSAL

Provided you have been in the job for more than two years, you can take action against your employer if you feel you have been sacked without good reason.

Unfair dismissal claims are made to win compensation and they are handled by an industrial tribunal. Wrongful dismissal claims seek to recoup wages owed and are heard in civil courts.

Unfair dismissal

Anyone who feels he has been unfairly dismissed, or is not receiving the redundancy money he is entitled to, can appeal to an industrial tribunal for compensation. This should be done within six months of losing your job or you might not be able to claim.

Reasons for fair dismissal

If your employer can prove any of the following against you, you could lose your unfair dismissal claim:

- [ ] misconduct, which includes:
  drunkenness
  violence
  dishonesty
  disobeying orders
  poor timekeeping
  non co-operation
- [ ] incompetence or lack of qualifications
- [ ] it is illegal for you to continue working (eg a driver who has lost his licence)
- [ ] striking, as long as all the other strikers were dismissed
- [ ] some other 'substantial' reason: this is not defined by the courts and, for example, can be used against someone who simply upsets his colleagues

Calculating compensation for unfair dismissal

This is calculated in the same way as redundancy payments and the maximum basic award is £4740. On top of this you can claim compensation for loss of earnings and benefits such as pension rights up to a maximum of £8500.

If the tribunal orders your employer to reinstate you and your employer refuses, you are entitled to an additional payment of up to £4108, depending on earnings.

Wrongful dismissal

Even if the dismissal is 'fair' you can claim 'wrongful' dismissal if you feel the contract of employment has been broken. For example, you were given insufficient notice or dismissed before the end of a fixed-term contract.

Successful cases
These are instances where employees have won claims for unfair dismissal:

☐ someone sacked without being given the opportunity to defend complaints or improve his behaviour
☐ someone sacked for alleged stealing who was given no opportunity to clear his name
☐ someone whose job was changed and the most interesting element taken away
☐ someone sacked on the grounds of ill health without a full medical report being obtained.

If you win an unfair dismissal claim, the tribunal can award you either:

☐ your old job back, that is reinstatement
☐ re-employment but in a different job, which is re-engagement
☐ a cash sum

EQUAL PAY
Both men and women must now receive the same money and same conditions as their colleagues in the same job, or if a woman's job has the same value as a man's under a job evaluation scheme.

EQUAL RETIREMENT AGE
Companies must allow female employees to continue working after the age of 60 if they wish to. They cannot be forced into retirement at an earlier age than men.

SEX DISCRIMINATION
You can claim discrimination on these grounds:

☐ you are passed over for promotion because of your sex
☐ the job you apply for has an unreasonable sex-biased qualification
☐ you are treated less favourably because you are married
☐ the conditions of the job make it difficult for married people
☐ you are treated less favourably because you have already claimed unfair treatment

If you feel you have been unfairly treated, appeal to your employer, or the industrial tribunal, or failing that, the Equal Opportunities Commission.

NATIONAL INSURANCE CONTRIBUTIONS
Your national insurance contributions entitle you to sick pay, a pension, unemployment benefits as well as various other benefits and allowances.
   There are four categories of contributions:

Class 1

You and your employer will pay at this level if you are employed; earn more than the lower earnings limit; are over 16 but have not reached retirement age. In this context, company directors count as employees. See DHSS leaflet NI 35.

Just how much you pay depends on whether you are contracted in or out of the earnings-related pension scheme. For more information on pensions see Chapter 15.

Contracted in

employee:	5 to 9 per cent of your salary between the lower and upper earnings limits (UEL)
employer:	5 to 10·45 per cent of your salary above lower earnings limit (LEL)

Contracted out

employee:	2·85 to 6·85 per cent of your salary between the lower and upper earnings limits
employer:	0·9 to 6·35 per cent of earnings above the lower earnings limit.

Married women who are still paying the reduced contributions pay 3·85 per cent of all earnings up to the UEL.

In 1988–89, the lower earnings limit (LEL) is £41 a week and the upper earnings limit (UEL) for employees only is £305.

Class 2

This applies to the self-employed, who may have to pay Class 4 contributions as well. The rate is £4.05 a week unless your earnings are below £2250 a year (1988–89).

If you work as an employee, and also have a self-employed job, you may have to pay both Class 1 and Class 2 contributions.

Class 3

These payments are voluntary and will maintain your contribution record for a few entitlements if you do not pay Class 1 or Class 2 contributions. Ask the DHSS for advice if you come into this category but it is rarely worthwhile paying. The amount is £3.95 a week.

Class 4

This class again is for the self-employed who have to contribute unless they are under 16 or over retirement age. The rate is 6·3 per cent of annual profit between £4750 and £15,860 (1988–89).

Contribution credits

If you are out of work through no fault of your own, you will receive credit contributions for Class 1 or Class 3. But married women still paying the reduced contributions cannot be credited.

Home responsibility protection
While you are looking after a child or an invalid, and not paying contributions, you are covered by home responsibility protection which means you will not lose the widowed mother's allowance, widow's pension or retirement pension. However, no year before April 1978 will count.

FRINGE BENEFITS
To tempt you some employers offer various fringe benefits on top of your normal salary. These range from luncheon vouchers to private education for the children. In some cases the benefit will be completely tax free; in others you will pay full tax. See p. 193.

The sort of perks that are offered, and which you may be able to negotiate if you are in a strong position, are:

- [ ] luncheon vouchers
- [ ] season ticket (or interest-free loan to buy one)
- [ ] car
- [ ] petrol
- [ ] private medicine
- [ ] living accommodation
- [ ] board and lodging
- [ ] television
- [ ] television rental or licence
- [ ] telephone rental
- [ ] cheap rate mortgage
- [ ] life insurance
- [ ] working clothes
- [ ] meals in canteen
- [ ] professional fees and subscriptions
- [ ] hairdressing expenses
- [ ] entertainment expenses
- [ ] shares or participation in share option scheme

Cheap loans
You will be taxed on the difference between the rate of interest you pay and an official rate, currently 9.5 per cent.

Profit sharing
You may work for an employer who allocates you shares in the company. There are tax advantages in taking these up. The company provides the money to buy the shares, which are held by trustees.

You cannot sell the shares for two years but then you will be taxed on the value of the shares (either the original value or the sale price, whichever is lower). After that, the tax gradually decreases until, if you hold the shares for more than seven years, you pay no tax on the benefit. The rules are about to be reviewed.

Share option schemes

Your company may run a share option scheme which gives you the right to buy an agreed number of shares at a fixed price. You pay nothing at the time but you have the option to buy the shares, at the same fixed price, in three years' time when, hopefully, they will have risen in value. You do not have to buy the shares and pay no income tax if the scheme is approved by the Inland Revenue.

SAYE share option schemes

Another way of investing in the company you work for is by a regular savings plan. See p. 37.

Bonuses

Any extra money your employer pays you is taxable at your top rate (the highest rate of tax you pay).

Commuting costs

These can be a very large element of your regular outgoings and it is worth finding any way you can to cut the costs:

- ☐ ask your employer for an interest-free loan
- ☐ if possible, travel in a cheap-rate period
- ☐ buy a long-term season ticket but time it so that you do not pay for holiday periods (see p. 14)
- ☐ share a car (see p. 226)
- ☐ walk or cycle short distances

CHAPTER · 12

BEING SELF-EMPLOYED

Advice on how to invest your spare money is all very well. But most people's financial problems start long before reaching this stage.

'Never mind about saving, how can I get my hands on the money in the first place?'

Apart from those lucky enough to inherit, the only way is to knuckle down and earn it.

There is a great deal of encouragement and financial help around for budding entrepreneurs these days. From those who want to build their own conglomerate, to others just making a bit of spare cash from their hobby.

IS SELF-EMPLOYMENT FOR YOU?
Make no mistake, this is hard work. Before taking the first step, you must be sure that you have the commitment to work long hours, overcome setbacks and keep on top of the accounts.

Your intention is to build a proper, lasting business. It is a waste of effort, and totally disheartening, to start a new business and then fail a year later because of lack of commitment.

THE DIFFERENT TYPES OF BUSINESS
There are a number of ways you can set up your own business:

- ☐ sole trader
- ☐ partnership
- ☐ limited company
- ☐ co-operative
- ☐ franchise

Sole trader
This is anyone who is totally responsible for their business, though not

necessarily working alone. Everything you own, including the house, can be taken away from you to pay debts.

Partnership

Two or more people sharing the profits and losses together form a partnership. From the outset, a partnership agreement is vital. This details who receives how much, and what happens if the partnership turns sour.

Limited company

Any losses will be limited, so your home is not at risk. But, in exchange, a company must comply with stricter accounting and public disclosure rules.

A limited company can be public or private. A public company puts 'plc' after its name and anyone can buy its shares, which are quoted on the stock exchange.

A private limited company writes 'Ltd' after the name and the shares are held by just a few people. A limited company is a separate entity from the person who owns it. It costs £50 to register a new company; £40 to change the name and £20 a year to file accounts.

Co-operatives

Co-operatives can be organised in various ways, including a partnership or limited company. But the basic principle is that the members, who are mostly the employees themselves, share the profits and have control over the way the company is run. Each member has one vote.

There are several organisations which help co-operatives to get started:

- ☐ Co-operative Development Agency
- ☐ Industrial Common Ownership Movement
- ☐ Industrial Common Ownership Finance
- ☐ Job Ownership Ltd
- ☐ Scottish Co-operative Development Committee

and the Registry of Friendly Societies will help on the basics of registration. See pp. 248–50 for addresses.

Franchise

A half-way stage between going totally alone and working for someone else is to buy a franchise.

Franchising is a system whereby the owner of a business (the franchisor) allows other self-employed people (franchisees) to sell its products, such as fast food, or service, such as carpet cleaning. For this the franchisees pay a fee.

The franchisor makes sure all the shops have a uniform appearance, provides the stock and gives help with finding premises, employing staff and generally running the business.

Many well-known high street names are franchises: Wimpy; Pizza Express; Kentucky Fried Chicken; Tie Rack and British School of Motoring.

The cost of buying a franchise ranges from £5000 to £3 million for a Holiday Inn hotel. Then there is an annual cost. Some franchisors charge a percentage of turnover, typically 10 per cent, called a management service charge. Others take a mark up on each product. Either way, the cost works out the same and, in return, franchisees receive continued support including further training as necessary and advertising.

Most franchisors belong to the British Franchise Association, which can provide you with a list of members. See p. 248 for address.

WHICH BUSINESS?

You will probably know whether you are going alone, want to be part of a co-operative or buy a franchise. But the most difficult choice is between setting up a partnership or starting a limited company.

PARTNERSHIP OR COMPANY?

The main consideration is tax, although there are other differences that may be important to you.

Partnership	*Limited company*
pays personal income tax twice a year after the business's year end	directors taxed on PAYE. Company pays Corporation tax which is cheaper for highly profitable companies
pays on previous year's profits up to 20 months later; useful when profits rising	pays PAYE monthly. Company pays on profit 9 months later
losses can be offset against future profit and other personal income of husband and wife	losses can be offset against one previous period; future profits and Capital Gains Tax
personal assets can be seized to pay debts; can be made bankrupt	liability limited to share capital
easy to start up	must register; can buy off the peg company for under £100
accounts can be kept simple	must file audited annual accounts
cheaper national insurance contributions but entitled to fewer benefits	directors pay higher national insurance plus company also pays

| can put up to 17·5% of earnings into pension | can put up to 15% of salary into pension plus contribution from company |
| pays Capital Gains Tax on business assets | can pay Capital Gains Tax on capital gain |

WORKING FROM HOME

If you are starting in a small way, working in a spare room saves rent and commuting time. But you should be aware of the consequences.

☐ you may need planning permission, especially if your project involves noises, smells or frequent visitors. Give your neighbours nothing to complain about
☐ if you only claim expenses for heat and light you pay no Capital Gains Tax when selling the house
☐ but if part of the house is used exclusively for business, you pay Capital Gains Tax on that proportion

PRICING

There is one recurring fault from which all self-employed people suffer: they under-price themselves at the beginning. Don't fall into this trap, even though pricing your goods or services is one of the hardest skills to learn.

Find out how much your competitors charge and, if you are giving a better service, you can charge more (but make sure your customers appreciate the quality of your service). Of course, you may feel you need to undercut until you get better known.

For example, if you are selling home-made cakes, however much you enjoy making them, your time must be valued fully. Do not think: that is what I must charge to show a profit. Always aim to charge the rate the market will stand.

INVOICING

Small businesses can be squeezed at both ends. They may have tight payment rules from their suppliers but find it hard getting money out of their customers. This has been the downfall of many self-employed.

Send your invoices out promptly and do not be too shy or insecure to hassle for payment. You need to keep money coming in regularly.

This creates your cash flow which is the life blood of any business.

SELLING YOUR DEBTS

This is called factoring and can provide a way out of trouble if a lot of people owe you money.

Factoring companies (often part of one of the large banks or finance houses) will take over your debts and give you a cash sum. Obviously, you have to pay for this service and it can be very expensive.

You will receive around 80 per cent of the value of invoices still outstanding and the rest when (and if) the money is finally paid up. But the factoring company will take a commission for their work.

However, you need a turnover of at least £100,000 a year before any factor will take you on.

BUSINESS PLAN

Even the smallest business needs a sense of direction. At the start you should write down your business objectives for the next five years and then review them regularly.

The bigger your business, the more detailed this business plan must be.

PROFIT

To stay in business you must make a profit. However much you enjoy the work and being self-employed, you must not lose sight of the fact that you need money to live on and money to plough back into the business.

Every new business starting out will find some customers; the problem is continually attracting new customers and then to create a lasting business which will grow year by year.

MONEY QUESTIONS

You need money to get going and more money to keep in business. This is 'start up' capital and 'working' capital.

Start up capital

You will almost certainly need to buy equipment of some sort before you start. You will also need to pay for wages, stationery, a telephone, possibly premises and perhaps publicity.

Even if you have enough in savings, you may be better advised keeping hold of that and taking a bank loan. This is where you need an accountant's advice. An accountant will also give guidance on how much capital you need to start up with.

Working capital

As well as the money to get started with, you will need money to keep going. Your working capital covers the gap between paying out for raw materials and receiving payment for the end product.

How much you need depends on what type of business you run. If you have to carry large stocks, you will need more working capital. Then you may need extra funds when you want to expand.

Some businesses have a better chance of negotiating credit terms with their suppliers. Others may persuade their customers to pay cash on the nail. Ideally, you should delay paying for materials as long as possible but get the money from your customers as quickly as you can.

Usually, it works the other way round which creates the gap in cash flow.

CASH FLOW

Accepting a lower priced job which pays promptly can, on occasions, be more profitable than taking a highly priced order where you have to wait months for your money.

You need cash flowing in regularly. Without that, however good or large the business, it will go bust.

A cash flow chart will help clear your brain about the money coming in and going out of the business and will show in advance the months when you will be overdrawn. A bank manager will expect you to have a forecast such as this before you ask for a loan.

You should draw up a cash flow forecast for at least a year at a time, even longer if you can. Include absolutely everything you can think of; over-estimate your outgoings and underestimate your receipts. Be realistic about how quickly customers will pay up.

Cash flow forecast

Month	January Forecast	actual	February Forecast	actual	March Forecast	actual
EXPENDITURE	£	£	£	£	£	£
Materials bought						
Rent, rates						
Heat, light						
Wages						
PAYE						
NI						
VAT						
Payments to creditors						
Repairs						
Vehicle costs						
Insurance						
Telephone						
Postage						
Packaging						
Bank interest						
Accountant						
Advertising						

Cash flow forecast

Month (*cont.*)	January Forecast	actual	February Forecast	actual	March Forecast	actual
EXPENDITURE (*cont.*)	£	£	£	£	£	£
Stationery						
Loans						
Pension						
Drawings						
Equipment bought						
....						
....						
....						
TOTAL EXPENDITURE (A)						
INCOME						
From sales						
From debtors						
Commission						
Investments						
Repayment of VAT						
Sale of assets						
Capital						
....						
....						
....						
TOTAL INCOME (B)						
SURPLUS = B − A (C)						
DEFICIT = A − B (C)						
OPENING BALANCE (D) (from previous month)						
CLOSING BALANCE = C + D						

YOUR COSTS

The everyday outgoings you face fall into two categories:

☐   direct costs
☐   overheads

Direct costs are the expense of buying raw materials and producing your product or service.

Overheads are the costs of keeping the business going, such as rent and heating.

BORROWING

Small businesses can borrow in the same way as individuals, by:

☐   overdrafts
☐   loans both short term and long term

(see Chapter 4 for more information on borrowing).

Banks are now very tuned in to small businesses. Ask at your local branch and you will almost certainly find they have special arrangements and a separate small business department. (See p. 58 for advice about how to deal with your bank manager.)

But there are other sources of finance as well, and grants in particular are very useful.

GOVERNMENT LOAN GUARANTEE SCHEME

This guarantees 70 per cent of a loan up to £75,000 made over two to seven years. It is available on bank loans made to most types of small business.

Then, if the business totally fails, the Government picks up 70 per cent of the tab and the bank only has to carry the rest. However, both will try to recover the money from you if they have any chance of getting it back.

The disadvantage is the cost. On top of the normal bank's rate of interest (around 2 per cent over base rate), the borrower has to pay an extra 2·5 per cent on the Government's 70 per cent.

BUSINESS EXPANSION SCHEME

This is a Government scheme to encourage outside investors to put money into new private UK businesses by giving them tax advantages.

There are restrictions about which small businesses can qualify as a Business Expansion Scheme (BES). Details are available from the Inland Revenue, booklet IR51. (See also p. 53.)

Businesses can raise up to £500,000 a year under a Business Expansion Scheme and this will qualify for tax relief. But if the business is to build privately rented property on assured tenancy terms (see p. 100), the ceiling is £5 million.

GRANTS

Various grants are available to small businesses, most of them local. Get in touch with your local enterprise agency or local authority who will know what is around.

Redevelopment areas also give grants to encourage new businesses to move into their area and create employment.

Grants are always worth having because, unlike loans, you do not have to pay them back.

ENTERPRISE ALLOWANCE

This is another Government scheme. It is available to unemployed people all over the country who start up their own business. The grant is £40 a week and it continues for 52 weeks.

To qualify, you must have been receiving unemployment benefit or income support (the enterprise allowance will replace this); be at least 18 years old but under retirement age; and unemployed for at least 8 weeks before you apply.

You must work full time in the business and show you can invest at least £1000 in the business.

YOUR ACCOUNTS

Keeping accounts may seem a chore but it does show you a regular picture of the health of the business. Ideally, you should keep weekly and, at the very longest, monthly figures. This keeps you in control and can give warning if you are running into trouble.

A sole trader does not have to submit formal accounts whereas a limited company does. But you must account to the Inland Revenue for income tax and you will appear better organised and well run if you show proper accounts.

Don't worry if you are unable to cope with accounts yourself. Whatever skills you have to run your own business, these are unlikely to include accountancy. It is money and time well spent to use an accountant.

A small local accountant will be cheaper to employ than a large city firm. Or you may find a retired accountant who will spend a couple of days a week, even one day a month, sorting out the paperwork for you.

TAX

This is what accounting leads up to. Immediately you become self-employed, inform the Inland Revenue.

Limited company

You as a director are an employee of the company and subject to the PAYE system. You decide at the beginning of the year how much you are going to pay yourself and deduct income tax before taking the money.

If, at the end of the year, there is a profit left, you can take this profit as extra bonus (less tax). Any profit you do not take is subject to corporation tax.

Sole trader or partnership
All profits are taxed as your income under Schedule D.

How tax is assessed
Tax is due twice a year on 1 January and 1 July.

In your **first year** of operating, you pay tax on the actual profits you earn. In the **second year** you can choose between paying tax on the profit you earn **or** on the profit you made in the first year.

This second option will usually be the best because in your first year you will have all the start up expenses, which can be offset against tax. And, hopefully, your profits will be increasing year by year so you can delay paying extra tax for a year.

In the **third year** again you can choose to be taxed on the actual profit you make, or on the previous year's profit. If this time your profits are lower than the year before, you should ask to be assessed on the real profit.

This system is designed to be helpful to new businesses. Once the company is up and running, you will be assessed on a preceding year basis.

When to take your year end
The accounts of a **sole trader or partnership** have to be made up annually and one of the first decisions you should make is when to strike your year end.

There are various ways of picking this date:

☐ using the calendar year
☐ the anniversary of your starting date
☐ your quietest trading period
☐ the tax year ending 5 April

You can pick any date you like.

If you have no special reason for choosing any particular one, then you should go for the date that gives you the longest period in which to pay tax. And that is the end of April.

The taxman's year runs from 6 April. Whatever your company's financial year, the tax you owe is due on 1 January for the first instalment and 1 July for the second.

Look at the difference, once the company has been going for a few years, between having a year ending on:

☐ 31 March
☐ 30 April
☐ 30 September
☐ 31 December

31 March, 1989: half the tax is due on 1 January, 1990, **nine months** later, and the second instalment on 1 July, 1990, **15 months** later.
30 April, 1989: half the tax is due on 1 January, 1991, **20 months** later, and the second half on 1 July, 1991, **26 months** later.
30 September, 1989: half the tax is due on 1 January, 1991, **15 months** later, and the second half on 1 July, 1991, a delay of **21 months**.
31 December, 1989: first tax due 1 January, 1991, **12 months** later, and the second bill on 1 July, 1991, **18 months** later.

You can see how much valuable extra time an end April date gives.

Preceding year basis

This means that you pay tax on the profits from your accounting year which ended in the taxman's previous year.

Limited company

A limited company pays tax nine months after the end of the financial year.

Expenses you can offset against tax

All the costs involved in running your business can be offset against income tax. But they must be incurred wholly and exclusively for the business.

With the car or telephone, for example, which is partly for business and partly for private use, you can claim a proportion for business use.

When it comes to claiming costs arising from using part of your house as an office, be careful that the room is not used exclusively for work, otherwise you could be liable to Capital Gains Tax on that part when you sell the house.

Other expenses which can be offset against tax:

- [ ] anything you buy to run the business, from paperclips to rent
- [ ] cost of selling and advertising
- [ ] books and magazines
- [ ] professional subscriptions
- [ ] car
- [ ] staff wages including wife's
- [ ] interest charges
- [ ] insurance premiums, except life insurance
- [ ] legal fees

What you cannot claim

- [ ] legal expenses on forming the company or partnership
- [ ] your living expenses
- [ ] business entertainment
- [ ] depreciation on equipment (but see capital allowances)

Capital allowances

You can claim separate tax relief on writing down the cost of equipment you buy, such as machinery, cars and buildings.

You can claim usually 25 per cent (less for buildings) of last year's cost of the item each year. A business in an enterprise zone can claim higher capital write downs.

VALUE ADDED TAX (VAT)

VAT has to be paid on almost everything we buy and every service we use. It is like a sales tax and the rate is 15 per cent.

VAT is administered by Customs and Excise who have very strict rules about how promptly you must account for VAT, keeping proper tax invoices and seeing receipts for everything.

There is no time delay advantage as there is with income tax. VAT must be settled quarterly, although small businesses that have been going for more than a year can opt to pay a fixed monthly amount and settle at the end of the year. If you are late they can, and will, fine you.

Cash accounting allows businesses to pay VAT only on payments they have received, rather than the invoices issued, which may not have been settled by the date VAT is due.

Some items have a zero VAT rate; others are exempt. It is important to know the difference for accounting purposes.

Exempt items:
☐ food and drink, apart from crisps and hot take-away food
☐ books and newspapers
☐ heat and light
☐ children's shoes and clothes
☐ transport, apart from taxis and hire cars
☐ exports
☐ new building

What you cannot reclaim

You cannot reclaim VAT you have paid on:

☐ buying a car
☐ business entertainment
☐ personal use of any equipment

Who has to register for VAT

Once your earnings reach £22,100 a year or £7500 in one quarter you should register for VAT.

You can voluntarily register for VAT, which means you can reclaim the VAT you pay out for company-related purchases, including telephone bills and petrol.

But you can only volunteer if Customs and Excise accepts you make taxable supplies as part of your business.

> You account separately for VAT and income tax. You can claim income tax relief for more items than you can offset against VAT.

KNOW WHERE YOUR MONEY IS

A barrow boy can be more astute than a businessman. Over and above your weekly or monthly accounting, you should have a pretty accurate idea of how much you owe and which of your customers owes you what, and when it is all due.

INSURANCE

You will need insurance for a variety of reasons:

- [ ] employer's liability
- [ ] public liability
- [ ] product liability
- [ ] business premises; fixtures and fittings
- [ ] motor insurance (see p. 221–4)
- [ ] private health (see p. 125)
- [ ] key person

Do not be dismayed at your responsibilities and expense. You may not need all this insurance.

Employer's liability

You are legally required to have this insurance for anyone who works for you. The only exceptions are members of your family, although it would be sensible to include them as well.

You could be sued by any of your employees who injured themselves or became ill as a result of working for you.

The cost depends on how risky the work is, whether it is purely clerical or involves heavy machinery. And how many are on your payroll.

Public liability

You do not have to take this but it covers you if a member of the public is injured because of your work. It could be that, while showing a customer the product, you drop it on their toe. Or one of your employees runs into a customer with a fork lift truck.

Product liability

This insurance is for any injury suffered because of a product you have manufactured or serviced.

Business premises

As with your own house, you should insure your premises and the fixtures and fittings against theft or damage.

You can include tools, equipment and the stock both while it is on your premises and on the way to customers.

Motor insurance

Just as with a private car, this is legally required. You should make sure your drivers are all covered, whichever vehicles they are driving.

Private health

Self-employed people believe they can never go sick. It can certainly throw a small business into confusion if the boss is ill for a long time.

There is permanent health insurance which will pay you an income if you become totally unable to work. But there are also other types of accident insurance: personal accident and hospital cash insurance.

For full private health treatment you need private health insurance. This could be particularly useful for the self-employed because it will entitle you to early treatment at a time that is convenient to you.

See pp. 123–6 for more information on all these types of insurance.

Key person insurance

The usefulness of this type of insurance is becoming recognised by both big and small businesses. The insurance is for directors, partners or any senior employees who are crucial to the business. If one of them dies, and in a partnership of 12 only ten will live long enough to retire, the insurance pays out a substantial sum.

This can help in a number of ways: to tide the business over a dip in profits, to buy the widow's shares or to employ extra temporary help.

PENSION

Self-employed people now buy the same personal pensions which are available to everyone. See pp. 212–14.

You can offset your pension contributions against tax at your highest rate, up to 17·5 per cent of net relevant earnings, and even more if you are over 50.

If you have not paid into a pension in recent years, you can make up the lost tax relief going back six years.

Choose a pension which allows you to pay in different amounts year by year as your profits change and to make lump sum payments or regular contributions as you wish.

You can then use this pension to back a mortgage (see p. 73) or to get a loan later on (see p. 214).

Those who have old Section 226 policies can keep them going.

EMPLOYING OTHER PEOPLE

Once the business expands from a kitchen table operation, roping in the rest of the family and neighbours in a crisis, you move into a whole new ball game.

Employees' rights are protected by law and must be strictly respected. And as with all things, you can save yourself many problems later by starting out on the right foot. Make sure the employee knows exactly what is expected and has written conditions of employment.

This contract will show:

☐ name of both employer and employee
☐ starting date
☐ wages or salary and when paid
☐ normal hours
☐ holiday entitlement
☐ pension arrangements if any
☐ period of notice required on either side
☐ disciplinary procedures

Slightly different rules apply to part-time workers employed for less than 16 hours a week, although there is no reason why they should not be treated in the same way.

Your overwhelming responsibility is to pay employees punctually. This involves deducting tax and national insurance contributions from their wage packets.

The Inland Revenue will tell you how to deduct PAYE and the DHSS can advise on the right amount of national insurance to take.

For more details see Chapter 11, In Work and Out Of It.

WHERE TO GO FOR HELP

There are numerous agencies which will help a small business. These are some to approach, the addresses are on pp. 248–50:

☐ Department of Trade and Industry small firms service has regional centres around the country
☐ London Enterprise Agency (LEntA)
☐ Business in the Community publishes a list of enterprise agencies
☐ Council for Small Industries in Rural Areas (CoSIRA)
☐ Welsh Development Agency
☐ Scottish Development Agency
☐ Local Enterprise Development Unit (LEDU) in Northern Ireland
☐ Highlands and Islands Development Board
☐ local authorities in many areas give help – ask at your local town hall

WHERE TO GO FOR FINANCE

Anyone putting money into a new business knows they are taking a risk. But there are specialists who provide this start up money, often called 'venture capital':

☐ your bank, or another bank if you have no response there
☐ 3i or Investors In Industry
☐ British Technology Group
☐ a Business Expansion Scheme, details from Inland Revenue or Department of Employment's small firms' service
☐ British Venture Capital Association

CHAPTER · 13

WILLS

A solicitor will charge about £30 to £40 to draw up a will; if you die intestate, that is without having made a will, he will charge about £500 to sort out the mess. Even if you think you own nothing worth worrying about, your family might still squabble over your possessions after you die.

It is worthwhile for everyone to write out a will. By having a will you ensure that the people, or charities, that you want to receive your worldly goods will, and anyone you dislike who might otherwise be entitled to a share, is cut out. There are, however, a few circumstances in which a properly drawn-up will can be challenged.

You can, if you wish, write a will on any old scrap of paper. If it is correctly signed and witnessed, it will be perfectly legal. You must be confident, however, that your wording is completely clear. Of course, you know very well which is your 'favourite charity' and everyone else knows that you love cats. But this is not good enough to ensure that the money reaches the right people. In these circumstances, lawyers can spend many expensive hours debating just what you had in mind.

Do not assume that once you have made out a will you can forget about it forever. Circumstances change and you should, if necessary, amend your will from time to time. You can do this by adding paragraphs, called codicils.

Printed forms
You can buy ready-printed will forms at many stationers or from HMSO. A plain form costs only £1.50.

If your affairs are straightforward, you can save the cost of a solicitor by using a will form. Or, if you are confident that you can make your intentions completely clear, you can even save that cost and write out your own will.

Solicitors
If you have any doubts about what you want to say, use a solicitor. It is better to pay a few pounds now rather than run the risk of having much of your estate disappear into a larger bill later on when your beneficiaries start arguing over their inheritance.

A solicitor will charge about £40 to draw up a simple will, but you can compare prices first by telephoning several. For advice on how to choose a solicitor see p. 245.

Making your own will

If you decide to do it yourself, these are the points to remember:

- [ ] keep it simple and absolutely clear:
    'I leave £500 to my children.' Does this mean £500 each or £500 between them?
- [ ] mention the people you wish to inherit by name:
    'I leave £500 to my sister-in-law.' Your brother might have divorced and remarried before you die and then both sisters-in-law could claim the £500
- [ ] sign in front of two witnesses, who must not be beneficiaries
- [ ] appoint two executors, who can be beneficiaries
- [ ] date the will
- [ ] say on the will that you are revoking all others. In any case, actually destroy any previous will when you make out a new one
- [ ] keep it in a safe place: with your bank (which can charge), with a solicitor, or in a safe drawer and tell your executors where it is. The bank manager does not have to charge you, but it could cost you about £3 a year

Executors

In your will, you must appoint executors who will be responsible for administering the estate when you die. You need, in fact, appoint only one executor, but people usually appoint two, or sometimes more, so that the work is not too great a burden for one person, and also as a precaution in case one of them dies before you. This also helps to ensure fair play and that there is no opportunity for bias.

Do check with the executors that they are prepared to take on the work before you commit them and remember, executors are fully entitled to inherit under the will.

You can ask a bank to act as executor. The banks gladly accept this work, but they charge steeply for it. The scale rises according to the value of the estate, regardless of how much work goes into it. The banks work to a fixed scale, something like this: first £50,000, 5 per cent; next £50,000, 3 per cent; everything over £100,000, 2 per cent. There will be a minimum charge of about £500 but the bank manager can exercise a certain amount of discretion if the estate is extremely simple.

A £100,000 estate, which is not particularly wealthy these days if a house is involved, will cost around £4000 in bank fees. Neither do the banks have a reputation for being very efficient or speedy.

Solicitors will be cheaper than banks. You can appoint one as an executor in your will or your executors can decide after your death to go to a solicitor for help. A large firm of solicitors in the City of London will be very expensive, but a small firm in London will be cheaper. In the provinces the cost will be even less. The bill is assessed according to the value of the estate, the amount of time involved and the number of documents being handled.

Witnesses

Two witnesses must be present when you, and then each other, actually sign the will. It is not even enough for them simply to be in the house at the time. If they do not watch you sign it, then the will can be declared invalid. Unlike executors, neither witnesses nor their husbands or wives can benefit from a will.

How can you leave your money?

You can leave your money to whomever you wish, but you cannot tell them what to do with it. If your heirs wish to turn the money over to a cause of which you strongly disapprove, there is no way you can stop them.

But you do not have to leave your money outright. For example, you can bequeath just the interest being earned on a sum of money to one person for as long as they live. Then you can leave the capital sum itself to someone else after the death of the first person.

If any of your beneficiaries dies before you, unless it is your son or daughter, the bequest is cancelled and their share is divided between the others. If your son or daughter predeceases you, then that inheritance is passed on to their children.

You can, of course, bequeath individual items from your estate to specific people. These are called legacies. To avoid any misunderstandings it is worth listing the items, however many, and naming the recipients, with an alternative choice in case they die before you.

Whether you have made out your own will, or paid a solicitor to do it for you, make sure that several people know where you keep it. Then they can begin to administer your estate without delay.

What happens when you die

Before the money from your will can be shared out, your executors must obtain probate. This means that the will is valid. The executor adds together all the assets, values them and satisfies himself that he has missed nothing out. He then contacts the Probate Office in London. If the total in any one account falls below £5000 there is no need to ask for probate. With a small estate, he simply contacts those holding the deceased's money, whether it is in National Savings, a building society, a bank, or an insurance company, and asks them to pass it on to him.

Certain charges are deducted from the final estate before the beneficiaries can receive the money. One of these, not surprisingly, is the solicitor's own fee; then the cost of the funeral and any bills that are left outstanding, such as gas and electricity bills, telephone, mortgage, etc.

If there is not enough money in the estate to meet these bills, then it is hard luck on the debtor. Your surviving family does not have to pick up the tab if your estate is insolvent.

Writing out a will

Although you can make corrections to a will as long as they are initialled by you and witnessed, if you do make a mistake it is advisable to start again on a fresh sheet to avoid any possible queries later on. In the first place, draft the wording so you need only to copy it on to the formal documents. See below for how to word a will.

A simple, straightforward will could be worded like this:

THIS IS THE WILL OF ....
I, Mary Elizabeth Jones, revoke all previous wills and codicils. I appoint to be my executors John Edward Jones of 1 Railway Cuttings, London NE6, and John Philip Brown of 2 Railway Cuttings, London NE6.

I leave everything to my husband, John Edward Jones. If he predeceases me, my estate is to be divided equally between my sister, Susan Smith of 9 Green Park, London NE9, and my brother, Peter Harold Smith of 46 Blue Street, London NE9.

Signed by Mary Elizabeth Jones ....
on the .... day of .... 19......

Witness's signature ....
Full name ....
Address ....
....
....
Occupation ....

Witness's signature ....
Full name ....
Address ....
....
....
Occupation ....

Administering an estate

Do not panic if you are the executor of a friend's estate when they die: your duties are straightforward. But if at any stage you cannot cope, you can always consult a solicitor.

First you may have to take care of the funeral arrangements. Then the essential task is to 'prove' the will. For this, you need to obtain probate by applying to the Probate Office in London.

However, if the estate is made up of cash and personal belongings, you do not need to obtain probate. And if there are several savings accounts with less than £5,000, again no probate is required.

In this case you write to the company concerned saying what has happened and ask for the money to be paid out. The company will send you a form to complete.

In the case of joint accounts, the surviving owner simply takes over the total use of the account.

If probate is required, you must collect all the details you can about the value of the total estate. This will include all assets and liabilities and involves having the property valued. If the deceased owed more than the value of the estate, including all the legacies, then you had better ask for professional advice from a solicitor. Otherwise, you can complete the probate forms. You will have to arrange to pay a probate registry fee and possibly inheritance tax.

Once probate has been granted, you advise the companies concerned to release the money.

You also need to settle any capital gains and income tax bills.

Your next action is to sell whatever assets are necessary to raise the money to pay any debts and the beneficiaries according to the terms of the will.

Provided everybody is happy, you can then distribute the assets among the beneficiaries.

Challenging a will

Usually, if a will has been properly drawn up, none of the beneficiaries or would-be beneficiaries, can challenge your wishes, however ridiculous or unfair others may find them.

But there are certain circumstances when a bona fide will can be challenged, and successfully.

One instance is when a dependant, usually a widow, is left insufficiently provided for. If a man dies and leaves all his money to his brothers and sisters and nothing, or very little, to his widow, then she has a right to more of the estate, providing she can prove she was dependent on her late husband. The court decides just how much. She can apply for legal aid to pay the cost of fighting, but she may find that if she wins a large sum of money she has to pay some of it back in legal fees.

The other instance when a legal will can be overturned is if anyone can show undue influence. If it can be proved that someone who benefited under the will used pressure to persuade the deceased to leave money to them, the right to the money can be rejected.

What happens if you die intestate

If you die without having made a will, there are strict guidelines about how your money is divided.

First, if you are married and have less than £75,000, everything goes to your husband or wife. It will not go to a divorced spouse. If you have more than £75,000, the spouse receives all the personal belongings and the first £75,000. Half the remainder is divided equally between the children (including adopted and illegitimate children) and the spouse receives the income on the remainder for the rest of his or her life. On the spouse's death, the capital is distributed equally among the children.

If there are no children, the spouse receives the personal belongings and the first £125,000 and the parents of the deceased share half the remainder. When there is no surviving spouse, or it is the estate of a single parent, the children share the estate equally. If the deceased was not married and had no children, the estate goes first to his or her parents; if they are no longer alive to brothers and sisters, or if they have died to their children; failing that to grandparents; and then to aunts and uncles.

If everyone who can benefit, whether or not a will was written, has already died, the estate then goes to the crown, that is, to public funds.

If a husband and wife die simultaneously, then the law assumes that the elder died first.

Scotland

The laws of testacy are different in Scotland. A surviving wife and children have an automatic right to part of the estate at least, regardless of what has been written in the will.

If there is no will, 'prior rights' apply which gives the widow or widower a large part of the estate, the house, contents and a large amount of cash. If there is a will, the widow or widower can either abide by the terms of the will or claim their legal rights. The spouse is legally entitled to one-third of the movable estate, the children to one-third and the remainder fulfils the terms of the will. If the spouse has claimed legal rights, he or she forfeits any further inheritance under the will.

In Scotland, if you have written the will in your own handwriting, it does not need to be witnessed. If it has been typed, you should have two witnesses; they do not need to see you sign it, or see the contents of the will, but they must hear you declare the signature to be yours. Alternatively, you could handwrite 'adopted as holograph' above your signature, which obviates the need for witnesses.

Also in Scotland, witnesses are able to benefit from a will, though the will could be challenged if the family thought a witness was inheriting unfairly.

If you made out a will while you were living in Scotland, but spent the next 30 years until you died living in England, the will is still valid. But it is advisable to write on the will that you want it administered under Scottish laws so that your executors are entirely clear about your intentions.

Trusts

At the time of making a will, solicitors often used to advise clients to set up a family trust. The purpose was to pass on money before you die, usually to grandchildren, to avoid paying one level of capital transfer tax. The money was held in trust so that the young beneficiaries did not control the money.

Now that CTT has been abolished, there is no need to set up a trust to avoid tax because you can give away all your possessions during your lifetime without paying any tax, as long as you live for seven years afterwards and do not retain an interest in the gift.

Under the inheritance tax (IHT) rules, it makes sense to give away as much as you can afford right away, to maximise your chances of living for a further seven years after you have made the gift and because a change of government could change the rules. Also, if the gift did become subject to IHT, its value is assessed at the time you made it, not at the time you die.

If you do not want the recipient to get their hands on the money, you can still set up a trust for the purpose.

C H A P T E R · 14

TAX

To evade tax is an illegal offence: to avoid it is legitimate. There are no options about tax; unless your income is very low indeed, you have to pay.

Three main types of tax affect private individuals: income tax; capital taxes; and Value Added Tax (VAT). You pay income tax on money you earn and income from investments; capital gains tax on any capital profit you make when you dispose of an asset, inheritance tax when you die or if you die within seven years of making a gift; and VAT on almost everything you buy.

If you try to escape paying tax that you owe, the taxman can take you to court. But you do not have to pay a penny more in tax than you absolutely need and you should be aware of all your entitlements because the taxman will not always award them to you automatically.

The Chancellor of the Exchequer announces how much tax you will have to pay each year in his Budget, just before the tax year starts on 6 April. Sometimes the Chancellor has an additional 'mini' Budget later in the year.

The tax year runs from 6 April to 5 April. This is the 'fiscal' year, or year of assessment.

The amount of tax you pay varies depending on which income bracket you fall into: the more you earn, the higher your rate of tax. The Chancellor of the Exchequer can introduce whatever rates he feels appropriate. At present, the basic rate of tax is 25 per cent and most people pay tax at this level only. The higher rate is 40 per cent.

But you do not pay tax on every penny you earn. Everyone is entitled to various allowances and outgoings which are deducted before tax becomes payable.

TAX REFORM
From 6 April 1990 the whole system of personal taxation will change. Then, for the first time, married women will be responsible for their own tax affairs with total privacy.

Until that date, a husband is responsible for completing his wife's tax return and must pay tax on her investment income. That will all change.

At present, wives can ask to fill out their own tax returns or, if the couple is well paid, be taxed separately, although that still does not affect investment income.

Both these options will go because under the new system women will automatically handle their own tax affairs.

Also disappearing under this new system of independent taxation are the married man's allowance and the wife's earned income allowance. Everyone will have the same single person's allowance.

If the Government stopped at that, it would leave married couples with a lower allowance than they have now. So there will be a new married couple's allowance equal to the difference between the existing single and married allowances.

This married couple's allowance goes to the husband first. But if he does not earn enough to use it, any unused part can be transferred to his wife.

Older taxpayers will have higher allowances. But for the first time, elderly married women will have an age allowance in their own right.

The changes also mean that married women can offset any income from savings against their own personal tax allowance. At present this is not possible, even if the wife has no other income, and her husband has to pay higher rate tax on it.

Lastly, wives will win their own capital gains tax exemption. At present, husbands and wives have one annual limit between them before they have to pay tax. From 1990, they will have the same amount of exemption each, just as single people. But gifts between husbands and wives will remain free of capital gains tax.

INCOME TAX
Income tax is divided into separate schedules:

Schedule A: covers income from letting property

Schedule D: case I covers income from being self-employed
              case III covers money from investments
              cases IV and V cover income from overseas
              case VI covers miscellaneous income

Schedule E: covers earned income and most pensions

Tax bands in tax year 1988–89

Taxable income	rate
first £19,300	25%
over £19,300	40%

You pay tax on what is called your 'taxable income':	£
Earned income	15,000
Investment income	2,000
Less outgoings e.g. charitable covenants	500
Total income	16,500
Less single person's allowance	2,605
	£13,895

So, your taxable income would be £13,895

The calculation is broken down into:
- ☐ earned income
- ☐ unearned income
- ☐ outgoings
- ☐ allowances

Your income is split into earned income and unearned income (investment income). Your earned income is your salary or wages or, if you are self-employed, it is the profit from your business. If you receive a state pension, then that is also treated as earned income.

Your main source of unearned income will be dividends, bank and building society interest and maybe rental income if you let out a property.

One quirk of the tax system is that the amount on which you are taxed for a given year is not necessarily the amount that arose in that year. As far as your salary, or your wife's salary, is concerned, and also any investment income from the building society and dividends, then the amount taxable will be the amount that you received in the relevant year. It is called 'current year' basis taxation.

But for business profits and for investment income received gross, such as National Savings interest, you are taxed on the income received in the previous year of assessment. That is the 'preceding year' basis.

Your outgoings (or charges as they are known) consist of any actual payments out of income that you are contractually required to make.

Giving to charity

If you give money to charity under covenant, you can claim tax relief at the highest rate you pay. Charitable donations can also be deducted from your salary with tax relief. The scheme is called 'give as you earn' and must be organised through your employer.

Covenants

Until March 1988, you could claim tax relief on regular payments made under covenant to children or any non-taxpayer. These covenants were commonly used by parents supporting student sons and daughters in further education and by grandparents to younger grandchildren.

There is now no tax relief at all on money given under covenant to individuals, whether young children, students or elderly parents. The only time there is tax relief on covenanted donations is when giving money to charity.

Investment income

If a wife has a large element of investment income but little earned income, the couple cannot save tax by electing for separate taxation, see p. 191. Even if their earnings are taxed this way, a wife's investment income will always be included with her husband's earnings, although this will change when independent taxation comes in April 1990.

TAX ALLOWANCES

Allowances are the amounts you can subtract from your total income before working out the tax. Looking at it another way, your allowances represent the amount that you can earn before you have to pay any tax at all. Allowances are not amounts of money which are handed over to you.

At present (1988–89 tax year), these allowances are:

Single person's allowance

£2605. This is granted to everyone who is single, from the day you are born. Every child can earn the single person's allowance, from either investments or working, before paying tax.

If you are widowed, divorced or separated, both men and women will revert to claiming the single person's allowance. Also, if a husband and wife opt for the wife's earnings separate election, both will receive the single person's allowance.

Married personal allowance

£4095. A married couple will receive this allowance.

Government proposals on personal taxation recommend that every individual should be able to claim allowances in their own right regardless of marital status. At the moment, the husband can also claim the allowance if they are separated but he is still wholly maintaining his wife. In the year you get married, the wife continues to be treated as a single person and will receive the single person's allowance for the whole tax year.

The husband is also treated as a single person but he can increase his single personal allowance by one-twelfth of the difference between the single and married personal allowances for each complete or part tax month they are married.

So, if you marry in the middle of August, the husband will receive the single person's allowance plus eight-twelfths of the difference between the single and married personal allowances.

Wife's earned income allowance

£2605. In straight figures this is equal to the single person's allowance. But it can be offset against the wife's earned income only, and not her investment income. The normal single person's allowance can be set against total income, earned and investment.

Any investment income a wife receives (for example, from savings) is always, even if she has opted for wife's separate taxation, added to her husband's income for tax purposes. This will change with independent taxation in 1990.

Where you are entitled to a wife's earned income allowance, it is given to the wife under her PAYE coding system which, effectively, puts her in the same position as a single person.

In the year that a couple are separated or get divorced, the husband is entitled to the full married personal allowance for the whole year and the couple are also entitled to the wife's earned income allowance in respect of her income before separation. In addition, the wife is given the full single personal allowance against her income after the separation.

If you have been separated or divorced during the past six years, remember that you can claim that far back if you missed out on this full allowance.

Additional personal allowance for children

£1490. Anyone with children who is not entitled to the married personal allowance, such as a single parent or a widow, can claim this instead. A 'child' must be either under the age of 16 at the beginning of the tax year or until they are 18 a full-time student.

The category includes legally adopted children and stepchildren. You can also claim for a child who is not your own but who you financially support, provided the child was adopted before the age of 18.

You can claim this amount only once, however, regardless of how many children you have.

A divorcee can claim this allowance in the year of divorce if she has custody of the children. The figure of £1490 is the difference between the single and married personal allowances.

Age allowance for those 65–79

£3180 for a single person; £5035 for a married couple. This is higher than the single and married allowances and is available to everyone, men and women, once they reach the age of 65.

A married man can claim the married age allowance when his wife reaches 65, even if he is younger. You can claim the allowance for the whole of the tax year in which you, or your wife, become 65, even if your birthday is only a few days before the end of the tax year in April.

However, there is a limit to the amount of age allowance you can receive if your earnings exceed a certain figure. In the tax year 1988–89, the point is £10,600 whether you are single or married. With independent taxation in 1990, husband and wife will be entitled to the income limit each.

Once your total earnings, husband's and wife's together, exceed this figure, the age allowance is reduced by £2 for every £3 of income. So, if you are earning more than £11,463 as a single person, or £12,010 as a married couple, the allowance drops to the same level as a younger person.

When assessing your income, the taxman will include any building society interest you receive and, moreover, at the grossed-up level and not the amount after tax that the building society actually pays you.

Age allowance for those 80 and over

£3310 for a single person; £5205 for a married couple. This higher age allowance is also reduced by £2 for every £3 earned over £10,600. In this case the benefit runs out when income reaches £11,658 for a single person and £12,265 for a married couple.

Tax trap

People receiving the age allowance can very easily fall into an iniquitous tax trap. If your earnings are only a few pounds over the £10,600 limit, you will be taxed at a high rate on the money.

For instance, if your income is £10,900

	£	£
Earnings	10,600	10,900
Age allowance for couple under 80	5,035	4,835*
	5,565	6,065
Tax at 25%	1,391.25	1,516.25

The age allowance reduced by £2 for every extra £3 of earnings over £10,600; for the extra £300 of earnings you lose £200.

So, you have paid an extra £125 in tax on just an extra £300 of income. In other words, you are paying tax at 41.6 per cent on the £300 even though your total income is well within the basic rate tax band.

In fact this is the highest rate of tax anyone has to pay now that the top rate has been cut to 40 per cent.

Widow's bereavement allowance

From the date that a woman becomes widowed, she is entitled, for two years, to an additional allowance worth £1490, to offset against her income. The allowance is available in the year of death and the year following but no unused allowances can be carried over.

Blind person's relief

£360. Anyone who is registered as blind can claim this allowance of £360. It is available to anyone who is single or if one partner in a marriage is registered as blind. If a married couple are both blind, they can claim twice the allowance, £720.

To register as blind, you do not have to be completely sightless. If your partial sight prevents you from working, you may be able to register.

Allowances for a dependent relative, housekeeper and son or daughter have all been abolished.

HOW TO CLAIM TAX ALLOWANCES

If you are not receiving an allowance that you think you are entitled to, write to the tax inspector who looks after your affairs. If you do not know who this is, contact the tax office nearest to your home or place of work (the address is in the telephone directory). The tax office will then send you a form telling you how to claim.

Do not forget that you can claim back relief for up to six years. If you have missed receiving an allowance, you will get a tax rebate plus the interest owed to you at 7.75 per cent a year.

HOW TO FILL OUT A TAX RETURN

The first rule is: honesty.

If your tax affairs are simple, you will be asked to fill out a tax return, a P1, about every three years. If your finances are more complicated, you may have to do so every year on a form 11P or, if you are self-employed, form 11.

If you have received any additional income one year and the taxman has not sent you a form, you should ask for one. Conversely, if your income goes down, unless covered by a PAYE code, you should complete a new tax return to ensure you are not paying too much tax.

Tax returns, which are sent out during April, ask for information about the money you earned in the year just ended and the allowances you want to claim for the new tax year. The subject headings cover: income, outgoings, and capital gains for the past year and allowances for the coming year.

If you are a married couple the form is sent to the husband to fill in until this changes in 1990. Married women can ask to be assessed separately (see p. 191). Anyone else who is single, widowed, divorced or separated should complete the 'self' column on the tax return.

If you receive the simple form, a P1, you need only sign the form and give the name and address of your employer. If not, you must write down all the money you have received in the previous tax year.

This includes your salary or wages, overtime, holiday pay, sick pay, bonuses, commission, fees, advances, tips, free gifts, share options, maternity pay, fringe benefits, leaving and compensation payments.

If you are employed and have no other earnings, the figure is the same as the one on form P60, supplied by your employer at the end of the tax year.

Also, your 'income' includes any money from pensions, letting property, untaxed interest, dividends and building society interest.

The next section concerns the outgoings on which you are allowed tax relief and includes qualifying loans, such as those used to buy an annuity or a share in a partnership.

Then, add on money paid under covenants and maintenance payments if you can still claim tax relief. The capital gains section must include details of all the gains both husband and wife have made in the year.

What is called your total income equals all your earned income plus investment income minus allowable deductions (charges or outgoings).

When filling in the tax form, you do not need to specify pennies for most entries. You round each sum down to the nearest pound. Only with dividends and tax credits should you be more precise.

You can claim for certain expenses which are incurred as part of your job. These include:

- protective and functional clothes
- tools and musical instruments which you have to provide
- books and stationery if they are essential to your job
- if you work from home, part of the cost of heating, lighting, etc
- interest on loans to buy equipment necessary for your work
- travelling costs but only those incurred in the course of your job and not the cost of getting to work
- sometimes the cost of a spouse accompanying you
- hotel and meal expenses incurred while working
- union or professional association fees if a condition of your employment

Once you have filled in a tax return, and sent it back to your tax office, the Inspector of Taxes will give you a code number on a notice of coding. Your employer uses this coding to make the correct deduction from your pay each week or month.

The inspector adds together all your allowances and deducts taxable state benefits such as the state pension. He then crosses off the last figure in the number he is left with, adds a code letter, and this is your tax code for the year.

The code number indicates the allowances you receive; the code letter indicates your tax status, that is whether you are single, married, on emergency tax, etc.

For example:

Married man's age allowance	£5035
Less pension	£3426
Tax code	160V

QUERYING YOUR TAX BILL

If you do not agree with the taxman's assessment, you have 30 days in which to appeal. If, after writing and querying his workings, you still disagree, you can appeal to the General Commissioners or the Special Commissioners (address on p. 250).

The general commissioners hear local appeals and are not usually tax experts themselves. But special commissioners are tax experts and they hear the more complicated cases.

If you are still unhappy with the findings, you can appeal to the High Court and then to the House of Lords. However, you cannot appeal to the High Court about a PAYE coding.

Although filling out a tax form is a chore, it is a duty and you should do it as quickly as possible. In practice, the taxman will allow you longer than the statutory 30 days to react before sending you a reminder. He may, however, decide to take his own action and put you straight on to emergency tax, which means he will take away all allowances of any kind. This invariably prompts a quick response from the taxpayer.

PAYMENT DATES

Tax is generally due to be paid on 1 January in the year of assessment. This includes investment income not taxed at source, Schedule A and Schedule B tax. Profits made from being self-employed are due in two tranches on 1 January and 1 July. Capital gains tax and higher rate tax on investments should be paid by 1 December in the year of assessment.

If you are on PAYE, the tax is taken away from your salary before you receive it.

If you have missed claiming an allowance, you can claim as far back as six years. If for whatever reason you have not paid tax you owe, the taxman can also claim back tax for up to six years but if he suspects you have deliberately evaded paying, there is effectively no limit to the time over which he can delve back.

On top of this he can fine, or sue you. In any case, he will charge interest on what you owe (a sum which he decides) at 7.75 per cent for the period since the tax became due.

ACCOUNTANTS

You may decide that the whole business of filling out a tax return is too tedious and prefer to hand the whole job over to an accountant. You will have to pay for his services, of course, but you hope that an accountant can squeeze a bit more out of the taxman than you could yourself. However, this is not necessarily the case.

When looking for an accountant, one tip is to use a small- or medium-sized firm because large firms of accountants, with more expensive overheads and higher-paid staff, will need to charge more to cover their costs.

The cost also depends on whether your affairs are handled by a partner, a senior manager or a junior.

How do you find an accountant if you have never used one before? The best method is word of mouth: ask your friends and colleagues if they can recommend someone. Otherwise, your bank manager or solicitor will be able to put you in touch with someone.

The local district branch of the Institute of Chartered Accountants will give you a list of accountants in your area.

HOW THE INLAND REVENUE TREATS WOMEN

At present, and until 1990, a woman loses all responsibility for her own tax affairs when she marries. In the first year of marriage, the rules do not apply. For that year only, a woman who continues working still gets the single person's allowance.

Her husband will receive the married man's allowance for a full year if they marry before 6 May (one month after the start of the tax year). After that date, he is docked one-twelfth of the difference between the married man's allowance and the single person's allowance for every month before the marriage. See p. 185.

Once the new tax year starts, the wife is granted the wife's earned income allowance on her husband's tax return. This is the same figure as the single person's allowance but can be used only against earnings and not against investment income.

Her earned income in this case includes the state pension if she has made her own national insurance contributions.

But a wife can ask for her earnings to be taxed separately from her husband's if she wishes – and her husband agrees.

Separate taxation

There are two different methods of separate taxation and it is important to understand which is which. One simply means the wife fills out her own tax return; the other way she has her own personal allowances but these are still included on her husband's return. It is possible to have both methods of separate taxation.

The first way will not affect the amount of tax either partner pays and is called separate assessment. The wife receives her own tax return to fill out independently of her husband but, when both forms arrive back with the taxman, he adds them together again to work out the bill.

The second option is called wife's separate election and is worth while only if a husband and wife have sufficiently high income. In this case, the wife is assessed as a completely separate person and the joint tax bill will be lower than it otherwise would. In the tax year 1988–89, a husband and wife's joint income needs to be at least £28,484, with the wife earning at least £6579 to make this worth while. The husband has to agree to the change because his own tax position will be affected.

A wife paying tax under wife's separate election will receive the single person's allowance; her husband will lose the married man's allowance and receive the single person's instead.

Unless the couple ask for separate assessment as well, the tax return will still be sent to the husband.

But note that the wife's investment income will still be treated as her husband's income; even under the wife's separate election.

The time during which you can apply for separate taxation and separate assessment is limited. You must ask for separate taxation no sooner than six months before the tax year starts and no later than 12 months after the end.

If you want to be assessed separately, you must decide no sooner than three months before the tax year starts or later than three months into the tax year. This short time limit is imposed to allow the tax office time to sort out its paperwork.

DIVORCE

If you legally separate or get divorced you will revert to single person status for tax purposes. During the year of separation, the woman can claim a full year's single person's allowance; a man is entitled to the married man's allowance for the whole year plus the wife's earned income allowance against his wife's earnings until the date of separation. See p. 185.

If you separate but do not start divorce proceedings, the taxman will still treat you as a single person.

A divorced husband used to be able to claim tax relief on two mortgages as long as the total borrowed did not exceed £30,000 for his own house and the one his ex-wife occupied. He no longer can.

MAINTENANCE PAYMENTS

The system for paying maintenance was changed substantially in the March 1988 Budget. Any new court orders made out from that day must be on the new system and all payments must be made gross.

It allows tax relief up to £1490 a year to a man, or woman, who is maintaining their ex-spouse. This figure is the difference between the married and single allowances. However, there is no tax relief on any other maintenance payments. This includes payments made direct to children, although the children will not have to pay tax on them.

Neither does an ex-spouse have to pay any tax on the money, unless they remarry.

Existing maintenance orders will continue as before, with tax relief for the giver, but in 1989–90 tax relief will be no higher than in 1988–89. The first £1490 will be tax free in the recipient's hands. This includes payments to children.

A payer on the old system can choose to move over to the new system if they wish. But the recipient, who will be better off because there is now no tax to pay, cannot make the choice. In future years, a payer on the old system will be worse off because the tax relief will be eroded.

Unmarried couples with children, who have taken out maintenance orders against each other to get double tax relief, will no longer be able to do so.

FRINGE BENEFITS

You may receive a fringe benefit or perk from your employer which is not part of your monetary salary. In some cases, this will be taxable; in others it will not.

First, there are ruled to be two types of employee: one who earns less than £8500 a year, including the value of the benefits, and one earning more than £8500 or a director of a company. The first will be taxed more leniently than the second.

Cars

This benefit is taxable according to a fixed scale if you are a higher earner but tax free for others, as long as you do make some business use of it.

Rent-free accommodation

You are taxed on the annual value, unless it is a condition of your job that you live there.

Clothing

The higher paid will be taxed on the full cost of smart clothes but others on the second-hand value only. Working clothes are tax free to both.

Loans

The higher paid are taxed on the difference between the rate of interest you pay (if any) and an official rate of interest, 10·5 per cent. However, the charge is waived if the benefit is less than £200 a year.

Other

Other fringe benefits with varying tax rules include: private health insurance; interest-free loans; share options; luncheon vouchers; subsidised staff canteen; cash vouchers; season ticket and credit cards; assets at employee's disposal.

CAPITAL GAINS TAX (CGT)

Capital gains tax is payable on any gain you make by disposing of an asset but with certain exceptions. You can make gains up to a certain level before tax is due and some items are tax exempt.

If you are a resident of the UK, or normally live here, you will be liable wherever in the world you make the sale. However, you can offset a capital loss against any gains before calculating the tax due.

Tax is due not just from selling an item but 'disposing' of anything. 'Disposing' means giving away, or even accidentally losing. If an item is destroyed by fire, for example, then it is still regarded as a disposal. Also, if you sell the right to an asset, such as by granting a lease, you can be liable to CGT.

Transfers between husband and wife, as long as they are living together at the time, do not count for tax purposes. But they will have to pay tax on any subsequent disposal.

This is how to work out your CGT liability: add up all the chargeable gains less allowable losses during the tax year. The first £5000 is tax free; any excess is added to your earned income and taxed at the same rate as you pay income tax. A large capital gain can put you in a higher tax bracket.

In dealing with the losses you can bring forward any earlier losses and use them to offset the gains to the level of £5000, at which point you do not have to pay CGT. Husbands and wives currently have one limit of £5000 between them. From 1990, they will have an exemption limit each. You can ignore the gains you make on items worth less than £3000 both at the time of acquisition and at disposal.

CGT is indexed for inflation. You calculate the gain by taking the original cost away from the proceeds and you also make an allowance for the effect of inflation on the original cost. The allowance is calculated by taking the percentage increase in the retail prices index from 12 months after the date of acquisition up to the month of disposal and applying this percentage to the original cost. The Inland Revenue will supply the formula.

This is to ensure that the gain on which you are charged is a gain in real terms and not just a rise caused by inflation. You must have owned the item for at least one year to benefit from the index-linked relief.

Only gains or losses from 31 March 1982 need to be counted.

ITEMS FREE FROM CAPITAL GAINS TAX

- [ ] private motor cars
- [ ] gains from gifts to an individual up to £100 in a tax year
- [ ] goods sold for less than £3000 each
- [ ] your own home (but only one)
- [ ] National Savings certificates
- [ ] gambling winnings
- [ ] gilts
- [ ] an asset with a limited life (not more than 50 years) such as a boat or a horse

- [ ] gifts to the National Trust or otherwise given to the nation
- [ ] compensation for damages
- [ ] foreign currency for your personal use
- [ ] gifts to charities
- [ ] shares held in a Personal Equity Plan
- [ ] life insurance policies

INHERITANCE TAX (IHT)

The tax you pay on your estate when you die is called inheritance tax (IHT). This replaced capital transfer tax (CTT) which was abolished along with the liability to pay any tax on money or assets that you give away during your lifetime.

However, there are two provisos. You must not retain an interest in the items you give away (for example, you cannot give away the Picasso but keep it hanging on your wall; more crucially, you cannot pass on the family home to your children while continuing to live there yourself). The other restriction is that you must live for seven years after making the gift. If you (or the beneficiary) die within that time, then the recipient will have to pay tax on a sliding scale. You could take out term insurance for the seven-year period to cope with a potential tax bill.

Number of years you live after making the gift	% of IHT to pay
up to 3	100
up to 4	80
up to 5	60
up to 6	40
up to 7	20

There is no inheritance tax to pay if your estate is below £110,000 and then just one rate of tax, currently 40 per cent.

£	tax %
up to £110,000	0
above £110,000	40

If you can afford to, it obviously makes sense to give away as much as you can during your lifetime. If you were to die and the gift became taxable, it would be taxed at its value when handed over, not the value when you died.

ITEMS FREE FROM INHERITANCE TAX

- [ ] transfers between husband and wife
- [ ] total transfers in any one year of £3000, the unused portion of which can be carried forward for one year and offset against a charge if you die within seven years of making a gift
- [ ] small sums up to £250 in addition to the £3000

- ☐ gifts to charity
- ☐ gifts to the nation
- ☐ gifts to political parties
- ☐ wedding gifts from parents of the bride or groom up to £5000 each; from grandparents up to £2500

There are special concessions for business property, agricultural land and woodland, and for an asset transferred twice in short succession because of death.

HOW TO REDUCE YOUR TAX LIABILITY

- ☐ buy your own home: there is tax relief on the mortgage interest repayments and your home is a tax-free investment
- ☐ take out a large pension if you are not in an occupational scheme; there is tax relief on pension contributions. See p. 201.
- ☐ each year you can give away £3000 plus £250 in small gifts free of IHT. But do not give away money unless you have sufficient to live on and your spouse will be well provided for
- ☐ do not spoil your way of life just to save tax
- ☐ remember that the law can (and will) change; do not make inflexible arrangements that mean you might be caught out in future
- ☐ tax planning involves spending capital sometimes, as well as saving income

VAT

The tax you pay on your income is known as 'direct' tax. There is also 'indirect' taxation which is value added tax, commonly called VAT. You have to pay this on nearly everything you buy.

There are some VAT free or zero-rated items such as children's clothes, food, books and gas and electricity. The rate of VAT is 15 per cent and you pay it at the same time as you buy the goods.

See also p. 170 for VAT and the self-employed.

Finally

If you are worried about tax problems and cannot afford, or do not want to see, an accountant, you can call into a PAYE enquiry office near your home and ask questions free of charge. The address is in the telephone directory under Inland Revenue.

The Inland Revenue has published a large number of leaflets on all aspects of tax which you can pick up at PAYE offices. Or you can call into a Citizens Advice Bureau which can give you advice on simple problems.

TAX-SAVING TIPS
For everyone

- ☐ make sure you claim all the allowances you are entitled to. Basic rate taxpayers can save £25 in tax on every £100 of allowances they claim. Higher rate taxpayers can save £40
- ☐ make sure you claim all the outgoings and allowance expenses you can

- [ ] if you think you may have previously missed out on some of these allowances, write to the taxman. You can claim back for the last six years to rectify a mistake. You may even receive interest on the money from the taxman
- [ ] check your PAYE code
- [ ] apply for any new relief immediately. Inform the taxman as soon as your circumstances change so you will receive any rebate as quickly as possible
- [ ] you do not need to include genuine gifts of money in your tax return: the donor is responsible for declaring tax

Married couples

- [ ] a wife can earn an amount equal to the married woman's allowance before she pays tax. If her husband is self-employed, she can earn up to that amount by working for him without paying tax. Or she can earn the same amount from another source
- [ ] if the husband has no income, the wife can claim the married person's allowance*
- [ ] similarly if a husband and wife could both command a similar salary by working but one has to stay at home to look after children, it pays for the woman to work. She can offset both the wife's earned income allowance and the married person's allowance against her earnings. But a man cannot claim the wife's allowance*
- [ ] a wife earning a reasonable salary should opt for the wife's earnings separate election*
- [ ] but consider divorce if the wife has a large element of investment income. Under no circumstances can this be assessed separately from her husband's money*
- [ ] in the year a woman is divorced she can claim the single person's allowance in full in her own right, regardless of when she and her husband part. The same applies to widows*
- [ ] if you receive any money net of tax but pay little or no tax yourself, claim a rebate from the taxman

* this will change with independent taxation in 1990

Savings

- [ ] if you pay tax at a higher rate, look for tax-free savings such as National Savings certificates
- [ ] alternatively, go for an investment that gives a capital gain rather than income (you can make £5000 gains a year before tax) but beware of paying a higher rate of tax
- [ ] if you do not pay tax but your interest or dividends are taxed before you receive them, make sure you claim the money due to you. But remember, you cannot reclaim the tax on building society or bank interest

Gifts

- [ ] gifts made to charities are free of inheritance tax
- [ ] gifts between husband and wife do not usually attract capital gains or inheritance tax

- ☐ there is no tax to pay on gifts made during your lifetime provided that you live for seven years and do not enjoy a benefit
- ☐ for the elderly, buying an annuity will provide an income and, at the same time, reduce the value of the estate

At work
- ☐ could you become self-employed? If so, you could claim far more expenses and settle your tax bill later
- ☐ pay in lieu of notice, as long as it is not stated in a service agreement, is tax free up to £30,000
- ☐ consider taking a fringe benefit as part of a wage rise. Many are tax free, or at least taxed favourably
- ☐ if you travel abroad on business, you can avoid paying tax if you stay away for longer than one year. This means no visits home during that time
- ☐ tell the taxman in the year before you retire that you are about to start drawing your old age pension. This will save paying too much tax and having to reclaim it later

These reliefs are deducted from your income before assessing the amount of tax you pay 1988–89

	£
Personal allowance: married person	4095
single person	2605
Wife's earnings allowance	2605
Additional personal allowance for children	1490
Blind person's allowance	360
Widow's bereavement allowance	1490
Age allowance: married person 65–79	5035
single person 65–79	3180
married person 80+	5205
single person 80+	3310
Age allowance limit	10,600

You do not have to pay any tax on the following:
- ☐ gambling winnings, such as football pools
- ☐ premium bond and lottery prizes
- ☐ interest on National Savings certificates; SAYE contract bonuses
- ☐ wedding or other presents from an employer as long as they are genuine presents and have nothing to do with your work
- ☐ retirement or redundancy pay-offs up to £30,000
- ☐ scholarships or educational grants
- ☐ war widows' pension
- ☐ the following social security benefits:
    income support
    sickness benefit (not statutory sick pay)

     attendance allowance
     child benefit
     family credit
     mobility allowance
- [ ] housing grants from local authorities
- [ ] disability pensions
- [ ] allowances paid for extra service in the armed forces
- [ ] the first £70 of interest from a National Savings ordinary investment account
- [ ] allowances paid under a job release scheme
- [ ] additional pensions paid to holders of gallantry awards

Pensions are, however, taxable.

You can claim tax relief on the following:
- [ ] loan to buy your home up to £30,000
- [ ] loan to buy an annuity if you are over 65 and the loan is secured on your main residence
- [ ] money given to charity under covenant

PAYE CODE LETTERS
L   single person's allowance or wife's earned income allowance
H   married person's allowance
P   single person's age allowance
V   married person's age allowance
T   your employer will not know how much tax allowance you are entitled to
F   taxed at a higher rate
D   higher rate tax
BR tax collected at basic rate on part-time casual jobs

> Your marginal rate of tax is the highest rate of tax you pay. The basic rate is 25 per cent, but if you have a larger income and pay tax at 40 per cent, then that is your marginal rate. If you are on the borderline between two rates of tax, you are on a tax 'threshold'.

CHAPTER · 15

PENSIONS

Pensions have recently undergone a monumental shake up which has freed the entire working population to make new pension arrangements. Now, all employees have the right to set up personal pensions for themselves. Previously, about half the workforce was pushed into a company scheme, regardless of how good or bad it was. The other half had no company pension arrangements at all.

A potential new market of 22 million people was created. Insurance companies responded by developing, and heavily advertising, new policies. But they did not hold the field to themselves. As part of the pension shake up, the Government allowed building societies, banks and unit trust companies to sell pensions as well.

The changes stemmed from the Government's original plan to scrap the State Earnings-Related Pension Scheme (SERPS). But, in the event, instead of total abolition SERPS benefits were cut back.

The reason for watering down SERPS was that the country could no longer afford it. Pensioners were living longer but the number of young people contributing to the state pension was shrinking because of the falling birth rate and high unemployment.

DIFFERENT TYPES OF PENSION

Pensions fall into three very general categories:

- ☐ the state pension
- ☐ company pensions
- ☐ personal pensions

The state pension subdivides again into:

- ☐ basic pension, which everybody who has paid national insurance contributions receives
- ☐ state earnings-related pension scheme (SERPS) which only goes to those who are 'contracted in'

Company pensions and personal pensions come in many guises (see below).

TAX

Unkindly, all pensions, including the state pension, are taxable. If you receive no more than the flat-rate pension, you will pay no tax because your income will be no higher than the personal allowance. But you will pay tax on any income you receive above that.

The company responsible for paying your occupational pension will have to make sure you pay all your income tax through the code number allocated to you. Since state pensions are payable gross and the DHSS has no way of deducting tax, your occupational pension will appear to bear an extortionate amount of tax because the tax due on your state pension will be taken off your occupational pension. If you have no occupational pension you will deal with the taxman direct.

One great bonus of pension contributions is that you are allowed tax relief on the money you invest. Your own contributions are deducted by your employer from your gross salary before calculating the tax. And you do not, of course, have to pay tax on your employer's contributions. So, if you put £10 a week into a pension scheme it is really costing you only £7.50, and even less if you pay tax at the higher rate.

Your employer qualifies for tax relief on his contributions. Moreover, the interest which both contributions earn is free of income tax and capital gains tax.

THE STATE PENSION

Nearly everyone will receive this. If you paid enough contributions while you were working you will receive the full basic state pension. If you have not paid enough, you will get a scaled-down amount.

Women are entitled to receive the state pension when they reach 60 and men at 65. However, you do not have to stop working at these ages and, if you delay drawing your pension, you will receive more when you finally give up work. But you cannot delay past 65 for a woman and 70 for a man.

How the state pension is made up
The state pension comes in several segments:
1. Flat-rate basic pension
2. State earnings-related pension (SERPS)
3. Income support
4. Graduated scheme

The basic pension
This is paid to both the employed and self-employed. The basic pension (April 1988) is £41.15 a week or £2139.80 a year for a single person and £65.90 a week (£3426.80 a year) for a married couple when the wife has no state pension rights of her own. To receive this you must have made sufficient national insurance contributions during your working life.

The minimum calculation is an average of 50 contributions a year between the ages of 16 and retirement. If you missed making contributions because you were ill at some stage, or were unemployed, or (in some circumstances) still in full-time education, then you will have received a 'credit'. But if you have been working abroad, or if as a married woman you either did not work or paid the lower rate national insurance contribution, then you will receive nothing in your own right.

If necessary, married women can claim a pension based on their husbands' national insurance contributions. Until the tax changes in 1990, this is taxed as his income. After that it will be taxed as hers and she can offset her personal allowance against the income.

The state pension pays today's pensioners from contributions made by today's workers. This is called an unfunded scheme or a pay-as-you-go scheme. Most private pension schemes work differently and are 'funded', that is, contributions are paid during an employee's working life and, together with the investment returns, are used to pay for the pension at retirement.

The state earnings-related pension scheme (SERPS)

SERPS has undergone a fundamental shift in significance since the Government diluted its role. The change was designed to encourage as many people as possible, either individually or through their employer, to make their own private pension arrangements.

Since April 1988, every employee has had the right to leave their company pension scheme. From July 1988 the new form of personal pensions came on sale.

Who should stay in SERPS?

This is the big question. For those just starting work, you will do better leaving SERPS and making your own personal pension arrangements.

Those just coming up to retirement age should stay put. It is too late for them to build up enough in a new pension fund. But anyone in their forties has a difficult decision to make. There is no exact formula to use but, broadly, men over 45 and women over 40 should stay in their existing pension scheme. Younger workers should think about making new arrangements.

But all of this depends on your individual circumstances. If you want to find out how much SERPS you have already earned, you can ask the DHSS for a calculation.

You can change your mind about contributing to SERPS year by year. You are not stuck with your first decision.

A factor that could swing your choice one way or another is whether your employer will continue contributing the company's money to your new personal pension. If he does you are fortunate, but it is most unlikely that employers will donate to workers' personal pensions if they leave the company scheme.

Check also whether you are entitled to the Government's 2 per cent incentive. This is a very attractive element of contracting out, but without it you need to think more carefully about starting a personal pension.

Transitional arrangements

As the new SERPS levels will not be fully in force until the next century, there are interim arrangements for those retiring between now and 2009. These are complex formulas to ensure that those who retire soon after the new terms start do not lose out.

Existing pensioners are not affected, nor is anyone who retires before the year 2000. But, after that, younger employees should not depend on SERPS for their pension.

The changes to SERPS

- [ ] maximum payable down from 25 to 20 per cent of average earnings
- [ ] amount calculated from best of lifetime earnings instead of best 20 years
- [ ] spouse will inherit only 50 per cent of partner's pension instead of 100 per cent
- [ ] transitional arrangements for anyone retiring before 2009

Timetable

November 1986	Employees and spouses have right to information about company pension
March 1987	Tax-free lump sum on retirement restricted to £150,000 for new members
April 1987	No longer any tax-free lump sums with additional voluntary contributions
October 1987	Free-standing AVCs available to individuals outside company schemes
November 1987	Women cannot be forced to retire before men
April 1988	Membership of company pension scheme becomes voluntary, except for non-contributory death benefits. Contracted out schemes must provide widower's graduated minimum pension. Must also provide pension increases up to 3 per cent a year. Company schemes must have an AVC facility. Schemes must provide pension after two years' service
July 1988	Personal pensions on sale to employees and self-employed. New pension providers in the market

Under the old plans, SERPS paid a pension based on an average of the 20 best years' salary. This was not total salary but the band between the upper and lower earnings limits (see p. 156). The maximum pension was 25 per cent of band earning after 20 working years. And, when a pensioner died, the spouse continued to receive the full pension.

Under the new plans, from April 1988, the benefits will be cut back although they will not affect anyone retiring until the turn of the century.

The new system of SERPS is based on an average of life time earnings. These include all the years when your salary was low, or even non-existent, and obviously this substantially reduces how much pension you will get. The maximum in any case will be only 20 per cent of band earnings. And a surviving spouse will receive only half the pension.

Women

Like men, if women are to claim a basic state pension in their own right, they need to have clocked up an average of 50 contributions for each year of their working life, between the ages of 16 and 60, and paid the full national insurance contributions.

It is highly unlikely that the older generation of married women, in particular, will have made so many contributions. It will not be a problem if they are still married and their husbands are five years older than they are, because then the husband would be entitled to draw his pension and the married couple's allowance just as his wife retires at 60. But, if the gap is less than five years or he is younger, she will have to wait until he reaches 65 before she gets any money on his pension.

A married woman may have devoted her middle years to staying at home and bringing up a family. If she has a full record over the rest of her working life, she is entitled to spend time at home bringing up a family without losing her pension rights. But she will need to have been paying full national insurance contributions during the outside years. Married women who, in the past, chose to pay reduced rate national insurance contributions will not be earning any pension rights at all on their own behalf. Since 1978 only those who had already opted to pay lower contributions can continue to do so.

Even if she had been working, and paying full contributions she may not have been entitled to join an occupational pension scheme, because it is only recently that employers had been forced to give women doing the same jobs as men equal access to company pension schemes.

But even single women who have worked all their lives will almost certainly be worse off than men at retirement because women's average salaries are lower than men's.

Widows

Widows are entitled to a pension when their husbands die, within certain limitations. If a woman is widowed after she is 55 she will receive the full state widow's pension of £41.15 a week; if she is between 45 and 54 when her husband dies she will get a smaller pension unless she has dependent children in which case she will receive the widowed mother's pension.

Widows have more help from the state than widowers. There is a lump sum widow's payment for women under 60, a widowed mother's allowance for those with dependent children, and a widow's pension for those without children.

If your husband had belonged to a company pension scheme, you will be entitled to a widow's pension from that, depending on the terms of his particular scheme. For more details of widow's benefits, see p. 145.

Ask your husband now who to get in touch with at his place of work should he die. If your husband dies and you do not know whether he belonged to a pension scheme, contact his employer anyway, to find out if you are entitled to anything. Do this even if your husband has already retired. There may also be some benefits from your husband's previous employers.

What it costs you

A percentage of your pay is deducted automatically by your employer for national insurance contributions. Your employer then chips in with a larger percentage in national insurance contributions on your behalf. The amounts are laid down by the Government.

At present, employees pay between 5 per cent and 9 per cent of their gross income, above the lower earnings limit. If you earn less than the lower earnings limit, you pay no national insurance contributions. You pay nothing on earnings over and above the upper earnings limit. Employers contribute up to 10·45 per cent.

Anyone contracting out of SERPS will get a rebate worth 2 per cent to individuals plus 3·8 per cent to employers.

How to claim

Four months before you reach retirement age, the DHSS will contact you with a claim form. If you are nearer to the date of your retirement and you still have not heard from them, get in touch with your local DHSS office quickly. Then you will be sure of receiving your pension as soon as it is due. You should do this even if you intend to carry on working.

When to retire

Men can retire at 65 and women at 60 and claim the state pension from that date. But you do not have to. You have two choices. You can draw the pension at that age and continue to work, or you can delay receiving it until you actually stop work.

You will not make any more national insurance contributions after 65 for men or 60 for women but you will get a larger pension when eventually you do start drawing it.

Once men reach the age of 70, and women 65, then there are no longer any penalties for working and they must take the state pension then or lose the money. There is no advantage in delaying, even if you are still working.

Men between the ages of 65 and 70 and women between 60 and 65 whose earnings are over £75 a week (April 1988) will have their state pension cut back. **This is known as the earnings rule and it works in two stages.**

Stage 1   Your basic state pension is cut by 5p for every 10p earned between £75 and £79 a week.

Stage 2   Your basic state pension is cut £ for £ for earnings over £79 a week.

So the pension disappears altogether once your earnings reach:
£140.25 a week married couple
£116.50 a week single

It is worth holding back and waiting for the higher pension later, because the earnings rule disappears at age 65 for women and 70 for men. Then you can earn as much as you like.

Retiring early

Unless you are disabled, you cannot claim the state pension any earlier than 65 for men or 60 for women. And also, if you stop making national insurance contributions, your pension may be considerably smaller when you do come to draw it. It may be worth while continuing to pay the fixed-rate national insurance contribution to make sure you receive the full basic state pension. If you retire close to retirement age, then check with your local DHSS office to see whether you have already paid enough contributions to qualify for the full rate of basic state pension.

Income support

If you have only the basic state pension to live on you are entitled to income support, even if you have £6000 in savings. In fact, if you are in this position it is worth while bringing your savings down so that you can claim income support. The DHSS allows you to make certain purchases to reduce your savings as long as they do not raise your standard of living. So, you would be allowed to trade in your old Ford Escort for a fairly new one but you could not replace it with a Rolls Royce.

Graduated Pensions

These were in existence from 1961 to 1975 and when you retire you will be entitled to a pension calculated on any contributions deducted during those years. At the very best, the sums involved are extremely small.

COMPANY PENSION SCHEMES

These can be either contracted out of SERPS or contracted in.

If your scheme is contracted in, then you will pay towards the earnings-related part and you will receive both elements of the state pension when you retire. You will also pay towards your company pension, unless the company meets the whole cost itself.

If your company has contracted out, you will not receive an earnings-related pension from the state. Instead, your company scheme must give you a pension which is at least as good. If you are contracted out, both you and your employer will pay less in national insurance contributions.

To be contracted out, your company scheme must fulfil certain minimum conditions:

☐ the pension must provide at least 1/80th of an employee's 'final earnings'
☐ the pension must be at least the same as the state earnings-related pension and the scheme must always guarantee that it has the financial resources to remain so
☐ employees must be able to start claiming the pension at the ages of 65 for men and 60 for women
☐ if the employee leaves the job before retiring the part of the preserved pension which is equivalent to the state earnings-related pension must rise in line with the level of earnings generally over the years to retirement. Anyone who is not entitled to a preserved pension will be brought back into the state earnings-related pension
☐ whether an employee dies in service or after retirement, widowers and widows over 45, or with children in full-time education, must receive a pension
☐ women must have the same right to join a scheme as men if they do the same kind of job. This condition applies to all schemes, not just those that are contracted out

Scheme benefits

The precise terms of pension schemes vary quite considerably. This is partly because the schemes are tailored to each company and also because some schemes have larger funds than others.

Whenever you change jobs ask closely about the new pension scheme. It may seem a totally unimportant facet of your salary (particularly when you are young) but really it is not. The money you will be paid when you retire is just as much part of your salary as the money you receive today. It is often difficult to see just how good a pension scheme is without showing the rule book to a pensions expert. Your trade union, if you belong to one, should be able to help.

However, here is a typical private sector scheme against which to measure your own. In this scheme, women are treated the same as men, except that they retire at 60, not 65, and are not covered for widowers' pensions.

☐ it promises a pension of 1/60th of your final salary for each year you work with the firm. Final salary is defined as the basic salaries of the best three consecutive years in the last ten years before retirement
☐ it increases pensions after retirement at a guaranteed rate of 3 per cent.

Occasionally, when the firm's profits have been allowed, discretionary supplements have been added
☐ it allows you to take part of your pension as a tax-free lump sum
☐ for death in service, it pays out a tax-free lump sum to your family of two years' salary plus a widow's pension of half your prospective pension
☐ for death after retirement, it pays out a widow's pension of half your actual pension, or what your pension would have been if you had not taken part of it as cash

What it costs you

With some schemes you contribute nothing at all – your employer meets the whole bill. But a scheme where you pay nothing, though it sounds good, is not necessarily the best deal because you might find yourself receiving cut-price benefits.

The more usual system is for the employee to pay 5 per cent of his earnings and the employer to pay whatever balance is needed to fund the scheme, usually between 7 and 12 per cent of earnings.

The most you yourself are allowed to put into a company pension scheme is 15 per cent of your gross salary although your employer can add as much as he likes. This limit only becomes a real constraint if you want to boost your pension by hefty extra voluntary contributions. (See p. 210.)

WHAT TYPE OF COMPANY PENSION?
Final salary scheme

The amount of pension you will receive under a final salary scheme is based on how much you are earning when you retire, or in the few years just before. Most schemes covering more than 20 employees or so use this formula. It is sometimes called a 'final pay' scheme.

Make sure you know exactly what the term 'final pay' refers to in your pension scheme: it could be the last year you work before you retire, or it could be the average earnings over the last few years, which will probably be less. You might find that any commission you earn, or bonuses, are excluded when your pension is calculated.

Your pension will be expressed either as a percentage or a fraction of your final salary for each year of service. If it is a percentage, say 1¼ per cent, and you have worked for the company for 30 years before you retire, your pension will be 30 × 1¼ per cent which is 37½ per cent of your final salary. If you are quoted fractions, the fraction will usually be either 1/60th or 1/80th, according to the terms of the scheme. Say it is 1/60th, and you worked for the same company for 30 years then you will receive 30/60ths of your final salary; in other words half.

Average earnings scheme

This kind of scheme quotes you a percentage or a fraction too, but it averages your earnings as you go along year by year, rather than waiting until the final years. You will be told each year how much you have earned towards your pension and, when you retire, you will receive each year's amount totalled together. Some such schemes copy the state earnings-related pension by revaluing the averages in line with some index, such as earnings or prices. There are very few average earnings schemes.

Flat-rate scheme

Here you will be quoted a flat rate and you simply multiply this number by the number of years you have worked for your firm, or more accurately, the number of years which count as pensionable service. Assuming the flat amount is £10 and you have worked there for 30 years, you will receive a pension of £300 a year. Again, there are very few such schemes.

Money purchase

New personal pensions will all be money purchase schemes. They work differently from the other schemes: instead of deciding how much pension will be paid at the end, a money purchase scheme decides how much the company and, often, how much you contribute to the scheme (usually a certain percentage of salary) and you have to wait until the time comes to see how much pension this will provide. Money purchase schemes are popular with companies that have small numbers of employees.

WHEN YOU LEAVE A JOB

One of the recent improvements made to pensions helped those who changed jobs. Until then, these early leavers, as they were called, suffered a severe setback by moving jobs. Any pension left with the ex-employer would not keep up with inflation over the years.

Now, all pensions which have been frozen on leaving a job must rise each year by the rate of inflation or 5 per cent, whichever figure is lower.

In times of low inflation, this is tolerable. But if inflation rose again to double figures, the pension will still only rise by 5 per cent per year.

Your rights when changing jobs

You may be entitled to a refund of your contributions when you leave a job if you have fewer than two years ranking for pension rights. This saves you having a number of extremely small pensions coming in when you retire.

But you can take out only the money you yourself have put in. You will not receive the contributions made by your employer. If you were contracted out you will have to be bought back into the earnings-related state scheme and part of the cost will be deducted from your refunded money. You will also have to pay tax at the rate of 20 per cent on any money refunded to you.

You can transfer your pension rights to your new employer. It does not necessarily follow that you will receive exactly the same rights from the new employer (they may be better or they may be worse). It depends on how the two companies' actuaries have based their calculations and on differences between the two schemes' benefit features.

Even so, you can transfer a pension only if both pension schemes' trustees agree. There are three ways that it can be transferred. Most probably your old employer will put a 'transfer value' on your pension rights. This is a formula which tells him how much they are worth in his scheme today. He passes on this transfer value to the new employer who in turn interprets it into the new pension scheme where it might buy less pension or more. So, you may have been entitled to a pension of £1000 in your old job. You might get more or less than this in the new one.

Another possibility is that your new employer will translate the transfer value into 'added years'. If you stayed in the old job for 15 years, the new employer may agree to credit you with ten years in his scheme. Remember, though, that these ten years will produce extra pension based on your final salary at retirement. Your new employer is not likely to credit you with more years than you had in the old job.

Or you can use the money to buy a personal pension.

RIGHT TO INFORMATION

Employees have the right to see full details about their pension from the company on request. And, by right, they must receive copies of annual statements.

This mandatory disclosure of information has only been a requirement since November 1986. It extends to prospective employees and spouses.

Some companies are better than others at volunteering pension information to employees. Even now, companies need only forward many details if a member of staff or trade union asks. And you can only make one request a year.

The annual statement, which must be completed within 12 months of the financial year end, must show the investment strategy used by the fund managers.

RETIREMENT AGE

Traditionally, men have retired at 65 and women at 60. But now employers cannot force women to retire if they do not wish to. Women employees can continue working for as long as men.

But companies can still choose how the pensions are treated. Employees may be allowed to continue contributing; or their pension may be frozen.

ADDITIONAL VOLUNTARY CONTRIBUTIONS

You can boost the pension you will receive when you retire by making Additional Voluntary Contributions (AVCs). Some employers have made AVCs available for a long time. And now, regardless of what arrangements the company has, you can take out a separate policy for AVCs through any provider you choose.

These will include:

- [ ] insurance companies
- [ ] banks
- [ ] building societies
- [ ] unit trusts

These are called Free Standing Additional Voluntary Contributions (FSAVCs). However, when you retire you will not be able to take a tax-free lump sum from your AVCs as you can with your pension.

The amount you pay into a company scheme will be set down by your employer. The maximum you can pay in is 15 per cent of your earnings, but your employer is unlikely to allow as much as this. So you can top up to 15 per cent with AVCs.

The new rules also relax AVC requirements. You can now take out AVCs as and when you want; previously you were committed for at least five years.

WHAT YOU SHOULD KNOW ABOUT YOUR PENSION

The Company Pensions Information Centre recommends the following questions as those which workers should ask about their pension schemes:

- [ ] who is eligible to join?
- [ ] if there are changes to a scheme, who is affected?
- [ ] how is the pension calculated at normal retirement?
- [ ] what length of service ranks for pension?
- [ ] what contributions, if any, are payable by the members?
- [ ] what benefits are payable on death before retirement?
- [ ] what benefits are payable on death after retirement?
- [ ] what provision is made for early retirement in ill health?
- [ ] what provision is made for early retirement not in ill health?
- [ ] what provision is made for late retirement?
- [ ] what provision is made for 'commuting' some or all of the pension for a cash sum?
- [ ] what provision is made to increase pensions in course of payment?
- [ ] what benefits are available to anyone leaving service?
- [ ] who can provide advice for individuals if it is needed?
- [ ] is the scheme contracted out?
- [ ] when does the scheme start?
- [ ] in the case of a change, when does the change take effect?
- [ ] what arrangements are made for collecting contributions from members?
- [ ] what tax relief is allowed on contributions?
- [ ] what provisions are made for approval by the Inland Revenue and what effect does this have?
- [ ] how are the various benefits taxed?
- [ ] what is the basis for calculating the employer's payment?
- [ ] what options are available to provide benefits for widows and/or dependants?

☐ what benefit is provided for a member who is disabled?
☐ what happens if a member is temporarily absent from work?
☐ what discretion, if any, arises over eligibility, calculation of benefits or the channels through which they are paid?
☐ are the benefits in any way modified to allow for state benefits?
☐ what is the position on discontinuance or partial discontinuance of the scheme?
☐ how is the pension money invested?
☐ how are the benefits paid for?
☐ how does one join?

PERSONAL PENSIONS

These are the new type of pension created to give every individual the right to make his or her own pension arrangements. Portable pensions are the same thing because whenever you change jobs, your personal pension stays with you.

The substantial difference between a personal pension and most company pensions is the way your eventual pension is worked out.

Personal pensions are 'money purchase', schemes which means that your contributions are invested and, when you come to retire, you will receive however much pension your money bought. You will not know until you retire exactly how much you will get.

Most company schemes are final salary, although they can now be money purchase if they wish. A final salary scheme takes contributions along the way, but you always know that your pension will be based on an average of the salary you were earning in your last few years' service.

Who can buy a personal pension?

Until the new pension legislation, only the self-employed and those with no company scheme were able to make their own pension arrangements. Now, in addition to these, any worker who wishes can take out a personal pension.

Any employee between the ages of 16 and 75 can have a personal pension; any aged between 16 and the state retirement age who pay national insurance contributions can contract out. You can even have a personal pension in addition to a company pension, whether this is contracted in or contracted out. If your company pension is contracted in to SERPS you can contract out through a personal pension and enjoy the incentives and rebates.

You can only claim these perks once, although you can have more than one personal pension at a time.

You can choose to leave a company scheme and not make any other pension arrangements. Then you will automatically be put into SERPS, which will only give you a very small pension to retire on.

How much can I put into a personal pension?
There are limits to the total amount you can put into a pension, but these are in any case higher than most people could afford. The limits are in addition to the extra Government incentives available for the first five years.

Age at beginning of tax year	Max contribution as % of net relevant earnings
50 or less	17·5%
51–55	20%
56–60	22·5%
60–75	27·5%

A personal pension is your little pot of money and, up to this amount, can include: regular contributions both from yourself and your employer; Government rebates, tax relief on your rebate; the extra incentive; and money transferred from another pension.

How little can I put in?
The minimum amount required to start a personal pension is:

☐ the national insurance rebate
☐ plus the 2 per cent Government incentive (see pp. 215–16)

Where can I buy a personal pension?
At the same time as making pensions more widely available, the Government allowed additional financial institutions to create and sell pensions. Until then, insurance companies had the market to themselves.
Now you can buy a personal pension from:

☐ insurance companies   ☐ larger building societies
☐ banks   ☐ larger unit trusts

However, only insurance companies can provide the pension at retirement. Others can look after your investment until that date, but then they must use the money to buy an annuity from an insurance company or subsidiary.
Personal pensions are heavily promoted and there are many on the market. **Do not be tempted to sign for the first pension you find.**

Deposit based pensions
These are offered by banks and building societies, though they are not necessarily the only type available from them. Instead of being put in a with-profits or unit-linked policy, your contributions are placed in a deposit account.

Tax relief

You receive tax relief on your pension contributions at the highest rate of tax you pay. You will pay the contributions after basic rate tax has been deducted and receive the rest later. Then, all investment income earned by the pension, and gains, are exempt from tax.

How to compare pension schemes

There is pressure from advertisers to buy personal pensions. You will find it difficult to compare one with another and they are all presented in expensive glossy brochures. You may get help from your employer or trade union. Or for a fee of about £40 to £60, you can get outside independent advice from a pension consultant.

For a list of members, write to the Society of Pension Consultants, address on p. 250.

Pension mortgages

A personal pension can be used as the basis for a mortgage. There are tax advantages but your eventual pension will be reduced. See p. 73 for more details.

Loanbacks

One added advantage of having a personal pension plan is the opportunity to borrow money. You are not actually borrowing your own money back, though it may feel like it. But, because the insurance company knows you to be a good risk, with security, it may agree to make you a loan out of its vast coffers.

This is a painless way of borrowing money because you do not have to pay it back until the pension falls due. The insurance company normally takes what you owe away from your tax-free cash sum at retirement. Any remaining balance must be paid back separately.

And there you can see the obvious drawback: your pension is going to be very diluted by the time you receive it if you have been borrowing money on it along the way.

Death in service

This is the only part of a company scheme where membership can still be made compulsory, provided it is non-contributory. Schemes that contract out must provide a pension for the spouse of a member who dies before retiring if the spouse is aged 45 or over or has a dependent child.

If there is no one in this category, the fund is paid in a lump sum to whoever the late employee has nominated.

With a personal pension, the same rules apply.

More can be paid out as long as the premiums do not exceed 5 per cent of net relevant earnings.

When you can retire

The usual retirement age is the same as the state scheme, 65 for men and 60 for women. Women can no longer be forced to retire before men, regardless of pension arrangements.

But you can choose to start taking the personal pension at any time between the ages of 50 and 75. This does not have to coincide with retirement if you can afford to leave the pension longer. The later you take the pension, the more it will be worth.

You may have the option of retiring early under your occupational scheme. If you do, the amount of money you receive will be less. The choice depends on what you want to do at the time. You may be able to take less money earlier, in which case you will be paid a smaller pension for more years, or your pension may be calculated as if you had left the firm, and held until you reach retirement age. If ill health forces you to retire early, you may find your scheme pays you what you would have received by staying on until the normal retirement age.

Pension increases after retirement

If you work in the public sector, the chances are that your pension will be increased each year in line with retail prices. There has been a great deal of debate about this highly valuable feature, largely because it is very rare in the private sector.

Otherwise, you may be lucky enough to be in a scheme which manages to increase your pension each year at, say, two-thirds of the inflation rate even when this is high. Personal pensions must rise by at least 3 per cent, or the rate of inflation if that is lower.

Taking cash

When you retire you may have the option of taking a cash lump sum and then receiving a lower pension. The maximum lump sum you can take is 25 per cent of the total value up to a maximum of £150,000. The advantage is that the money is tax free whereas, if you take the money in a pension, it is taxable.

But remember that you may not just be giving up part of your pension. You would also be forfeiting the future increases that might be given, though you would not normally lose any widow's pension.

If you do take cash, you could use the money to buy an annuity to increase your income later on. See p. 129.

PERKS FOR CONTRACTING OUT

To encourage individuals and companies to contract out of SERPS and thereby release pressure on the state pension, the Government has added financial incentives:

☐ 2 per cent special incentive
Government contributes 2 per cent of band earnings for the first five years of personal pensions, that is until April 1993.

Personal pensions taken out between July 1988 and April 1989 can backdate one year to April 1987 and claim an extra year's 2 per cent incentive.
The incentive does not go to those who have already been contracted out for at least two years.
☐   2 per cent rebate
Another 2 per cent is given as a rebate on national insurance contributions.

Both incentives can be put straight into a new personal pension as the minimum payment.

MAIN CHANGES TO PENSION RIGHTS
☐   all employees can leave their company scheme to make their own arrangements with personal pensions
☐   right to full detailed information about company pension
☐   early leavers must receive increases of 5 per cent or the level of inflation, whichever is lower
☐   Government giving 2 per cent incentive to contract out of SERPS
☐   Government adding 2 per cent rebate on national insurance contributions
☐   additional voluntary contributions available to everyone
☐   women cannot be forced to retire before men
☐   transferring from one pension to another is easier
☐   more companies able to offer pensions

GLOSSARY OF PENSION TERMS
Accrued pension   The amount you are entitled to when you retire for the years worked so far
Actuarial report   Shows the financial state of your pension fund at a given date. It also recommends to the employer what contribution he should make. It is expensive to produce so is done every few years only
Actuary   The person who works out how much has to be paid in to meet the cost of the pensions that will eventually be paid out
Added years   When you move jobs, you sometimes gain additional benefits in the new scheme in terms of more years in exchange for transferring the value of your old pension scheme rights
Additional voluntary contributions (AVCs)   You may have an option to buy extra benefits by paying in more money as AVCs
Annuity   In this context, it means the same as your pension
Approved scheme   To qualify for tax relief, your scheme must be approved by the Inland Revenue
Average salary scheme   There are not many of these around. They assess your eventual pension on the average salary you have earned over the whole of the time you have been part of that particular scheme
Band earnings   Earnings between the lower and upper earnings limits
Castle plan   The state earnings-related pension now in operation which was introduced by the Rt Hon Barbara Castle

Commutation   or cash option. Your option to take a tax-free cash lump sum when you retire and a lower pension

Contracting out   An employer who provides a pension at least as good as the state earnings-related pension can contract his pension scheme members out of that part of the state scheme if he chooses

Deferred pension   The pension from a job you have left which will be paid to you at some date in the future; or the pension you will receive later because you have delayed retirement beyond the normal date

Defined benefit scheme   The rules dictate the benefits to be paid

Defined contribution scheme   Same as money purchase

Early retirement   If you stop working before the normal retirement date you may be able to draw an occupational pension, but it will probably be less than you would receive by waiting

Final salary scheme   The most common form of pension which bases the amount you receive on your salary in the last year, or few years, that you worked

Free standing AVCs   Every worker can make additional contributions to boost their pension, regardless of any company arrangements

Frozen pension   The amount held for you, when you retire, from a job you have left some time before

Graduated pension   This is what you receive from a scheme run by the state between 1961 and 1975. It is added to the rest of your state pension.

Guaranteed minimum pension (GMP)   If your employer is contracted out of the state scheme, he is required to provide at least a minimum amount of pension which is roughly the same as the earnings-related state pension

Insured scheme   Any scheme that has an insurance company looking after it and gives guarantees on investment

Late retirement   If you retire after the normal age, your pension will build up and when you draw it you will receive a bigger pension than you would otherwise have done. Or you can take your pension and carry on working

Lower earnings limit   Only people earning less than this figure do not have to pay national insurance contributions

Managed fund   A fund managed by any outside institutions such as a bank or insurance company. This money is pooled with money from other pension funds and invested as the organiser decides, often in consultation with the pension scheme trustees

Money purchase   This scheme dictates how much money is paid in rather than how much is paid out. You will not know how much pension you are going to receive until you retire

Net relevant earnings   Roughly, gross earned income from non-pensionable employment, before deducting income tax

Occupational Pensions Board   Supervises contracted out schemes

Paid-up pension   A pension which is totally paid for in advance but will not be paid out until a future date

Pay as you go   This is how the state pension works. Today's pensioners are paid out of the money today's contributors make

Pensionable earnings or pensionable salary   The amount of your earnings used to calculate your pension; it may be different from your total earnings. For example, your bonuses, commission and overtime may be excluded

Pensionable service   You may not be eligible to join the company pension scheme until you have worked for the company for a number of years. Those early years may not then count towards your pension

Personal pension   An individual pension for self-employed and employees; it can be used to contract out of SERPS

Portable pension   One that you take with you whenever you change jobs and is not tied into an employer's scheme

Preservation   When you leave a job, if you have worked there for five years, any pension you have earned will be 'preserved' until you retire

Protected rights   Part of the personal pension bought with minimum contribution of national insurance rebates and incentive payment

Rebate   Given on national insurance contributions to contracted out schemes

Self administered scheme   A scheme which the employer runs himself without outside help

SERPS   or state earnings-related pension scheme. For employees who are not contracted out of the state scheme

Superannuation   Pension

Transfer value   When you move jobs, if your new employer agrees to accept the pension rights you have built up already into his scheme, the amount handed over is called a transfer value

Trustees   Those responsible for looking after the pension fund

Upper earnings limit   You pay no further national insurance contributions on any earnings above this figure

Widow's or widower's pension   This is paid to the widow or widower of a member.

A CAR

A new car loses 20 to 30 per cent of its value in the first year; by the end of year three its value will have halved. But, despite the expense, more people are buying cars every year.

Your first decision is whether to buy a new or a second-hand car, and the deciding factor will be how much you can afford. For the same amount of money you can choose a smaller, brand new car or a larger, faster, second-hand one.

BUYING NEW

It is easy to compare prices of new cars: the car you are buying should be in immaculate order, though it may not be in practice. But, if it is not, then you are covered by the manufacturer's guarantee.

Certain extras such as a radio, or carpet, may be included in the basic price or they may cost extra; if a garage is running a special promotion, it might pay a year's road fund licence for you, or fill up the car with petrol. These are incidental perks which are simply meant to catch your attention.

You will probably have to pay extra for seat belts, which are compulsory, a delivery charge and number plates.

The disadvantage of buying new cars is that they drop so much in value in the first year. And, if there are any inherent faults in the car, you will have the hassle of getting them put right as well as being without the car while the garage works on it.

BUYING SECOND HAND

This is an extremely tricky exercise. If you do not know much about cars yourself, make sure you have the advice of a friend who does.

Better still, if you are a member of the AA or RAC, you can ask them to check over a second-hand car for you. A vehicle inspection for ordinary family cars costs £48 and for this they give your car a two-hour inspection including road test.

If the inspector finds any faults, the seller is under no obligation to put them right but you are in a stronger bargaining position to ask. However, if you go ahead and buy the car knowing that there are faults, you have no case for complaining later.

The test will be carried out at a garage or, if it is a private deal, at the owner's house. The tests are recommended even if the car is less than a year old so that you can pick up any likely faults before the manufacturer's warranty runs out.

Again, if the car has been involved in an accident, it is worth while having a test carried out in the hope of showing up problems which otherwise might not become apparent for some time.

But be careful if you are buying privately. There will be very little you can do if anything goes wrong with the deal, whereas if you buy from a garage or dealer you are covered by a range of consumer protection laws. See p. 236.

SELLING PRIVATELY

You will almost certainly be able to obtain a higher price if you sell your old car privately rather than trading it in at the garage. The drawback is the time and expense of advertising, seeing prospective buyers, and receiving the money safely.

Make sure you have the cash before handing over your car or, if payment is by cheque, make sure the cheque is cleared.

Then, if you cannot manage without a car for a day or two, there is the problem of co-ordinating the selling and buying dates.

HOW TO PAY

You have several choices when it comes to finding the money for a car, some more advantageous than others.

Cash

If you offer a garage cash, you will very likely be able to negotiate a discount. This will depend on how well car sales are going at the time and how anxious the garage is to shift its stock.

You may have an old car to sell, in which case you can either negotiate a part exchange or sell privately. The part-exchange deal you agree will depend on how keenly you fight for what you consider to be the car's value and how anxious the garage is to sell.

Prices offered by the trade for second-hand cars are based on *Glass's Guide* which lists all cars in all stages of decrepitude. You will be lucky if you can look at a copy yourself because garages obviously do not want to show their hand in negotiations.

But you can get an idea of current second-hand car prices by looking at car magazines.

Hire purchase

If you do not have enough cash to buy a car, or simply do not want to pay in cash, the garage will be more than happy to arrange hire purchase for you.

It works out as an expensive way of borrowing money but the only thing you have to do towards arranging it is to sign your name. The garage will have an arrangement with a particular HP company and will do all the paperwork for you.

Garages are not just providing an efficient service; they receive commission from the HP company for every contract they sign up. When the garage is quoting the rate of interest, make sure you know what the Annual Percentage Rate (APR) is, see p. 55.

There is now no legal requirement to put down a deposit but, in practice, garages will ask for one, just to make sure you are serious about going ahead.

You can repay the loan over any agreed period but the usual time is two or three years. To be covered by consumer credit law, the amount of credit must be no more than £15,000.

You do not have to agree to use the HP company suggested by the garage. Telephone several to see if anyone else is offering a better deal and make sure you know how much is being charged for arranging the loan. Also, ask how much it will cost if you repay the loan earlier than stated in the agreement: it can become surprisingly expensive.

But always work out the figures for yourself. Do not take anyone's word that he is giving you a bargain, either by offering more for the trade-in of your old car, charging you less for a new one, or providing you with 'free' credit.

The important sum is the total cost to you of buying that car, allowing for all the incidentals.

Bank loan

A cheaper way to borrow to buy a car can be to ask your bank for a loan. The principle for evaluating the cost is just the same as with HP: find out the APR. This figure will be lower than the HP company charges.

It is worth putting a little spade work in before you see the bank manager, deciding exactly what you want, and how you are going to repay it.

As with HP, you will repay the loan in equal monthly instalments.

ROAD FUND LICENCE

This is car tax which is a compulsory charge. See p. 14 for details.

INSURANCE

A minimum amount of cover is required by law but you can opt for some additional cover which is more costly.

So, is it worth paying out for extra insurance cover over and above the minimum you need? In practice, very few people opt for the minimum cover and, if they do, it is probably because their driving record is so bad that they cannot obtain any more.

There are four types of motor insurance to choose from:

- [ ] the minimum legal cover
- [ ] third party
- [ ] third party, fire and theft
- [ ] comprehensive

The insurance company is the 'first party', you are the 'second party' and 'third party' means anyone else. If you have an accident, and injure someone, he or she is the 'third party".

Minimum cover

This does not include the cost of damage to your car if you have an accident. Neither will it pay the cost of repairing another car which you may hit, nor the replacement value of your car if it is stolen.

The cover is limited to accidents which happen on the public roads – not even those in your own driveway. All it does is to insure for the liability of the driver in case they injure or kill someone.

The amount of this liability is unlimited. However, these policies are very rarely issued.

Third party

If you have an accident, a third-party policy covers you for injury to others, including passengers, and damage to other cars or property.

Additionally, there is an indemnity to passengers in your car. So if they cause an accident, perhaps by opening the door carelessly, your policy will pay out to the injured person and for any damage.

Third party, fire and theft

This type of policy goes further and covers loss or damage to the car by fire, explosion, theft or attempted theft. The policy will also cover the theft of accessories fitted to the car.

Comprehensive

Comprehensive policies cover everything mentioned so far plus accidental damage to the car whoever is to blame, although they will not cover you for breakdown. There is limited cover for personal accident benefit.

Cost

How much you will have to pay in insurance premiums depends on a mix of factors:

- [ ] the type of car
- [ ] where you live
- [ ] your driving experience
- [ ] what you use the car for
- [ ] any accidents or claims you may previously have had

The money the insurance company collects in premiums is pooled to pay out when drivers make a claim. Very simply, the actuary gauges how much he will need by equating the number of accidents against the cost of repairs.

If you use your car in the course of work, the rating is higher. And if you want to use your car for motor rallies or competitions, you will have to pay an even larger premium.

No-claims discount

Insurance companies reduce their premiums to more experienced, safer drivers by allowing a no-claims discount, the amount of which depends on your number of claim-free years. In practice, very few drivers, except the young and totally inexperienced, or extremely bad drivers, have no discount at all.

The usual penalty for making a claim is to go back two steps on the discount scale. You then move back up the scale one step at a time each year when you renew your policy.

When you reach the top rung, usually a 60 or 65 per cent discount, for a small additional premium you can obtain a protected no-claims bonus which will allow you, for example, two claims every five years without the penalty of losing some of your discount.

Your comprehensive policy should allow you to claim whenever you break a windscreen without affecting your no-claims discount. Some companies allow you only one free windscreen claim a year.

Cutting the cost

To cut the cost of motor insurance you can limit the scope of the policy. Restricting driving to yourself is the first step, and here it is female drivers who earn the greatest discount. If you have just one driver and a spouse named on the policy, this will save about 10 per cent over a policy which allows anyone to drive the car.

But think carefully before asking for these discounts. Circumstances may arise when you need someone else to drive your car.

Then, if you agree to a voluntary excess, that is paying the first agreed amount of any claim yourself, you can reduce the premium by up to 25 per cent.

Some insurance companies give a special discount to the over 50s or the over 60s and to women drivers.

A standard private motor insurance policy might cost something like this a year:

Driver: aged 35 years; comprehensive cover; nil accident damage excess; driving a new Ford Escort 1300L (Group 3); with full no-claims discount; any driver

living in Cornwall	£175
living in Nottingham	£208
living in Watford	£267
living in Central London	£304

Driver: aged 55 years; comprehensive cover; with a £35 accidental damage excess; driving a new Ford Escort 1300L (Group 3); with full no-claims bonus;
His wife also drives the car; is aged 55; and has had a full licence for more than three years

	with no-claims discount protection	without no-claims discount protection
living in Cornwall	£164	£144
living in Nottingham	£196	£172
living in Watford	£252	£220
living in Central London	£286	£250

LEGAL EXPENSES INSURANCE

Increasingly, you will be offered legal expenses insurance with your motor insurance policy. This will cover areas that a basic car insurance misses. For example, after an accident you can pursue a claim for personal injury, hire charges, loss of use of your own car, motor prosecutions. And you can defend a dispute with your garage over buying, hiring or repairing your car.

With legal expenses insurance you will also be able to recover your losses if you have an accident with an uninsured driver.

The cost is about £5 a year.

See p. 131.

HIRING A CAR

Even if you own a car, you may need to hire one on occasions: you may need a larger car than you own, or yours may be in for repair.

If you do not use a car very often, it may be cheaper to hire one when necessary rather than buying a car which sits in the street or in the garage rusting away for most of the year.

Shop around to compare rates. Obviously, you will pay more for larger and newer cars and you will pay twice as much if you hire one at an airport.

Rental companies will ask you to pay a deposit before you take the car away, unless you pay by credit card or charge card.

Outside Central London you will pay around £20 a day to hire a car, with unlimited mileage. You should add on insurance and VAT to this and you will have to pay about £40 in advance. The weekly rate will be about 20 per cent cheaper.

COSTS OF RUNNING A CAR

The AA produces figures showing how the total running costs add up:

	Engine Capacity (cc)				
	Up to 1000	1001 to 1400	1401 to 2000	2001 to 3000	3001 to 4500
Standing charges per annum (£)					
Car Licence	100.00	100.00	100.00	100.00	100.00
Insurance (i)	392.80	462.90	557.60	900.00	1115.20
Depreciation (based on 10,000 miles per annum)	698.56	975.37	1214.08	2447.77	3286.78
Subscription to AA	42.00	42.00	42.00	42.00	42.00
	1233.36	1580.27	1913.68	3489.77	4543.98
Cost per mile (in pence)					
5,000	24.667	31.605	38.273	69.795	90.879
10,000	12.334	15.803	19.137	34.898	45.440
15,000	9.153	11.835	14.376	26.528	34.675
20,000	8.262	10.827	13.210	24.792	32.580
25,000	7.727	10.222	12.511	23.750	31.323
30,000	6.439	8.518	10.425	19.791	26.102
Running cost per mile (in pence)					
Petrol*	4.300	4.914	5.733	7.818	8.600
Oil	0.440	0.440	0.468	0.517	0.845
Tyres (ii)	0.463	0.586	0.713	1.381	1.905
Servicing	0.808	0.808	0.808	1.055	1.574
Repairs and Replacements	4.849	5.133	5.999	9.076	11.280
	10.860	11.881	13.721	19.847	24.204

*At £1.72 a gallon (37.9 per litre). For every penny more or less add or subtract

	0.025	0.028	0.033	0.045	0.050

Total of standing and running costs (in pence) per mile based on annual mileages of:

5,000	35.572	43.486	51.994	89.642	115.083
10,000	23.194	27.684	32.858	54.745	69.644
15,000	20.013	23.716	28.097	46.375	58.879
20,000	19.122	22.708	26.931	44.639	56.784
25,000	18.587	22.103	26.232	43.597	55.527
30,000	17.299	20.399	24.146	39.638	50.306

(i) Insurance: this is the average cost for a fully comprehensive policy. No allowance is made for no-claims discount

(ii) Tyres: estimated tyre life of 30,000 miles

© The Automobile Association

POOLING LIFTS

It used to be against the conditions of motor insurance policies to accept money for giving people lifts. This is no longer the case, as long as you do not make a profit out of it and the lift is for a social purpose.

So, if several of you want to share a car to get to work, you can each use your car in rotation and save money.

But you must take no more money than necessary to cover the price of petrol and the other costs of motoring, otherwise you will still invalidate your insurance policy.

IF YOU HAVE AN ACCIDENT

First, talk to any witnesses who may have seen the accident. Before they disappear, write down their names and addresses so they can back up your story later. If anyone has been injured you must exchange insurance details.

Then, take the name and address and car registration number of any other drivers involved in the accident. They are legally required to give you this information but, in case they give false names and addresses, make sure you have the licence number.

If the other car does not stop, try to take down his licence number and report him to the police immediately.

Next, make notes describing the scene of the accident, including the position of all other vehicles and the road conditions at the time, the weather, and the speed at which you were travelling.

Lastly, admit to nothing. It is difficult not to keep saying 'sorry, sorry' just after an accident but you really should not. In fact, your insurance contract forbids you to accept liability.

Call the police if anyone has been injured and, if necessary, an ambulance. If someone else was to blame for the accident, he will either have to pay out of his own pocket or through his insurance policy.

If you have to pay, you may find it less expensive to pay for the repairs yourself rather than claiming on your insurance policy and losing part, or all, of your no-claims discount. If you decide to claim, or even if you think you may, telephone or write to the insurance company and they will send you a claim form to complete. In any case, you should inform them that you have had an accident, even if you do not claim.

Most insurance companies have knock-for-knock agreements to reduce the administration costs of dealing with motor claims. Under these agreements each insurance company pays for the damage to the car it insures without apportioning blame. This saves the time otherwise spent in establishing blame and it costs the insurance company less money. Therefore, do not expect an insurance company to pursue a claim on your behalf very aggressively.

If you have an accident, the insurer may ask you to take the car to one of its approved garages to have it repaired, or they may ask you to supply them with two quotations before sanctioning payment.

If the repair work is going to be more expensive than replacing the car, then it will be written-off and you will receive what the insurance company decides was the value of your car at the time. If you had a new radio or very low mileage, make sure you tell the insurer because your car will be worth more than the standard second-hand value.

CHAPTER · 17

HOLIDAYS

Brighton or Barbados? Blackpool or Biarritz? Once you have decided where, you will start wondering how. After agreeing where to go and how to book it, there are two more important issues to decide: do I need insurance, and what do I do about foreign money?

FOREIGN MONEY
You can take this in the form of cash, travellers cheques, Postcheques, eurocheques, credit cards. Each has its own advantages and disadvantages.

Cash
This is the most versatile and cheapest method but it is also the most risky. You can take sterling abroad with you (you will need some change when you come home anyway); you can buy the foreign currency before you go; or you can pick it up while you are travelling, at the airport or on the boat, although watch the rates here. Remember too that you will need some cash as soon as you set foot on foreign soil.

But, whether to buy the bulk of it before you leave or when you arrive is debatable. For the amount of money you will be taking on holiday, really you may as well buy wherever is most convenient for you because any potential gain will be too small to worry about.

Similarly, there is no point in buying your currency six months before you go away in the hope of beating the foreign exchange rates and making a killing. You just might. But, unless you put the money in a foreign currency deposit account, you will probably lose more by forfeiting the interest you could otherwise have earned.

Maybe you prefer to wait until you arrive to buy your holiday money. When deciding, remember you might get a marginally better rate if you buy 'hard' currencies before you go and 'soft' ones when you arrive. 'Hard' currencies are those that are doing better than sterling, so once you are abroad, sterling will be less welcome and the rate not so good. 'Soft' currencies are weaker than the pound, so sterling, as a stronger currency, will be wanted abroad.

Carrying large sums of cash around is extremely risky. But if you take out holiday insurance, you can claim on the policy if your cash is lost or stolen. However, do check the small print before you sign, to make sure you are covered and to see what the limitations are: you may have to pay the first £5 or £10 of the loss and you may not be able to claim more than £200. In any case, you will have to wait until you arrive home to claim for the money. You will also need proof that you really did lose the money; a statement from the local police is best.

Travellers cheques

You can buy travellers cheques from banks, some building societies, the post office and large travel agents. They come in various denominations, currencies and names. Each bank has its own; other well-known names are Thomas Cook, American Express, and Diners Club.

You pay commission when you buy them (1–2 per cent) and commission when you exchange them.

If you order travellers cheques in the currency of the country you are visiting, you may not have to pay anything to cash them but each bank in each country has its own scale of commission charges. Sterling travellers cheques will cost about 1 per cent to exchange but, conversely, you will suffer if you have any unused foreign currency travellers cheques to bring back.

You can buy travellers cheques over the counter at bank branches with large foreign exchange departments. But usually you have to order them in advance, say ten days or two weeks. When you collect them you will be asked to sign each cheque in one corner before leaving the premises. Once this is done, the money is guaranteed and will be refunded if you lose the travellers cheques.

To cash travellers cheques, you date them, insert the name of the payee and countersign them in the presence of a cashier who checks that your two signatures tally before handing over the money.

Sometimes you will be able to use travellers cheques to pay for goods in shops, as well as withdrawing cash from the bank. In the United States, you can receive change in dollars.

You can cash travellers cheques in various places: at banks, of course, where you will probably get the best rate; in large hotels where the exchange rate is not as good; and in some shops.

Postcheques

This is a facility offered by Giro systems throughout Europe. The main advantage is the enormous number of outlets where you can cash Postcheques – including small post offices in out-of-the-way villages.

You need to have an account with Girobank first because it is essential to have a cheque guarantee card. Then, some time before you are due to leave, ask Girobank to send a book of Postcheques printed with your name and account number. There are 10 Postcheques to each book and you can ask for as many books as you think you will need (and your account will stand).

Postcheques are accepted in 34 countries throughout Europe and the Mediterranean area. Each cheque has a maximum limit in the local currency of approximately £120 and you can cash up to ten cheques a day. You pay £5 for the book and 1 per cent of the value that you cash.

Eurocheques

You can withdraw cash from your own bank account nearly anywhere in Europe. You now need a special eurocheque encashment card to do so and special eurocheques.

With eurocheques you can pay for goods in stores as well as drawing cash, in the same way as you would with an American Express or Diners Club cheque.

The uniform eurocheque encashment card costs £5 a year and euro-cheques are 30p each plus 1·6 per cent of the amount you write out. You can use these cards in some cash machines on the continent.

Cash cards

Increasingly, you will be able to use your ordinary cash card in foreign machines to obtain local currency. When this becomes more widespread it will be the most convenient and safest way of getting money abroad and is a logical extension of the services available with plastic cards.

Meanwhile, you can use a credit card or Connect card (with your PIN) to obtain cash from machines in France, Spain, Italy, Norway and Sweden through link-ups with foreign banks. More countries are steadily joining in.

Credit cards

You can use Access, Barclaycard, Trustcard or any other credit card to pay for goods abroad and to obtain cash. Just look for the familiar Mastercard and Visa logos displayed in shop and bank windows. If you buy goods, you will pay for them when you receive the monthly bill at home and at the exchange rate ruling when the bill is presented.

You can use Access and Barclaycard to withdraw up to £350 worth of foreign currency a day at banks showing the Mastercard or Visa signs. With Access you pay the usual interest rate starting immediately you take the money; with Visa you pay a straight 1·5 per cent handling charge and then interest is due as usual when the bill arrives at home a few weeks later.

Access and Barclaycard are accepted in most countries, but if you intend visiting an out-of-the-way spot, make enquiries before you leave.

Charge cards

You can use American Express or Diners Club charge cards almost anywhere in the world. These cards do not allow you credit; you have to pay the full bill when it arrives back home, probably six weeks after you have had the goods. The cards can be used to pay for goods and to get cash at their companies' offices.

If you lose your card, or it is stolen, you should report it as soon as you can to the company through the local office.

INSURANCE

Should you take out insurance before going abroad on holiday? Yes, probably you should. The highest risk you will run is having to pay for medical treatment abroad and this can quickly grow to staggering amounts.

The most useful advice before taking out holiday insurance is to read the small print. **Make sure that you are covered for all the eventualities you want and that there are no exclusion clauses cutting out anything you might need or any activity you might take part in.**

If you are buying a package holiday, the brochure will almost certainly include an insurance application on the back page. It could be that the insurance is reasonably priced and comprehensive, but do not assume that it is. You should shop around.

If you have an all risks policy for your house contents, you may find that this covers your possessions while you are on holiday abroad and you may not need any extra insurance. It will be worth while putting a little effort into finding insurance that meets your needs for the least cost.

If you have been ill or consulted a doctor recently, you might find that the insurance company says this invalidates a claim. They call it an 'existing' condition and may not pay out if you were already ill before you went on holiday, even if you are claiming for a quite different problem.

It is a question of what the insurance companies call 'material' facts. The onus is on you to declare all information about yourself and your state of health that might affect the company's decision to insure you. Even if there is no specific question on the application form, it is your responsibility to tell them. This is unsatisfactory, but it is the way the companies are allowed to operate.

To find out more about holiday insurance, call into an insurance broker and ask for several quotations. Or contact an insurance company direct. The Association of British Travel Agents (ABTA) recommends its own comprehensive insurance policy following complaints a few years ago about the inadequate policies available.

You should expect to pay about £47.50 for two weeks' cover worldwide under a policy giving £500,000 worth of medical expenses, cancellation compensation, delay, lost baggage, money, personal liability, and personal accident. Two weeks' holiday insurance in Europe will cost about £21. You will have to pay at least twice as much if you are going on a high-risk holiday such as skiing, so be sure you have the appropriate cover. Some holiday insurance policies include a get-you-home air ambulance service.

The insurance company arranges a tie up with an air ambulance organisation which provides emergency repatriation.

If your plans do not fit in with a 'package' insurance, ask for 'selective' travel insurance which allows you to insure for exactly what you want.

Before you leave, make sure you know how to claim, should you need to. If you are unlucky enough to have an accident, while you are lying unconscious is not the time to start wondering where the insurance policy is and how you set about making a claim.

Make sure, before you go on holiday to an EEC country, that you know what to do if you fall ill. Some EEC countries have reciprocal arrangements under which UK residents can receive free, or reduced cost, medical treatment. Pick up a leaflet SA30 from your local social security office. This is called: 'Medical costs abroad: what you need to know'.

Four weeks before you are going to an EEC country, complete a form E111 which comes complete with an explanatory leaflet. This will entitle you to medical treatment in EEC countries. You apply for form E111 by completing a form included in leaflet SA30. When E111 arrives, you will also receive SA36, telling you how to get medical treatment on holiday abroad.

Another useful leaflet is SA35 'Protect your health abroad'.

But even in EEC countries, private insurance cover is still recommended. You may be able to recoup only part of the cost of treatment. And worse, if you had an accident, there would be no time to look around for another doctor if the one treating you does not take part in the reciprocal arrangements.

Then, think of the extra hotel accommodation and travel expenses you might have to meet.

When motoring abroad, every country you visit will have its own insurance regulations and these will almost certainly demand a stated minimum level. All UK motor policies have some provision for the minimum requirements of EEC countries. But it is worth while taking out insurance beyond this minimum requirement, which you can do by extending your UK motor insurance policy. Only for driving in remote places will this not be possible.

When you ask for your UK insurance to be extended you will be issued with a Green Card. This is an internationally-recognised document indicating that you have the same level of cover abroad as you do in the UK. Without a Green Card you are covered only for the minimum insurance in the EEC.

In Spain, the police can detain a driver and his car after an accident unless a deposit is paid. For an additional premium, you can take out a Bail Bond, which acts as surety if this happens to you.

If your car is stolen abroad, or damaged beyond repair, you may have to pay import duty in that country. This is because the duty is payable on any car that is not taken back out of the country within a certain period of time.

If you have a caravan, your existing policy may include travelling with it abroad. If not, get the policy extended and note the caravan separately on the Green Card. In the UK, caravan insurance can either be taken out as a separate policy or as an extension to a package household policy.

Similarly, a household policy can be extended to cover horse riding. But more usually this insurance is taken out separately. The premiums will differ depending on the type of riding – the more hazardous, the more expensive.

Most of the large insurance companies will underwrite insurance for pleasure boats. Small craft under 16 feet, including speedboats and racing dinghies, can either be included in a household policy or treated separately.

Boats over 16 feet, including yachts and motor boats, have a more complicated rating basis and need a separate quotation.

TIMESHARE

A growing form of holiday is timeshare. You buy the right to stay one or more weeks of the year in a property for the next 50 to 80 years, depending on the agreement. Overseas or in Scotland you buy in perpetuity.

So, instead of booking into a hotel, or renting a holiday home, you buy your accommodation for a few weeks every year for the next so many years.

The timeshare companies make expansive claims for the advantages, but you should remember this is not an investment. When you come to sell, you may not even find a buyer, let alone make a profit. The trade association is the Timeshare Developers Association; address on p. 250.

The usual selling points given include:
- [ ] you are buying a good investment
- [ ] you are buying holidays for the next 80 years at today's prices
- [ ] you can swap your weeks with other timeshare holidays in other parts of the world
- [ ] you can rent out any unused weeks
- [ ] you can sell your timeshare weeks at any time you want
- [ ] you can live in more luxurious accommodation than you could afford at home
- [ ] you are inflation proofing your holidays

What the salespeople will not emphasise is:
- [ ] you are buying 'weeks'; you are not buying a property
- [ ] service charges will increase each year; and once the developer has sold all the weeks, this will be his only source of income
- [ ] you may not be able to swap with what you ideally want
- [ ] there is no guarantee that you can sell later on – you will have to find a buyer first and no one knows how much in demand timeshare weeks will be in a few years' time
- [ ] so there can be no guarantee that you will get any money back, let alone a higher price

- ☐ remember to add VAT to any prices you are quoted
- ☐ you still have to pay the fares to the holiday home
- ☐ you have to rely on the developer to maintain the standard of the property and, once all the weeks have been sold, he may not be so interested in the property
- ☐ other timesharers may not share your standards of cleanliness
- ☐ there is no control over timeshare developers
- ☐ the property should be completely closed for at least two weeks each year for maintenance and repair; make sure it is
- ☐ there will be legal fees to pay when you buy
- ☐ the developer might sell out after all the weeks have been sold
- ☐ timesharing may suit you and your family now, but will it when your children have left home?

DUTY-FREE ALLOWANCES

	goods bought in ordinary shops in EEC countries	goods bought outside the EEC, or in a duty-free shop in the EEC
TOBACCO		
cigarettes	300	200
or cigarillos	150	100
or cigars	75	50
or tobacco	400g	250g
ALCOHOL		
over 22 per cent	1.5 litres	1 litre
or fortified	3 litres	2 litres
or sparkling wine		
plus		
still table wine	5 litres	2 litres
PERFUME	90cc	60cc
plus TOILET WATER	375cc	250cc
OTHER GOODS	£250	£32

but no more than 50 litres of beer and 25 mechanical lighters.

CHAPTER · 18

THE LAW

If you buy a Japanese radio in a sale, can you take it back if it is faulty? Can you return an armchair if you find the colour does not match your curtains? If a pair of shoes falls apart, should you complain to the manufacturer or the retailer?

Your rights as a consumer are laid down by law but the interpretation of the law is sometimes unclear. The broad guidelines are designed to protect the consumer. However, they are effective only if you use them.

BUYING GOODS

Every time you buy something, whether you pay by cash or by credit, whether it is something as small as a packet of sweets or as large as a car or a house, your rights are protected. The consumer is able to buy goods knowing that, if they are in any way faulty, or if you have been deceived about the quality, you can complain with the full back-up of the law.

Different laws cover different situations, but the whole basis of buying is that you make a contract with the shopkeeper. He displays goods for sale; you offer to buy them; you agree the price; you hand over the money; he hands over the goods. In the eyes of the law, both of you have made a contract and if either of you breaks the contract, the other has redress.

If you find that the pair of shoes you just bought fall apart the first time you wear them, go back to the shop. And if your cheque bounces, the shopkeeper will come back to you.

You both have to agree the terms of the deal before a contract is struck. So, if the shopkeeper displays a video recorder in his window with a £244 price tag, that does not automatically give you the right to buy at that price. When you go inside the shop, the shopkeeper may say that the price ticket is wrong and the real price is £422. You then have to decide whether or not you will buy at £422.

But if the trader had no intention of selling at the lower price and was deliberately trying to mislead you to tempt you into the shop, then he is breaching the Trade Descriptions Act which is a criminal offence.

Sale goods

You have exactly the same rights if you buy goods in a sale as you do at any other time. Unless the items are specifically labelled 'damaged', the retailer cannot refuse to give you your money back simply because you bought them at a reduced price.

Even if he displays a sign saying: 'sale goods cannot be exchanged' or 'no refund on sale goods', if you were allowed to believe that they were 100 per cent sound, you can take them back if they turn out to be faulty. But you cannot expect exactly the same quality of goods as if you had bought them at the full price.

Changing your mind

You cannot ask for your money back simply because you have changed your mind about an item. Some retailers will allow you to do this for the sake of goodwill, but you do not have any statutory rights. Only if you change your mind before you hand over the money does the shopkeeper have to accept your decision. Similarly, the shopkeeper cannot withdraw the goods once he has accepted your offer to buy.

If you are buying on credit or mail order, the timing is a little different (see below).

Buying privately

Here, you do not have quite the same rights: the only responsibility of the seller is that the goods are 'as described' and correspond with any sample given. Beyond that the onus is on you to ask the questions which will establish the condition of the article.

Buying at auction

Here, it really is up to you to decide about the condition of what you are buying. You will have the opportunity to examine the items before the bidding starts and the catalogue will give some indication of condition. The initials A.F. mean 'as found' and are a warning that the goods are likely to be in a poor condition.

The contract on this occasion is made as the auctioneer's gavel hits the table and whoever has made the last bid (which will be the highest) has to buy.

Buying second hand

Unless you are buying privately, you are fully protected by the consumer laws. But they do take account of the fact that second-hand goods are not expected to have the same quality or length of life as new ones, and the older they are, the poorer in quality they will be.

There are a number of overlapping laws that protect the consumer. They cover the quality, condition and safety of the goods. If you buy on credit, you are further covered by the Consumer Credit Act, 1974.

The shopkeeper's side of the contract demands that he:
☐ sells goods that are suited to their normal purpose, even if you have bought them in a sale or second hand
☐ sells goods that are capable of doing what he says they will
☐ sells goods that conform to his description of them

In the first place, if you are not satisfied with any items you have bought, you should take them back to the shop where you bought them. You should not at this stage send them to the manufacturer because your contract was with the retailer.

If the object is too heavy to carry, tell the shopkeeper and ask him to come and collect it. If you are right and the item is seriously faulty, the retailer's only obligation is to give you your money back. If the goods are slightly faulty or damaged you may be able to negotiate a partial repayment and keep the goods.

The trader can offer to repair the item, or to replace it. But if he offers you a credit note in exchange for faulty goods, do not accept it. You are entitled to the cash and you may not see anything in his shop that you wish to buy with a credit note.

There are some instances when you cannot claim your money back for faulty goods:
☐ if you knew the fault was there when you bought the item
☐ if the salesman told you about the fault before you bought the goods
☐ if you bought an item in the hope that it would suit your purpose, even though the salesman had told you he did not know if it would or not

If you are given a present that turns out to be faulty, then the person who bought the item for you must take it back to the shop. Even if this is embarrassing, you do not have the right to return it yourself as you are not the person who has a contract with the retailer.

Disclaimers
If a tradesman displays a notice in his shop saying 'no money refunded', you can ignore it. In fact, this notice is illegal and you can report the shop to the Trading Standards Officer. A shopkeeper cannot escape his legal responsibilities this way and, despite any notices, you still have your usual consumer rights. For example, if the notice reads 'items left at owner's risk' in a dry cleaners, the trader can enforce it only if it is reasonable for him to do so.

Pay a deposit
There is no necessity to pay one, but it is a sign of your good intention to buy. You should expect to pay a deposit if you want to reserve a dress until you can afford it on payday, or if the shop is out of stock and ordering one

in your size specially for you. If you pay a deposit, the trader is obliged to reserve the dress for you until the balance is paid.

If you change your mind later about buying, the trader could keep your deposit because you have already made a contract. He could even sue you for the balance of the purchase price.

A builder adding an extension to your house may ask for a deposit, or money in advance, to buy the materials he needs. You will have to make up your own mind about paying it.

Guarantees
Some manufacturers give a guarantee with the goods they sell. This cannot in any way take away your statutory rights, but it may increase them. A television manufacturer might guarantee all parts for five years. But if you need to claim, read the terms of the guarantee closely. You may be better off returning the television to the shop (which you should do in the first place anyway) rather than paying postage or labour charges to the manufacturer.

Doorstep salespeople
Always be extremely wary of anyone knocking at your door trying to sell. They will be hoping to catch you off your guard and talk you into buying something you otherwise would not.

If you are tempted, make a note of the price he is charging and his name and address, then ask him to come back later. That will give you time to check his price against those of other retailers. If you do buy, you cannot change your mind afterwards, unless you bought on credit.

Mail order
To be safe, buy from well-known names only, or at least make sure you keep a copy of the original advertisement promising the quality of the goods. The descriptions must conform to the same standards demanded of retailers.

BUYING SERVICES
When you are paying for services rather than buying goods, you are protected by different laws. These say that the trader must do the work properly, as you have agreed. In most cases, it is obvious whether you are buying services or goods:

- ☐ you are buying a pound of potatoes; or you are paying a gardener to dig them up
- ☐ you are buying a pair of shoes; or paying to have them mended
- ☐ you are buying a new coat; or having it dry cleaned

But there are some instances where it is not so clear cut, or that involve buying both services and materials, for example if you are having your car repaired.

If you walk into an art gallery and buy an oil painting, are you paying for services (the artist's talent) or for goods (the paint and canvas)? The answer is that you are buying goods, unless you have commissioned the painting, in which case you are paying for the artist's skill.

The difference is important because, if it comes to a dispute, you are covered by different laws. Services cover such things as: dry cleaning; shoe repairs; hairdressing; travel agents; repairs; car servicing; taxis; hotels; solicitors; accountants; estate agents; builders; banking; and insurance.

When you pay someone to carry out a service for you, his responsibility is:
- ☐ to work to a reasonable or laid-down professional standard
- ☐ to use good quality materials which are suitable for the job
- ☐ to look after your property while it is in his care
- ☐ to carry out the work as agreed
- ☐ to charge a reasonable price (unless a price has been agreed)

If he fails in any of these areas, you have cause for complaint, although the terms are extremely vague. The 'reasonable standard' you would expect from a gardener trained by the Royal Horticultural Society would be different from the one you could fairly expect from an odd-jobman who will turn his hand to anything. And of course, you will pay accordingly.

What happens if your watch is stolen while it is at the jewellers for repair? If the jeweller can prove that he took all reasonable measures to secure his premises, he owes you nothing. Unless you can claim on an all risks insurance policy, you have lost your watch. But if the jeweller cannot show that he has taken proper care and so, in a way, contributed to the theft, then you can sue him for compensation.

Printed on the receipt you are given when you first leave the goods for repair, you may see words to the effect of: 'goods left at owner's risk'. This clause is an attempt by traders to avoid their responsibility. But, if you were not made aware of the clause at the time of the transaction, or if the court decides the wording is unreasonable, then it has no effect.

Estimates

Very often when you take in goods for repair, the shopkeeper will not be able to tell you exactly how much the job is going to cost. If you ask, he will give you an estimate before he starts work.

The difficulty is knowing how precise this figure is going to be. The trader can charge you more or less, when the work is finished and you have no firm basis for disputing the cost. If in doubt, always ask for a written estimate as this prevents the trader telling a different story later.

Quotations

These can be regarded as firmer indications of the eventual cost. And if the quotation is stated to be a fixed price quotation, then that is the figure, and the only figure, you will have to pay. The exception would be if you subsequently asked for more work to be done.

Disputing the bill

If you feel that the trader is charging too much, and you did not agree this price beforehand, then, to prove your point you should ask for quotations for the same job from other traders. But you must expect to pay a 'reasonable' amount, even if you are not satisfied with the job at the end. You must at least pay for the work that has been done.

For instance, should a builder walk off the site leaving your extension only half built, you do not have to pay the full agreed price for the job, because he has broken the contract. But you do have to pay him for the amount he has done (if he has the nerve to come and ask you) less an appropriate sum to compensate you for his breach of contract.

Completing the work

You should agree the time in which you expect the job to be finished so that, if it is unreasonably late, you can claim recompense. If you have not mentioned timing, you cannot complain as long as the time taken is 'reasonable'.

Descriptions

The Trade Descriptions Act rules also apply to services. The trader is liable if he knowingly or recklessly makes a false statement. Thus, '24-hour dry cleaning', 'same day service', 'repairs while you wait', and 'sea view' must mean exactly that.

BUYING FOOD

Very strict regulations cover the sale of food: it must be fit to eat; correctly labelled; and manufactured and stored in hygienic conditions. You cannot sell short-weight items.

Food labelling

Food labelling laws set out very strictly just what must be included on the label: all the ingredients for pre-packed foods must be shown in order of quantity and this includes water. If one ingredient is singled out for special mention: 'cake made with butter', then the amount of butter used must be shown: 'contains 10 per cent butter'.

Labels on all food that is advertised especially for slimmers must explain which ingredients are beneficial and also give the number of calories. Branded foods must say what the packets contain beyond a brand name.

The name and address of the manufacturer or distributor must be clearly shown and also the date by which the food is best eaten. It is illegal to fail to display a price on foods and no foods past their 'sell by' date should be on offer unless they are sold at a reduced price and clearly labelled as having passed the 'sell by' date.

BUYING ON CREDIT

Here again, strict rules have been laid down to protect the customer. Anyone selling goods on credit must display certain information very clearly:

- ☐ the rate of interest according to the APR
- ☐ the basic price without the interest
- ☐ the total cost including interest
- ☐ what the repayments are and how frequently they must be paid
- ☐ the length of the loan
- ☐ the deposit
- ☐ if you have to put down any security

For details of the various methods of buying on credit see pp. 61–2.

When you sign a credit agreement, you are signing a legally binding contract so be very sure you understand what you are doing. The agreement must show the relevant information as above. If it does not, the trader cannot enforce the contract.

You become absolutely bound to maintain the agreement once whoever is granting you credit approves your application. This will take several days while he checks out your references, so during this time you can, if you wish, change your mind and pull out.

If you sign the contract in your own home, or at least not on the shopkeeper's premises, and the trader has discussed the transaction with you face to face beforehand, you have extra time. This cooling-off period is designed to protect people against unscrupulous door-to-door salespeople who often have a very smooth line in sales talk.

With any agreement signed in your home, you have a five-day cooling-off period during which you are quite free to back out even if you have signed a contract. Moreover, the five days start from the time you receive a copy of the agreement in the post from the salesperson, which will be a few days after you have signed the contract.

He must leave a copy of the agreement with you at the time he makes the sale and then post another one later on. If you decide you want to back out, you should send a letter in writing to the company and, ideally, send it by registered post so there can be no argument about whether it arrived.

If you cancel an agreement, any money you have paid over must be refunded although under certain circumstances the trader is allowed to keep a £1 administration fee.

The consumers' watchdog is the Office of Fair Trading, or OFT. The

OFT looks after the interests of both consumers and businessmen, and protects them against unfair practices.

The Director General of Fair Trading keeps in contact with trade organisations, encouraging them to maintain Codes of Practice; he monitors traders who consistently offend; he issues licences to credit traders; he watches estate agents; and he looks out for unfair practices.

The OFT cannot take up individual complaints but this can be done through the Citizens Advice Bureau or a Trading Standards Department.

The Trading Standards Officers are also known as consumer protection officers; they are employed by the local council to enforce the Trade Descriptions Acts and consumer legislation.

Door-to-door salespeople

No one is allowed to knock on your door, or stop you in the street, and offer you credit. But what they can do is to knock on your door and offer to sell you goods which, surprise, surprise, you can buy on credit.

Faulty goods

You are protected against substandard goods when you buy on credit in the same way as you are with cash transactions. Moreover, whoever has provided you with the credit is, in some circumstances, liable equally with the shopkeeper for goods which cost between £100 and £30,000 including VAT.

But this applies only where you have borrowed the money to buy specific goods. An overdraft from the bank does not involve the bank in liability for the goods because the money has not been lent for any one item. But, if a personal loan is tied in with the purchase of a particular item, the bank is responsible with the supplier.

Paying off early

If you wish, you are fully entitled to pay off the whole amount for the goods at any time. And you should not pay interest beyond then.

Guaranteeing a loan for someone else

If a friend asks you to sign a guarantee enabling him to take out a loan or buy on credit, be very, very, cautious before agreeing. Remember, if he does not pay up, then you will have to pay – and moreover for goods which you have never received.

Unless you are happy to pay off someone else's debts, the best advice is DON'T SIGN.

Licences

Everyone who offers credit in whatever form must be licensed by the Office of Fair Trading. Before giving them your business you should check that the company is indeed licensed and, if you find someone operating without a licence, then you should report them.

If you have already signed an agreement with someone who is unlicensed, stop paying immediately but hold on to the goods. The agreement is not enforceable without a validation order from the OFT and it serves the company right for acting illegally.

But this applies only if the credit is below £15,000. A licence is not necessary if the trader only ever provides credit above this amount. And it is the amount of credit that matters, not the cost of the item. House purchase is always excluded.

Credit cards
When you buy goods using a bank credit card, such as Access or Barclaycard, the credit card company is liable too if the goods are faulty or if the service fails, and the credit is between £100 and £30,000.

Credit card responsibility
Until you receive the card and sign it, you have no responsibility whatsoever for the card. If it is stolen and misused, that is not your worry. But, once you have signed the card, you are theoretically liable for the first £25 or £30 if anyone uses your card without your permission. However, in practice, the banks do not penalise if your card is stolen and misused. But, if you have lent the card to a friend, you are totally responsible for whatever is spent.

Once you have notified the credit card company of the loss of the card, they take total responsibility for the debts run up. Obviously, it is crucial to notify them immediately you realise you have lost a card, and to make a note of exactly when you contact them.

Unsolicited goods
If goods are sent to you which you have not ordered, do nothing. You should not use the goods but put them to one side where they will not be damaged. You can, if you wish, write to the sender, saying that these goods were unsolicited, and ask him to take them back.

If you ask and he does not come to collect them within 30 days, the goods are yours. If you do absolutely nothing, the goods become your property after six months.

HOW TO COMPLAIN
The attitude you adopt when you first complain can make an enormous difference to the eventual outcome. If you are calm and reasonable when you talk to the people involved, you are far more likely to reach an amicable conclusion than if you rant and rave and force them into a defensive corner.

But you should never fail to complain when you have just cause. If you don't, you are making it easier for the slack standards to continue and so others will suffer.

First of all, take the item back to the shop where you bought it. If it is too large, telephone and ask them to come and collect it. Take the receipt or some other proof of purchase with you, if you have it, but the shopkeeper cannot wriggle out of his responsibility simply because you do not have one.

You can, if you prefer, write a letter. Address it to a senior person at the company and make sure you keep copies of all correspondence. Or you can telephone, in which case note down the name of the person you spoke to and what was said.

If you have a complaint about the quality of food, contact your local Environmental Health Officer immediately. The address is in the telephone directory under the name of your local authority.

Should you get no satisfaction at this stage, you can ask for further help from your local Trading Standards Officer, Citizens Advice Bureau or consumer advice centre. You might find that a letter from one of these bodies will persuade the shopkeeper to reach a settlement.

If you still cannot reach agreement, you should contact the trade association which monitors the business you are in dispute with. Many of them have a Code of Practice which the shopkeeper may be breaking. In any case, the trade association's staff will be anxious that you should be satisfied with the services of their members and will try to sort out the problem. They may have an arbitration scheme which will pronounce a binding decision.

The final resort is to go to court, though you cannot do this if you have already accepted binding arbitration. Going to the law can be expensive and time consuming so make sure this is what you want to do before starting. You may be able to apply for Legal Aid to help meet the costs, or for small amounts use the small claims procedure in the County Court.

Small claims

You may think it is not worth suing for a small amount of money because of the costs involved. But, if the value of the disputed item is £500 or less, then it is classified as a 'small value' claim and will not be as expensive as a full-scale claim.

The case will not be treated as a full trial: there is no judge or open court, simply an arbitrator. No legal costs are allowed and the only cost to pay is the court fees which are 10p in the £ up to a claim of £300; £37 between £300 and £500. The minimum fee is £7.

Where to go for legal advice

As well as using a solicitor (see below, for advice on how to choose one) you can go to a local law centre, Citizens Advice Bureau, or advice centre for help. Look in the local telephone directory for the address.

How to find a solicitor

You will probably feel quite bewildered wondering how to find a solicitor for the first time. You will want someone you find sympathetic; someone who has specialist knowledge of your problem; and someone who will not charge too much.

The best starting point is to ask friends, neighbours, and colleagues if they have used a solicitor and what they thought about him or her.

Your bank manager may be able to suggest someone he knows locally or you can write to the Law Society which will send you a list of solicitors in your area, although it cannot, of course, give you a recommendation. You may also see an advertisement in a local newspaper.

Before finally deciding, ask for an estimate of the fees and also ask if the solicitor regularly handles your sort of case. If you are fighting a divorce case, it is less use going to a solicitor working in a district of happily married people who deals only in commercial matters or with conveyancing and wills.

Citizens Advice Bureaux and local libraries keep a list of solicitors who operate legal aid schemes. The CAB will be able to give you the names of solicitors in the area that its clients have used satisfactorily in the past.

Law centres

These are voluntarily staffed by lawyers to help people in dire need and with little money. The service is free if they agree to handle your case.

LEGAL AID

There are four different schemes broadly known as legal aid and you need to ask for the one most appropriate to your circumstances.

Legal advice and assistance or green form scheme

This is for those with simple legal problems who have very little money. See p. 144 for divorce cases. If you qualify, you will receive free legal advice. You should look for a solicitor who displays the legal aid logo. In your local public library you will be able to find a list of solicitors who do legal aid work.

Anyone on income support is automatically entitled to free legal aid, unless you have more than £850 of possessions, excluding your house, furniture and clothes and minus an allowance for dependants.

If your weekly disposable income is below £58 you will also receive totally free advice. If it is between £58 and £122 you will have to contribute a certain amount on a sliding scale.

Civil legal aid

This is a common form of legal aid. Anyone who is involved in a civil case, whether they are suing or being sued, can apply. Whether or not you will be granted legal aid depends on your income.

Very broadly, you may be entitled to legal aid if your disposable income, that is your income after all your regular, essential outgoings, is less than £5765 a year and your disposable capital is below £5000. You certainly will if the figures are £2400 and £3000. The Law Society also needs to be satisfied that the merits of your case warrant legal aid. Generally, you must show that you are justified in bringing or defending the case and that you stand a reasonable chance of winning.

You may be entitled to receive all your legal costs free or just a proportion of them, depending on how much money you have.

Criminal legal aid

You can ask for this aid if you are defending a criminal case. Weekly earnings of less than £50 automatically entitle you to criminal legal aid. Then there is a means test to decide if you qualify.

Account will be taken of the seriousness of the offence with which you are charged and the likelihood of you losing your liberty. A rich man charged with murder may well be granted legal aid whereas he would not if charged with a trivial offence, say, giving short weight in his sweetshop.

£5 for half-an-hour scheme

As long as the solicitor agrees, anyone, regardless of means, can ask for an interview under the scheme. The first half hour will cost £5, including VAT, but after that normal rates apply.

BANKRUPTCY

You can be declared bankrupt if a court makes an adjudication order against you. But, before that can happen, you will already have passed through a long process of creditors trying to reclaim their money.

Before anyone can start bankruptcy proceedings against you, you must have committed one of the following acts:

☐ you have already been ordered by a court to pay a debt of £750 or more and failed to comply
☐ you have disposed of property in order to avoid paying your creditors
☐ you have fled the country to avoid paying your debts
☐ you yourself asked to be made bankrupt

If you start bankruptcy proceedings against anyone, you will have to pay court fees of £45 and a £1 search fee, plus a deposit of £200 for the official receivers. In total, £246.

If you are declared bankrupt, a trustee will sell off everything you own and distribute it to your creditors. All you can keep is your bedding and clothing for yourself and your family.

First, the legal fees are met; then secured creditors are paid (this will be a mortgage and any money you have borrowed against security); next come 'preferential' creditors which means paying tax to the Inland Revenue, rates to the local authority; and finally the ordinary creditors who may receive only so many pence in the pound rather than the full amount.

To declare yourself bankrupt will cost you £118.75 plus solicitor's costs.

Discharge

Once you have been discharged, which means that all your debts have been paid off, you can start again with a clean sheet. The disadvantages of being an undischarged bankrupt are:

- ☐ if you earn any money you must hand it over to the trustee; you keep only a small amount for yourself
- ☐ you cannot become a Member of Parliament
- ☐ you cannot obtain credit for over £50 without disclosing the fact
- ☐ you must tell the trustee if you want to open a bank account
- ☐ you cannot manage a company or become a company director

USEFUL ADDRESSES

Age Concern, Bernard Sunley House, 60 Pitcairn Road, Mitcham, Surrey CR4 3LL (01-640 5431)

Associated Scottish Life Offices, 23 St Andrew's Square, Edinburgh EH2 1AQ (031-556 7171)

Association of British Credit Unions, 48 Maddox Street, London W1R 9BB (01-408 1699)

Association of British Insurers, Aldermary House, Queen Street, London EC4N 1TT (01-248 4477)

Association of British Travel Agents, 55–57 Newman Street, London W1P 4AH (01-637 2444)

Association of Investment Trust Companies, Park House, 16 Finsbury Circus, London EC2M 7JJ (01-588 5347)

Association of Manufacturers of Domestic Electrical Appliances, Leicester House, 8 Leicester Street, London WC2H 7BN (01-437 0678)

Automobile Association, Fanum House, Basingstoke, Hants RG21 2EA (0256 20123)

Banking Information Service, 10 Lombard Street, London EC3V 9AP (01-626 8486)

Banking Ombudsman, Citadel House, 5–11 Fetter Lane, London EC4A 1BR (01-583 1395)

British Franchise Association, Franchise Chambers, 75a Bell Street, Henley-on-Thames, Oxon RG9 2BD (0491 578049)

British Insurance and Investment Brokers' Association, BIBA House, 14 Bevis Marks, London EC3A 7NT (01-623 9043)

Building Centre, 26 Store Street, London WC1E 7BT (01-637 1022)

The Building Societies Association, 3 Savile Row, London W1X 1AF (01-437 0655)

Building Societies Ombudsman, 35–37 Grosvenor Gardens, London SW1X 7AW (01-931 0044)

Business in the Community, 227a City Road, London EC1V 1LX (01-253 3716)

Child Poverty Action Group, 1 Bath Street, London EC1V 9PY (01-253 3406)

Citizens Advice Bureau, National Association, Myddleton House, 115–123 Pentonville Road, London N1 9LZ (01-833 2181)

Company Pensions Information Centre, 7 Old Park Lane, London W1Y 3LJ (01-493 4757)

Consumers' Association, 2 Marylebone Road, London NW1 4DX (01-486 5544)

Co-operative Development Agency, Broadmead House, 21 Panton Street, London SW1Y 4DR (01-839 2988)

Council for Licensed Conveyancers, Golden Cross House, Duncannon Street, London WC2N 4JF (01-210 4602)

Cruse National Widows' Association, 126 Sheen Road, Richmond, Surrey TW9 1UR (01-940 4818)

Domestic Coal Consumers' Council, Gavrelle House, 2 Bunhill Row, London EC1Y 8LL (01-638 8914)

DTI Tel 100 and ask for Freefone Enterprise

Equal Opportunities Commission, Overseas House, Quay Street, Manchester M3 3HN (061-833 9244)

Ethical Investment Research Information Service (EIRIS), Bondway Business Centre, 71 Bondway, London SW8 1SQ (01-753 1351)

Families Need Fathers, 39 Cloonmore Avenue, Orpington, Kent BR6 9LE (0689 54343)

Federation of Private Residents' Associations, 11 Dartmouth Street, London SW1H 9BL (01-222 0037)

Fimbra, 22 Great Tower Street, London EC3R 5AQ (01-283 4814)

Finance Houses Association, 18 Upper Grosvenor Street, London W1X 9PB (01-491 2783)

Gas Consumers' Council, Abford House, 15 Wilton Street, London SW1V 1LT (01-931 0977) (see local telephone directory for regional councils)

Gingerbread, 35 Wellington Street, London WC2E 7BN (01-240 0953)

Highlands and Islands Development Board, Bridge House, 27 Bank Street, Inverness IV1 1QR (0463 234171)

House Builders' Federation, 82 New Cavendish Street, London W1 (01-580 5588)

Housing Corporation, 149 Tottenham Court Road, London W1P 0BN (01-387 9466) and 24 Cathedral Road, Cardiff CF1 9LJ (0222 384611)

Incorporated Society of Valuers and Auctioneers, 3 Cadogan Gate, London SW1X 0AS (01-235 2282)

Industrial Common Ownership Finance, 4 St Giles Street, Northampton NN1 1AA (0604 37563)

Industrial Common Ownership Movement, 7 The Corn Exchange, Leeds LS1 7BP (0532 461737)

Industrial Tribunals, Central Office, 93 Ebury Bridge Road, London SW1 (01-730 9161)

Institute of Chartered Accountants in England and Wales, Chartered Accountants Hall, Moorgate Place, London EC2P 2BJ (01-628 7060)

Insurance Brokers Registration Council, 15 St Helen's Place, London EC3A 6DS (01-588 4387)

Insurance Ombudsman Bureau, 31 Southampton Row, London WC1B 5HJ (01-242 8613)

Job Ownership, 9 Poland Street, London W1V 3DG (01-437 5511)

Land Registry Headquarters, Her Majesty's, 32 Lincoln's Inn Fields, London WC2A 3PH (01-405 3488)

LAUTRO, Centre Point, 103 New Oxford Street, London WC1A 1QH (01-379 0444)

Law Society, 113 Chancery Lane, London WC2A 1PL (01-242 1222)

Law Society of Scotland, PO Box 75, 26 Drumsheugh Gardens, Edinburgh EH3 7YR (031-226 7411)

Lloyds Advisory Division, London House, 6 London Street, London EC3R 7AB (01-623 7100)

Local Authority Loans Bureau, Sterling Brokers, Colechurch House, 1 London Bridge Walk, London SE1 2SS (01-407 2644)

Local Enterprise Development Unit (LEDU), LEDU House, Upper Galwally, Belfast BT8 4TB (0232 691031)

Motor Agents' Association, 201 Great Portland Street, London W1N 6AB (01-580 9122)

National Association of Conveyancers, 44 London Road, Kingston-on-Thames, Surrey KT2 6QF (01-549 3636)

National Association of Estate Agents, 21 Jury Street, Warwick CV34 4EH (0926 496800)

National Association of Funeral Directors, 57 Doughty Street, London WC1N 2NE (01-242 9388)

National Consumer Council, 18 Queen Anne's Gate, London SW1H 9AA (01-222 9501)

National Council for One Parent Families, 255 Kentish Town Road, London NW5 (01-267 1361)

National Federation of Credit Unions, The Cottage, 18 The Downs, London SW20 8HR (no telephone)

National Federation of Housing Associations, 175 Grays Inn Road, London WC1X 8UP (01-278 6571)

National Home Improvement Council, 26 Store Street, London WC1E 7BT (01-636 2562)

National House Building Council, Chiltern Avenue, Amersham, Bucks HP6 5AP (02403 4477)

Office of Fair Trading, Field House, Breams Buildings, London EC4A 1PR (01-242 2858)

Personal Insurance Arbitration Service, Chartered Institute of Arbitrators, 75 Cannon Street, London EC4N 5BH (01-236 8761)

Post Office Users' National Council, Waterloo Bridge House, Waterloo Road, London SE1 8UA (01-928 9458)

Rating and Valuation Association, 115 Ebury Street, London SW1W 9QT (01-730 7258)

Registrar of Companies, Companies House, Crown Way, Maindy, Cardiff CF4 3UZ (0222 388588)

Registry of Friendly Societies, 15 Great Marlborough Street, London W1V 2AX (01-437 9992)

Royal Automobile Club, 49 Pall Mall, London SW1Y 5JG (01-839 7050)

Royal Institution of British Architects, 66 Portland Place, London W1N 4AD (01-580 5533)

Royal Institution of Chartered Surveyors, 12 Great George Street, Parliament Square, London SW1P 3AD (01-222 7000)

Royal National Institute for the Blind, 224 Great Portland Street, London W1N 6AA (01-388 1266)

Scottish Co-operative Development Committee, Templeton Business Centre, Templeton Street, Bridgeton, Glasgow G40 1DA (041-554 3797)

Scottish Development Agency, Small Business Division, Rosebery House, Haymarket Terrace, Edinburgh EH12 5EZ (031-337 9595)

Securities and Investments Board, 3 Royal Exchange Buildings, London EC3V 3NL (01-283 2474)

Shelter Housing Aid Centre (SHAC), 189a Old Brompton Road, London SW5 0AR (01-373 7841)

Social Security, freefone 0800 666 555

Society of Motor Manufacturers and Traders, Forbes House, Halkin Street, London SW1X 7DS (01-235 7000)

Society of Pension Consultants, Ludgate House, Ludgate Circus, London EC4A 2AB (01-353 1688)

Solid Fuel Advisory Service, Hobart House, Grosvenor Place, London SW1X 7AE (01-235 2020)

Special Commissioners of Income Tax, Turnstile House, 94 High Holborn, London WC1 (01-438 6622)

Sterling Brokers, see Local Authority Loans Bureau

Stock Exchange, London EC2N 1HP (01-588 2355)

Timeshare Developers Association, 23 Buckingham Gate, London SW1E 6LB (01-821 8845)

Unit Trust Association, Park House, 16 Finsbury Circus, London EC2M 7JP (01-638 3071)

Welsh Development Agency, Treforest Industrial Estate, Pontypridd, Mid Glamorgan CF37 5UT (044 382 1666)

Credit reference agencies:
CCN Systems, Lincoln Chambers, Lincoln Street, Nottingham NG1 3DJ (0602 410888)

UAPT Infolink, Coombe Cross, 2–4 South End, Croydon CR0 1DL (01-686 5644)

Self-employed advice:
Co-operative Union, Holyoake House, Hanover Street, Manchester M60 0AS (061-832 4300)

Council for Small Industries in Rural Areas (CoSIRA), 141 Castle Street, Salisbury, Wilts SP1 3TP (0722 336255)

Crafts Council, 8 Waterloo Place, London SW1 (01-930 4811)

London Enterprise Agency (LEntA), 4 Snow Hill, London EC1A 2BS (01-236 3000)

National Federation of Self-Employed, 32 St Annes Road West, Lytham St Annes, Lancs FY8 1NY (0253 720911)

Small Firms Centres, Freefone 2444 and ask for your regional centre

INDEX